Domestic Biographies

Studies on Themes and Motifs in Literature

Horst S. Daemmrich
General Editor

Vol. 105

PETER LANG
New York • Washington, D.C./Baltimore • Bern
Frankfurt • Berlin • Brussels • Vienna • Oxford

Elif S. Armbruster

Domestic Biographies

Stowe, Howells, James, and Wharton at Home

PETER LANG
New York • Washington, D.C./Baltimore • Bern
Frankfurt • Berlin • Brussels • Vienna • Oxford

Library of Congress Cataloging-in-Publication Data

Armbruster, Elif S.
Domestic biographies: Stowe, Howells, James,
and Wharton at home / Elif S. Armbruster.
p. cm. — (Studies on themes and motifs in literature; v. 105)
Includes bibliographical references and index.
1. Authors, American—Homes and haunts. 2. Home in literature.
3. Stowe, Harriet Beecher, 1811–1896—Homes and haunts.
4. Howells, William Dean, 1837–1920—Homes and haunts.
5. James, Henry, 1843–1916—Homes and haunts.
6. Wharton, Edith, 1862–1937—Homes and haunts.
7. Authors, American—19th century—Biography.
8. Authors in literature. I. Title.
PS141.A76   810.9'004—dc22   [B]   2010032708
ISBN 978-1-4331-1249-2 (hardcover)
ISBN 978-1-4331-1224-9 (paperback)
ISSN 1056-3970

Bibliographic information published by **Die Deutsche Nationalbibliothek**.
Die Deutsche Nationalbibliothek lists this publication in the "Deutsche
Nationalbibliografie"; detailed bibliographic data is available
on the Internet at http://dnb.d-nb.de/.

FSC
Mixed Sources
Product group from well-managed
forests, controlled sources and
recycled wood or fiber

Cert no. SCS-COC-002464
www.fsc.org
©1996 Forest Stewardship Council

Cover image: Harriet Beecher Stowe's winter retreat in Mandarin, Florida,
circa 1880, showing the author and her husband on the verandah.
Courtesy the Stowe-Day Foundation, Hartford, Connecticut

The paper in this book meets the guidelines for permanence and durability
of the Committee on Production Guidelines for Book Longevity
of the Council of Library Resources.

© 2011 Peter Lang Publishing, Inc., New York
29 Broadway, 18th floor, New York, NY 10006
www.peterlang.com

Printed in the United States of America

For my husband, Bill,
the keystone

CONTENTS

ILLUSTRATIONS

ACKNOWLEDGMENTS

This is a book about houses and how authors live behind closed doors; I am grateful to everyone who opened their doors to me. This includes the staffs at house museums, such as at The Mount in Lenox, MA, and the Stowe House in Hartford, CT, and also involves the owners of all the homes that remain privately owned—people who graciously showed me through their personal rooms and told me stories that in some cases have found their way into these pages. I am indebted in particular to Mr. and Mrs. E. Wilson Merrill of Redtop, in Belmont, Massachusetts, who were so welcoming to my husband and me on our visit to their home in 2004. Equally hospitable were the inhabitants at Stowe's Andover house, now owned by Phillips Andover Academy, and the renters of Howells's Kittery Point, Maine, cottage, now owned by Harvard University.

My research also brought me to countless libraries and archives; I was privileged to receive a research fellowship from the Huntington Library in San Marino, California, and from the Winterthur Museum in Wilmington, Delaware. My stays on the grounds of these beautiful landmarks were blissful, not least of all because of the helpfulness and interest of the many librarians and researchers who eagerly showed me the way to important letters and photographs, books and diaries, as I pursued the details of my four authors' lives. Likewise, librarians at Harvard University's Houghton Library and Schlesinger Library; at Yale's Beinecke Rare Book and Manuscript Library; at the Stowe-Day Foundation; Historic New England; and at Edith Wharton Restoration, diligently helped me find my way through folder upon folder of letters and photographs. I thank the estate of Edith Wharton and the Watkins/Loomis Agency, Smith College Archives, the William Dean Howells estate, and the Stowe-Day Foundation for permission to reprint the photographs in the book.

I am indebted to two anonymous readers whose thorough and thoughtful comments strengthened the manuscript in important ways (it bears mention, of course, that any shortcomings are my responsibility), and I am grateful to my dissertation committee members at Boston University who oversaw this project from the beginning: Susan Mizruchi, Keith Morgan, Anita Patterson, Bruce Schulman, and Adam Sweeting. Equally I owe an intellectual debt to Donna Cassidy, Joseph Conforti, Ardis Cameron, and Kent Ryden at the University of Southern Maine where my interest in the domestic interiors of American Realism was first realized.

I feel extremely privileged to be a part of the English Department at Suffolk University. Had it not been for the unmitigated support of the Chair of my department, Dr. Anthony Merzlak, and the Dean of the College of Arts and Sciences, Dr. Kenneth Greenberg, this project never would have come to fruition. I was very fortunate to receive from my department and the College of Arts and Sciences the financial and research assistance I needed so that I could better complete this project. Every day I feel grateful to be surrounded by my intellectually active and kind colleagues. Special thanks to Andrew Butler, Jeremy Solomons, and Keith Wise, who answered innumerable requests, large and small, with cheerful alacrity. Thank you to my students, off of whom I bounced many of the ideas in this book, for being such an important part of my work and for keeping me on my toes.

I am very grateful to my family, friends, and colleagues who read earlier versions of this project and whose comments helped improve its final shape. Especially helpful and close readings were provided by Katherine Wolff, Jeanne Slater, Sofia Gearty, and my mother, Paula Armbruster. I thank David Schuyler and Jill Lepore for their comments on earlier versions of the Stowe and Howells chapters, respectively.

I owe the origins of this project to my mother whose conception and meaning of home has infiltrated my psyche since I was a child. It was in my mother's house, thanks to her abundant aesthetic sense, that my interest in rooms and things first took hold. Later in life, my thoughts about home were solidified by the paintings and writings of my brother, Levni, whose domestic renderings have always touched me. My brother Murat has, for years, opened the doors of his own amazing homes to me graciously and generously; for that, I am thankful. My great aunt Elizabeth, who passed away on the same day as Edith Wharton, in 2004, inspired me from the time I was small. I owe my commitment to higher education to her. Finally, this book would nary exist without the love and support of my husband and best friend, Bill Cochrane, who has been there for me without fail since we met in March, 1997. We bought our first house together while I toiled on this project, and we welcomed our greatest collaboration into our home—Mary-Elizabeth Acadia—just before this book came out. My home-nest is complete because of them.

ABBREVIATIONS

ABG	Edith Wharton's autobiography, *A Backward Glance* (New York: D. Appleton and Co., 1934).
Beinecke	Yale Collection of American Literature, Beinecke Rare Book and Manuscript Library, Yale University, New Haven, CT.
CEN	Charles Eliot Norton is frequently but not always referred to in the footnotes by his initials.
DH	Edith Wharton and Ogden Codman, Jr. *The Decoration of Houses* (1897; rpt., New York: W. W. Norton & Co., 1998).

Edel, *Untried Years*
    Conquest of London
    Middle Years
    Treacherous Years
    The Master
	Five volume biography of Henry James, written by Leon Edel with the common title of *Henry James*, followed by a subtitle (Philadelphia: J. B. Lippincott & Co., 1953–1972).

EMH	Elinor Mead Howells, the wife of William Dean Howells, is frequently but not always referred to in the footnotes by her initials.
EW	The italicized *EW* refers to R. W. B. Lewis's biography of the author, *Edith Wharton: A Biography* (New York: Harper & Row, 1975).
EW	Edith Wharton is frequently but not always referred to in the footnotes by her initials.
EW Letters	*The Letters of Edith Wharton*, R. W. B. and Nancy Lewis, eds. (New York: Collier Books, 1988).
HBS	Harriet Beecher Stowe is frequently but not always referred to in the footnotes by her initials.
HBS: The Story of Her Life	*Harriet Beecher Stowe: The Story of Her Life*, by her son Charles E. Stowe and her grandson Lyman Beecher Stowe (Boston: Houghton Mifflin, 1911).
Henry James	Leon Edel, *Henry James: A Life* (New York: Harper & Row, 1985).
Historic Landscape Report	Refers to the unpublished *Historic Landscape Report for the Harriet Beecher Stowe House*. Prepared for the Harriet Beecher Stowe Center, 1999.
Historic New England	Historic New England (formerly the Society for the Preservation of New England Antiquities), Boston, MA.
Historic Structures Report	Myron Stachiw, Thomas Paske, et al. *Historic Structures Report for the Harriet Beecher Stowe House*. Prepared for the Harriet Beecher Stowe Center, December 31, 2001. (Hartford, CT: Stowe Center Library, 2002).

HJ	Henry James is frequently but not always referred to in the footnotes by his initials.
HJ Letters, followed by volume number	Four volumes of *Letters of Henry James*, edited by Leon Edel (Cambridge, MA: Belknap Press of Harvard University, 1974–1984).
Houghton	The Houghton Library, Harvard University, Cambridge, MA.
Huntington	The Henry E. Huntington Library, Art Collections, and Botanical Gardens, San Marino, CA.
Letters of EMH	*If Not Literature, The Letters of Elinor Mead Howells*, edited by Ginette de B. Merrill and George Arms (Columbus, OH: Ohio State University Press, 1988).
Life and Letters of HBS	*The Life and Letters of Harriet Beecher Stowe*, edited by Annie Fields (Boston: Houghton Mifflin, 1897).
Life in Letters	The two volumes of letters of William Dean Howells, *Life in Letters of William Dean Howells*, edited by his daughter, Mildred Howells (1928; rpt., New York: Russell & Russell, 1968).
NGFC	Shari Benstock, *No Gifts From Chance: A Biography of Edith Wharton* (New York: Charles Scribner's Sons, 1994).
OC	Ogden Codman, Jr. is frequently but not always referred to in the footnotes by his initials.
Portrait	Henry James, *The Portrait of a Lady*, ed. Robert E. Bamburg (1908; rpt., New York: W. W. Norton, 1995).
Schlesinger	Arthur and Elizabeth Schlesinger Library on the History of Women in America, Radcliffe College, Harvard University, Cambridge, MA.
Selected Letters, followed by volume number	The six volumes of *Selected Letters of William Dean Howells*, edited by George Arms et al. (Boston: Twayne Publishers, 1979–1983).
Stowe Center Library	The Harriet Beecher Stowe Center Library, Hartford, CT.
WDH	William Dean Howells is frequently but not always referred to in the footnotes by his initials.
WJ	William James, the brother of Henry James, is frequently but not always referred to in the footnotes by his initials.

"There is no one fact of our existence that has a stronger influence upon us than the house we dwell in."

—Harriet Beecher Stowe, *House and Home Papers*, 1864

"The nineteenth century, like no other century, was addicted to dwelling. It conceived the residence as a receptacle for the person, and it encased him with all his appurtenances so deeply in the dwelling's interior that one might be reminded of the inside of a compass case, where the instrument with all its accessories lies embedded in deep folds of velvet."

—Walter Benjamin, *The Arcades Project*, 1940

INTRODUCTION

From Romance to Realism:
New Houses and New Literature

Readers get to know their favorite authors primarily through their work; we imagine what they might be like based upon our reading of their fiction. Studying *Uncle Tom's Cabin*, we cannot help but envision its author, Harriet Beecher Stowe, as an uncommonly caring, concerned, and spiritual woman, mother, and wife. But a writer's fiction is just that: fiction, and not a reliable means of determining who an author actually is. Still, we want to know our beloved writers. We connect with them and wonder about the details of their writing lives: was there a particular type of desk, a specific time of day, a special view that they sought for their creative process? We speculate about their private lives: why did they marry or not; have children or not; prioritize their writing or not? Usually, we never know how right or wrong we are.

Today, most Americans are familiar with the novel *Uncle Tom's Cabin*, at least by name, but few know anything about the book's author (sometimes, not even her name). A still fewer number of readers can name the title of any other work Stowe published, though she went on to write nearly one a year for the rest of her long life.[1] That leaves a scant number indeed who know anything about the circumstances of her writing—let alone the domestic environment in which she worked. Where did she do her writing, and what was going on in her life while she was busy drafting her books? How did she integrate her professional work with her roles as wife and mother? These are the types of gaps that, at its most basic level, *Domestic Biographies* seeks to fill.

~   ~   ~

This book opens the door on four major American authors at home to examine how they lived when no one was looking: Harriet Beecher Stowe (1811–1896), William Dean Howells (1837–1920), Henry James (1843–1916), and Edith Wharton (1862–1937). For these realist writers, whose primary literary preoccupation was the world around them, houses played a vital and constant role, both in their lives and in their literature. Each of the four principal chapters presents a "domestic biography" of the writer in question, and takes the reader on a virtual tour of the author's most significant homes. By studying specific features of the authors' major residences and reading their personal documents (diaries, notebooks, account books), prized possessions (photographs, books, furniture), and the houses themselves, I reveal the types of domestic environments the authors sought, and what such spaces signified for and about them. This glimpse at four American realists behind closed doors offers readers a privileged view of domesticity and realist authorship that is rarely accessible.

As realist writers, the book's four subjects—Stowe, Howells, James, and Wharton—are particularly well-suited to this type of examination. The real world and its quotidian details—the very subjects of literary realism—mattered to them, that we know for certain; such specifics pervade their greatest works. Houses and belongings play central roles in each author's work, for example, Tom's cabin in Stowe's eponymous novel; the Beacon Street mansion in Howells's *The Rise of Silas Lapham*; the English country house Gardencourt in James's *The Portrait of a Lady*; and the numerous dwellings from Aunt Peniston's dreary brownstone to the boarding house where Lily Bart dies in Wharton's *The House of Mirth*. Everywhere we turn in these novels, we find a house, a parlor, an object that represents much more than its mere physical presence suggests.

In the authors' real lives, as in their fictional realms, houses play central roles. The foursome focused their lives on the creation of, and the search for, a domestic environment that facilitated their lives as authors. This was not the case for other groups of writers, whether because of the time period in which they lived, financial constraints, or their own preoccupations and inclinations. Ralph Waldo Emerson, Henry David Thoreau, and Nathaniel Hawthorne, themselves the subject of two recent group biographies, show far less concern for the actual houses in which they dwelled than Henry James or William Dean Howells, and the domestic realm does not dominate their writing either (except in the case of Hawthorne's novel, *The House of Seven Gables*).[2] Older generations of writers, such as the essayists and poets Oliver Wendell Holmes, Henry Wadsworth Longfellow, and James Russell Lowell (who functioned as mentors for William Dean Howells), came of age before American consumerism became gospel, and their preoccupations were moral and religious rather than domestic and personal.

For the group of authors that this book examines, the consumer and materialistic culture that followed the Civil War dominated their writing and their daily lives. The decades following the Civil War, known as America's Gilded Age, saw unprecedented economic, industrial, and population expansion. Stowe, Howells, and James were at the peak of their careers while Edith Wharton was coming of age during this period of excessive wealth and display. Due to both the era in which they lived and/or wrote and their personal preoccupations, the four authors featured in this work are especially important to the study of the search for home and home ownership in postwar America.

Because the book addresses four writers with highly different life circumstances, it exposes a variety of challenges: those facing a married woman with seven children (Stowe); a divorced woman with no children (Wharton); a married man with three children (Howells); and a bachelor (James). In spite of these differences, one of the book's greatest revelations is how fundamentally similar we all are. While each of these writers became in his or her lifetime a world-renowned intellectual and celebrity, each wrestled with the same issues at home as all of us: they fought with their spouses, struggled financially, wondered how to raise their children, and questioned their places in the world. As authors, they confronted writer's block, simultaneously craved and loathed fame, and often wanted to give up.

~   ~   ~

Domestic Biographies covers the one-hundred-year period from 1836 when Harriet Beecher Stowe was married to 1937 when Edith Wharton died. This was a critical century in our nation's history, encompassing the antebellum era; the Civil War period; the post-War, Gilded Age era; and the emergence of American Realism. The late nineteenth century saw a number of unprecedented advancements in the production of art and culture: the creation of photojournalism, the first American school of architecture, the first university department of art history, and the first professional interior decorators and landscape designers. The four authors of this study *alone* contributed unparalleled milestones to this epoch, all of which—and especially when taken together—were invaluable to the literary and cultural history of the United States: Harriet Beecher Stowe wrote the best-seller, *Uncle Tom's Cabin* (1852)—considered the most influential novel of all time; William Dean Howells assumed the assistant editorship of the newly-founded *Atlantic Monthly* (1857) in 1866 when he was twenty-nine, and went on to launch the careers of Henry James, Mark Twain, Bret Harte, and Paul Laurence Dunbar, among others; Henry James, one of America's greatest realists, helped introduce the "international" novel with *The American* (1877), *Daisy Miller* (1878), and *The Portrait of a Lady* (1881) and then the "psychological" novel with his later work, *The Spoils of Poynton* (1897); Edith Wharton co-authored one of the first manuals on interior decoration, *The Decoration of Houses* (1897), which sold 100,000 copies in its first year, and became an instant classic.

Furthermore, each author was born or married into a family whose other member(s) also played a pivotal role in American history, literary or otherwise: Stowe was the daughter of America's most renowned preacher of his day, Dr. Lyman Beecher, and the sister of the "the most famous man in America," Henry Ward Beecher, as well as of Catharine Beecher, a fervent pioneer in women's education and domestic reform; Howells married the sister of Rutherford Mead, a partner in the most important architectural firm of the Gilded Age, McKim, Mead, & White; James was the younger brother of William James, the late-nineteenth-century's most innovative philosopher and psychologist; and, Wharton was the aunt of Beatrix Jones Farrand, the first and only female charter member of the American Society of Landscape Architects.

These relations in part account for my selection of the four authors: they came from families who, like themselves, were among the most important culture-makers of the period. Perhaps because of the acclaim of certain family members—and for other reasons as well—the authors examined here wavered between confidence and insecurity in their work. This was certainly the case for Stowe and James who had the longest shadows cast over them by one or more siblings.

The quartet of writers that I treat lived during the long nineteenth century, as it has been called by historian Eric Hobsbawm, when the professions of writing for a living (professional authorship) and designing houses (architecture) came into existence.[3] While I do not purport to offer a history of these professions, the emergence of these fields provides a valuable backdrop for the authors and their works, literary and architectural. The concept of a personalized domestic architecture, and therefore, of a domestic interior—along with other byproducts of industrialization like intimacy, privacy, and domesticity—appeared on the national stage after the Revolution. Increasingly, over the nineteenth-century's course, the home became an expression of one's taste and wealth, and, as historians have argued, a theater upon which the individuation of a newly self-conscious social subject was displayed.[4]

At the same time that the house emerged as a locus for forging one's identity, it also became an increasingly privatized sphere. In the nineteenth century, labor moved outside of the house into the public sphere, a change which led simultaneously to the sacralization and the commercialization of the home; the home became a private sphere, but also the site for consumption. Literary writing (in contrast to journalism) was distinct in its domestic grounding; women as well as men could launch careers from home. All four authors discussed in this book entered the ranks of professional authorship from their homes, and yet were able, if they chose, to keep their writing entirely separate from their lives.

The literary tradition that was contemporaneous with the development of American domestic architecture proved consistently responsive to houses, their interiors, and the material world in general. Even when novelists focused on impoverished characters, as in Crane's *Maggie: A Girl of the Streets* (1893), the tenement and its sparse contents play central roles in the narrative. Or when Stowe, for example, wrote her trilogy of society novels—*Pink and White Tyranny* (1871), *My Wife and I* (1871), and *We and Our Neighbors* (1873)—she emphasized her characters' materialistic and avaricious tendencies, picturing home life as an excess of worldly possessions. Howells displayed his preoccupation with houses in *The Rise of Silas Lapham* (1885) and *A Hazard of New Fortunes* (1890), which chronicle two families and their desire for good—and better—places to live, as emblems of their social arrival. James too takes us into the residences of his characters; once there, he penetrates their minds. In *The Portrait of a Lady* (1881), for example, we are privy to Isabel Archer's domiciles and her most private thoughts.

We Are the Rooms We Live In: Authorship At Home

The book is organized around two parallel concepts: Part One emphasizes "writing to live," as was the case for Stowe and Howells; Part Two prioritizes "living to write," the more apt phrase to describe James and Wharton. These concepts provide a conceptual structure for the work and highlight the primary relationship that each author had with his or her craft. Chapter titles as well elucidate a key tenet of the author's lifestyle. Stowe, for example, as we see in the chapter entitled "The Cost of Domesticity," experienced firsthand this cost in her pursuit of home ownership, an enterprise that began with the design and construction of a behemoth called "Oakholm," which she eventually had to abandon for the more realistically priced and sized house on Forest Street. Howells, like Stowe, spent nearly his entire adult life searching for the perfect place to call home; always in motion, as the title of the chapter, "Realism in Transit," suggests, domestic stability proved elusive for Howells. His search was not complete until he found the ocean-side property in Kittery Point, Maine, where he lived part of each year from 1902 until his death in 1920. James, by contrast, was more of a dreamer and imagined his houses (in fiction) as the chapter, "Dwelling in the 'House of Fiction,'" exposes. Not until he was in his fifties did he buy the only house he ever owned, on the coast of England. Wharton, the most outwardly focused of the group, was very successful in her "constructions," whether of her public persona or her many homes, as the chapter "'A Beautiful Construction'" reveals.

Each chapter draws upon a variety of primary sources to help the reader picture the author at home and to assess the significance and meaning of home for that author. I quote from diaries, correspondence, and private notebooks in an effort to bring the authors to life as much as possible. I include, where possible, an image to enable the reader to visualize one principal domain of the author, and a photograph of the author him or herself.

Chapter One, "Harriet Beecher Stowe and the Cost of Domesticity," launches *Domestic Biographies* with the case of Harriet Beecher Stowe (1811–1896), arguably the most important and well-known domestic writer of the nineteenth century. In the 1960s, six decades after her death, Harriet Beecher Stowe was accorded her rightful position as an early practitioner of American realism by literary scholar and Stowe critic Kenneth Lynn, who considered her one of the nation's first realists.[5] As such, Stowe sets the stage for the realism of the authors who followed her: William Dean Howells and Henry James. She was also, along with her sister Catherine Beecher, hailed as a domestic reformer of the highest order and co-authored the bestseller *The American Woman's Home* with her sister in 1869. With the publication of *Uncle Tom's Cabin* in 1852, and the continued publication of almost one book a year for the rest of her life, Stowe was the first of the four authors of this study to meld the two spheres: domesticity and literary production. Writing in the 1860s about her next project, she exclaimed that her "train of thought and feelings

[were] tangled up with bills, kitchen, garden, pea vines, etc., so that [she] couldn't smooth [her writing] out."[6] For Stowe, the overlap between domesticity and writing could not have been clearer.

Part of the expansive and admired Beecher clan of Litchfield, Connecticut (father was preacher Lyman Beecher, brother was preacher Henry Ward Beecher), Stowe married preacher Calvin Stowe at age twenty-five, gave birth to seven children, and wrote *Uncle Tom's Cabin* when she was forty-one. This chapter uncovers the private reality of Stowe's life. In public, the celebrity author came across as a domestic doyenne—not unlike Martha Stewart today—but at home she was frantic, disorganized, exhausted, and wrote amidst a chaotic domestic life.

I begin with the Andover, Massachusetts, house that Stowe and her husband occupied soon after she published *Uncle Tom's Cabin.* This rented residence, which Stowe renovated and decorated, expressed her new interest in shopping for and acquiring objects of beauty—hobbies that coincided with the financial windfall of her first novel. Ten years later, when her husband was about to retire, Stowe designed and built her dream house, Oakholm, in Hartford, Connecticut, fulfilling a long-held desire. Yet because Stowe could not afford the maintenance of the large property, her dream of living there for the rest of her life was cut short; after six years, Stowe was forced to sell the property and move to a smaller house on Forest Street where she lived until her death in 1896.

By tracking Stowe's various moves, the hasty manner in which she bought her houses, and the ancillary role she assigned her husband, I convey aspects of Stowe's personality that do not come across in her writing. Letters to family members, friends, architects, and publishers reveal her multi-tasking—cooking, feeding children, overseeing servants and accounts, and writing—all in the name of a nineteenth-century ideal housewife. Stowe may have aspired to an orderly and well-appointed home, but hers was stressful and disorganized, an "undress rehearsal," as she called it in *House and Home Papers* (1864). Only in her published work was she able to realize her model of virtuous living. Whether detailing Uncle Tom's tidy slave cabin or prescribing rules for household management in *The American Woman's Home*, Stowe conveyed the importance of the home to the life of a family in terms she could not effect in reality.

Chapter Two, "William Dean Howells: Realism in Transit," concerns William Dean Howells (1837–1920), Stowe's closest chronological and literary successor. During his lifetime, he became the editor of the

Atlantic Monthly magazine, and near the end of his life he was dubbed the "Dean of American Letters." Today, Howells happens to be one of our more overlooked authors. The only one of the quartet to be entirely self-made, Howells began his career as a journalist in the small Ohio town from whence he hailed. As his career as an editor at the Boston-based *Atlantic* developed along with the novelistic career he coveted, he struggled to settle into happy domesticity with his wife and three children. Between 1866 and 1902—less than forty years— he lived in over twenty houses and apartments, primarily in the Boston area and New York City.

Howells's home life began ordinarily enough: he purchased his first house in Cambridge, Massachusetts, in 1866, four years after he married. He lived contentedly in the modest house for five years with his wife, Elinor, and firstborn child, Winifred. After his son John was born in 1868, the need for a larger and more prominent dwelling compelled the family to move to a new home, designed by Elinor, in a better neighborhood. This address did not offer enough of a refuge for the quiet, reclusive author who was now well-known, and the family moved further out to the then-secluded country town of Belmont. The handcrafted, Shingle Style house outside Boston proved equally untenable, requiring yet another move to a townhouse on Beacon Street. Howells and his family ultimately abandoned New England for New York City, where they rented numerous apartments before buying one in 1909. Not until Howells purchased a house on Maine's coast in 1902 did he find a haven of stability and peace.

The endless moves of Howells and his family, the hope with which they approached each new house, and the despair with which they departed, expose a side of Howells that is unfamiliar even to scholars of his work. A devoted family man, he relinquished many of his own wishes for his wife's whimsical fancies, while invoking the peripatetic lifestyle in his fiction. His journeys and struggles are mirrored in the lives of some of his most memorable characters, including the Marches in *A Hazard of New Fortunes* (1890) who spend days searching for a New York City apartment, and the Laphams in *The Rise of Silas Lapham* (1884) who build a mansion in the Back Bay neighborhood of Boston. Both novels are based upon events in Howells's own life and contain similar messages about the ultimate benefit of simplicity—the lesson that Howells seems to have gleaned from his years of itineration. Though the emphasis of the chapter is on Howells's private, domestic life, his novels are touched upon when their content stems directly from his life experiences.

Chapter Three, "Henry James: Dwelling in the 'House of Fiction,'" treats Henry James (1843–1916), whose life at home differed dramatically from Stowe's, Howells's, and Wharton's. Unlike the other authors, who occupied multiple residences in their quest for contentment, James kept his choices simple; his career always came first. He lived in England without a partner or children, which enabled him to concentrate exclusively on writing. His London apartments contained monastic interiors that afforded the financial freedom to travel and prevented distractions—these are detailed in the chapter. Throughout his first two decades in the European capital, James, like Charles Baudelaire's famous *flâneur*, spent hours walking, often several miles a day, observing the life that became the fruit of his fiction.[7] His "homes" were clubs, where he took his meals, wrote letters, socialized, and read; and the country estates and villas of aristocratic friends where he rested on weekends. At fifty-six years old, James purchased his first house in Rye, on the southeastern coast of England. Here at Lamb House, James became the domesticated adult he had never been as a young man: he bought a dog, a typewriter, and a bicycle. He planted a large garden, strolled through the rustic, seaside neighborhood with friends, and wrote (or dictated) for several hours each day. Finally, James was at home, and continued to be so, spending at least six months of every year at Lamb House until he died in 1916.

Even though literal houses were perhaps less important to James than to the other subjects of this study, James was preoccupied with the fictional house, and famously dubbed the writing process an act of building "a house of fiction."[8] James's novels are minutely constructed and pay inordinate attention to the details of houses, settings, and interiors. Because James's oeuvre is so large and the task of writing about houses and interiors in his work could comprise several books in itself, I emphasize the use of houses in one work, *The Portrait of a Lady* (1881). Houses abound in this novel, from the Albany, New York, home where Isabel Archer is raised, to Gardencourt, the English manor that belongs to the Touchetts, to the Italian villa of Isabel's future husband, Gilbert Osmond. These residences offer keys to their fictional owners and also reveal parts of James himself—for James, like Stowe, used his writing to create houses that he lacked in life.

Chapter Four, "Edith Wharton: 'A Beautiful Construction,'" considers Edith Wharton (1862–1937), a woman known for her houses and interiors, and herself the co-author of a best-selling decorating manual, *The Decoration of Houses* (1897). Unlike the other authors of this study, Wharton was financially independent from the age of twenty-six when she inherited $120,000 (more than two million dollars today), from a distant relative. She could now live as grandly as she wished. Upon receiving the money, she bought and renovated two major properties: Land's End in Newport, Rhode Island, and 882–884 Park Avenue in New York City. Wharton played a crucial role in the design and decoration of both residences, working closely with her architect and friend, Ogden Codman, Jr., with whom she co-authored the decorating book, and whom she initially enlisted to help her design the Mount, her best known house (and now a museum), in Western Massachusetts.

In spite of ample funds, beautiful homes, and impeccable taste, Wharton's personal life was lonely and sad: her father died when she was a teen; she was estranged from her mother and two older brothers; and her childless marriage ended in divorce. Each of these factors influenced how and where Wharton lived. For example, she did not like the proximity of her Newport and New York dwellings to her mother (who also owned homes in these locations), so she sold them and relocated to the distant Berkshires town of Lenox, Massachusetts. At the Mount, Wharton felt truly at home, and it is easy to see why: the house was large enough for both seclusion and socializing. She could write without disturbance in her second-floor bedroom and escape visitors in her meticulous formal gardens and the land beyond, which encompassed over one hundred acres of meadows, forests, hills, and lakes. In spite of her self-imposed isolation and love of solitude, Wharton also entertained lavishly and frequently invited friends and acquaintances for lengthy stays. When her husband, Teddy, grew increasingly unstable mentally, Wharton was forced to make a decision about her marriage; she divorced him and moved to France. There, Wharton again threw herself into the task of renovating and decorating two estates, and finally settled into a way of life that worked for her: spending six months of each year in her villa north of Paris and six months in her château on the southern coast of France.

Where Stowe was disorganized and frantic at home, Wharton was controlled and perfectionistic. But Wharton's carefully orchestrated interiors—the opposite of Stowe's "undress rehearsal"—belied an inner turmoil. Dubbed the "angel of devastation" by Henry James, whom she met when she was forty years old (he was sixty), Wharton used the beautiful constructions that were her houses to order an inner life of anxiety and impatience. Indeed, while Stowe was forced to change residences because of her husband's work or a lack of funds,

Wharton moved because she wanted distance from people she knew or because permanence made her uncomfortable. She found a balance in her fifties: two houses in France between which she traveled for the rest of her life. The self-imposed transience brought out the best in her writing abilities: in the last two decades of her life, Wharton earned a Pulitzer Prize for *The Age of Innocence* (1920) and an honorary Doctor of Letters from Yale University—honors never before bestowed upon a woman.

~   ~   ~

This book likewise seeks to travel distances: between the study of domestic architecture and domesticity; between dream houses and real homes; between the worlds of an author's fiction and the reality of his or her daily life. Houses *house* our most valued possessions, inspire our most private thoughts, and witness our most uncensored emotions. More than "architecture"—the concrete, fabricated, and structured—houses are animated, vitalized, and haunted by the people who live in them. Uniting the study of domesticity and domiciles, houses and lives, brings us closer to feeling at home with four great American realist authors and allows us to settle into their novels with greater understanding and perspective. Ultimately, touring the domestic and psychological interiors of these writers adds dimensions to our sense of our own.

PART ONE

Writing to Live

CHAPTER ONE

Harriet Beecher Stowe and the Cost of Domesticity

"[The home] is life's undress rehearsal, its back-room, its dressing-room, from which we go forth to more careful and guarded intercourse, leaving behind us much debris of cast-off and everyday clothing."
—Harriet Beecher Stowe, *Little Foxes*, 1865

Contrary to the popular image of Harriet Beecher Stowe as a successful novelist and house-reformer, at home she was a picture of chaos. Stowe cooked, cleaned, sewed, decorated, refurbished, gardened, painted, preached, raised her children, supported her husband, and oversaw her servants—all while writing prolifically for more than forty years. In spite of her many accomplishments, however, Stowe's household did not run smoothly: her finances were precarious and several of her children failed to live up to her example. Her home life more closely resembled the "undress rehearsal"—a phrase Stowe coined in her 1864 manual *House and Home Papers* (and which reappears in her 1865 book *Little Foxes*)—than the well-orchestrated performance that she promulgated in many advice manuals.

In her lifetime, Stowe wrote more than thirty books, including several domestic treatises such as *House and Home Papers* (1864), *Little Foxes*, and *The American Woman's Home* (1869), which she co-authored with her sister, Catharine Beecher. These books, like her novels, were instrumental in carving out Stowe's identity as a moral and domestic model for America's middle-class reading women. Whether detailing the homes of Southern slaveholding families in *Uncle Tom's Cabin* or instructing women in parlor-room decoration in *House and Home Papers*, Stowe's work—fiction and non-fiction alike—sets standards for American taste and behavior. In this regard, Stowe was a leader in the formation of "the cult of domesticity" throughout the early and mid nineteenth century.[1]

Unlike her published work, Stowe's personal writing (letters, journals, account books) along with her houses (in themselves physical, private texts), reveals a woman for whom the living was not easy. While Stowe espoused the highest of domestic and personal ideals, the moral, social, and domestic standards of the large and accomplished Beecher family, as well as the era in which Stowe came of age, were not easy to live up to. This is to be expected given the family into which she was born, particularly the example of her father, preacher Lyman Beecher, the member to whom she was most often compared and with whom she resided until she was married.[2] Trying to be many things to many people, Stowe struggled profoundly: she underwent "electricity" and water cure treatments and remained countless days in bed trying to recoup her energy; she bemoaned the helplessness of her two eldest daughters—twins Hattie and Eliza—and the dependency of her husband, the frequently unemployed Reverend Calvin Ellis Stowe. In addition to her daily struggles, Stowe lost four of her seven children in her lifetime.[3] Her life was informed by one great irony after another: she was raised in modest, rural homes amidst ministers who failed to earn as much money as they felt they deserved; she achieved material comfort through her portrait of a materially deprived and dispossessed slave named "Uncle Tom"; she became a "conspicuous consumer" who fought to reconcile this status with her firm religious identity. The schism between Stowe's literary production and her domestic life in the 1860s and 1870s reveals the impact of the United States postwar Gilded Age and its dominant consumer culture upon the author. Even more, a look at Stowe's private life, at the "undress rehearsal" that took place therein, animates one of the most popular writers of the nineteenth century, enabling twenty-first century readers to meet her at home on her own terms.

~   ~   ~

Born in 1811 in Litchfield, Connecticut, Stowe came of age in the decades following America's independence—an era of economic, political, and intellectual transformation. She died at the end of the nineteenth century, in 1896, at age eighty-five, and over her long lifetime, saw the world change dramatically from a relatively slow, faith-bound, producer economy to a fast-paced, increasingly secular consumer society. In the 1830s and 1840s, the United States forged significant inroads in technology and transportation, factors which made not only travel but also the dissemination of ideas faster and simpler. When Stowe married in 1836, the time of the country's Second Great Awakening, church membership in the United States was reaching new levels. Her father was a key contributor to the revival of Calvinism, a Christian faith that places the rule of God above all things, and to other influential reform movements such as temperance during the first half of the nineteenth century. As young adults, Stowe and her sister Catharine participated in missionary work as well, and traveled from Connecticut to Cincinnati in furtherance of the Christian cause. In the first half of the nineteenth century, the Beecher family embodied the most dominant reforming trends of the era: Lyman in awakening church membership; Catharine in elevating the woman's role in society; and Harriet in furthering the cause of abolition. Younger brother Henry Ward would soon carry his father's reins.[4]

After the Civil War, religion began losing its hold on Americans, and Stowe, like other members of her family, struggled with her own and her family's worldly desires. As an author, Stowe had gained a degree of financial security by the time the war broke out in April 1861 through the success of *Uncle Tom's Cabin*, *The Key to Uncle Tom's Cabin*, and *Dred*, all published in the 1850s. While Stowe and her family lived in a series of rented houses throughout the 1850s and early 1860s, the author oversaw the building of a custom-designed eight-gabled mansion, Oakholm, from 1862 to 1864. Perhaps in an effort to rekindle her religious zeal, Stowe, also in the 1860s, bought a house in Florida, which, she claimed, enabled her to convert newly-freed slaves in the area. Her writing too changed dramatically from the 1850s—when she was still in the early stages of a lifelong career—to the postwar years, by which time she was a well-known author. Her mid-century novels about slavery, which established her reputation and gave her the freedom to write about whatever she wished, were supplanted after the War by non-fiction travelogues such as *The Pearl of Orr's Island* (1862) about her life in Maine and *Palmetto Leaves* (1867) about her life in Florida; novels of sharp social commentary such as *Pink and White Tyranny* (1871); and autobiographical novels such as *Poganuc People* (1878), based upon her childhood in Litchfield, Connecticut. The differences among these works disclose several notable trends: the dwindling of the cult of domesticity by 1860, a preoccupation with European taste in the second half of the nineteenth century, and a shift in the notion of self from an interior conception to an external one. Stowe helped catalyze these changes and was herself shaped by them.

Stowe witnessed the boom of numerous professions throughout the nineteenth century: authorship, architecture, and interior decoration, among them. These developments also played a role in shifting Stowe's focus from abolition and religion to consumer and material culture. When she began writing in the late 1830s, in general, women's opportunities for education and careers were limited. By virtue of her class and position (her family was eminent among the clergy) Stowe had access to literary outlets such as the *New York Evangelist* and *Western Monthly Magazine*—both magazines to which she began submitting work in the 1830s. She also tapped *Godey's Lady's Book*, one of the earliest magazines for women, edited by a woman, Sarah Josepha Hale; and assisted her younger brother, Henry Ward Beecher, at the *Journal*, a small daily paper he edited in Cincinnati at this time.

While options were limited in the prewar years for women less fortunate than Stowe and her sisters, by the end of her life, women were writing for and editing a number of magazines as well as attending college. Before the Civil War, only three private colleges accepted women (Oberlin College, founded in 1833; Antioch College, founded in 1853; and Bates College, founded in 1855), and they offered a restricted curriculum compared to courses for men. By 1875, approximately fifty women's colleges had been founded.[5] Writing careers were solidified after the war by a 300 percent increase in average fees, enabling the first wave of "professional authors": men and women who made careers of writing for magazines. Stowe, William Dean Howells, and Henry James, whose many works were often first serialized in magazines, were all part of this early trend.[6]

In the postwar era, partly as a result of the arrival of the professional architect, the home emerged as the premier symbol of one's station in life. The formation of the first school of architecture at the Massachusetts Institute of Technology in 1865 launched careers in architecture and design. Before the war, the architecture profession did not formally exist; men were either "gentlemen architects" like Thomas Jefferson and acquired their knowledge through reading and travel or they were carpenters and builders. Other individuals such as Andrew Jackson Downing and Alexander Jackson Davis, who were not architects, but considered themselves designers, also published popular books in the prewar era that contributed to the enthusiasm for individualized home construction during and after the Civil War. Scholar David Schuyler, for one, considers Downing the preeminent shaper of American taste in house design in the two decades prior to the Civil War.[7] With monumental advances in technology and industry before and after the War came the development of specialized house design and the all-important architect—that arbiter of standards and taste whom American consumers could now enlist for a specified fee. Stowe's, her sister Catharine's, and her sister-in-law Eunice's work in dozens of home magazines and numerous best-selling books such as Catharine Beecher's *Treatise on Domestic Economy* (1841), like Downing's and Davis' work, awakened American women to the concept of a specialized, privatized home and to the notion that good taste could signify good character.[8] In due course, the manner in which people decorated their homes spoke volumes about the type of people they were.

Stowe was brilliant in her ability to anticipate trends, tapping into the national zeitgeist; she caught on to the national need for a return to the "home nest," as her letter to her *Atlantic Monthly* editor, James T. Fields, demonstrates: "The home nest is everywhere disturbed and the birds consequently flutter around that [...] Home is the thing we must strive for now; it is here we must strengthen the things that remain. I feel sure that *here* we could do something worth doing."[9] She proposed a collection of essays, *House and Home Papers*, to reinforce the importance of home for a war-torn nation. Stowe and her fellow wives and mothers witnessed firsthand the devastating effects of the Civil War on the nuclear family and home life. Her son Frederick, who quit his medical studies at Harvard to enlist in 1861, suffered multiple wounds in battle and became an alcoholic; shamed by his professional failures after the war, he eventually sailed around Cape Horn to San Francisco and was never heard from again.[10] His example, along with thousands of others like it, compelled Stowe to write her first domestic advice manual.

Stowe's career advanced in tandem with the Civil War and the professions of authorship and architecture; as such, it shifted from a preoccupation with the romantic and sentimental to an emphasis on the real. This chapter examines Stowe from within the private spheres of her houses, and it utilizes Stowe's postwar work to trace changes in her ideas about authorship and architecture from the mid to the late nineteenth century. As we witness Stowe and her family move from rented abodes in Brunswick, Maine, and Andover, Massachusetts, to a family estate at Oakholm and a winter haven in Florida, we simultaneously observe the woman who wrote *Uncle Tom's Cabin* change her authorial course in the 1860s with the publication of travelogues and society novels. Taking the whole of Stowe's professional life from the 1850s to the 1870s in hand with her private domestic life, we come to understand the tremendous weight that sat upon Stowe's shoulders, not only because of her family legacy and the cultural limitations of her time, but because of her far-reaching goals as a visionary nineteenth-century woman.

Bringing Culture Home to Andover, Massachusetts

One evening early in her marriage, when Stowe's husband Calvin was away on business, Harriet Beecher Stowe (Figure 1.1) was struggling at home with the chores. On a thin square of paper, she scribbled to her husband:

> It is a dark, sloppy, rainy, muddy, disagreeable day, and I have been working hard (for me) all day in the kitchen, washing dishes, looking into closets, and seeing a great deal of that dark side of domestic life [...] I am sick of the smell of sour milk, and sour meat, and sour everything, and then the clothes will not dry, and no wet thing does, and everything smells moldy; altogether, I feel as if I never wanted to eat again.[11]

As her letter suggests, Stowe was not fond of housework and often complained about the amount of effort various chores required as well as her children's reluctance to help her. Contrary to her prescriptions for "the good temper in the housekeeper" in the housekeeping manual she would coauthor with her sister Catharine, Stowe fought to appear happy to her husband and children.[12] The first decade and a half of Stowe's marriage—from 1836 when she married the Reverend Calvin Ellis Stowe, to 1852 when she published *Uncle Tom's Cabin*—was beset with financial worry and household drudgery. Stowe had seven children during this time and often felt as though she would collapse under the burdens of childbearing and childrearing. Because her husband, "a man rich in Greek and Hebrew, Latin and Arabic, and alas! rich in nothing else," was irregularly employed, he convinced Stowe to publish her stories to earn extra money for the family.[13] In this regard, the sexually lusty and often irritable Calvin Stowe (1802–1886), whom Harriet met in Cincinnati in 1832 when he was thirty and she twenty-one, was unusually supportive for the time period. A professor of theology at Lane Theological Seminary, where Harriet's father was the president, Calvin, like most of the other men in Stowe's life, was a minister and religious scholar; he did not make a substantial contribution to his wife's earnings until the late 1860s when he published the *Origin and History of the Books of the Bible* (1867).

In spite of Stowe's writing consistently about the importance of a stable and secure home for parents and children and about the successful management of a home for the self-esteem of a wife and mother, the Stowe family did not own a home for more than twenty-five years. Throughout the 1830s and 1840s, Stowe and her brood of young children lived with her father in Cincinnati while Calvin sought ministerial work in the Northeast; when he found a job at his alma mater, Bowdoin College, in Brunswick, Maine, in 1850, they rented a large white Greek Revival house on the main road in town.[14] In 1852, when Calvin took a job at the Andover Theological Seminary, in Andover, Massachusetts, the family leased a property from the school. Not until they moved to Hartford, Connecticut, in 1864, did the Stowes live in a home of their own. Throughout these years, from her marriage in 1836 to the completion of the house in Hartford in 1864, Stowe wrote amidst a flurry of activity in the kitchen, the parlor, or the dining room of rented houses. Most of the work that Stowe produced at this time was based closely on life around her. Though she scribbled at a frantic pace from 1836 to 1852—a period that culminated in the serialization of *Uncle Tom's Cabin* in 1851 and 1852—and well into the 1870s, and though her writing contributed much needed money to the family's income, Stowe told her loved ones that her writing was "the least of [her] cares."[15] Though Stowe did not prioritize her career as a writer in front of her husband and children—such a preoccupation would not have been in keeping with the approved roles of wife and mother in the mid nineteenth century—as a public celebrity and contracted author, she was very much aware of her power and position as a well-known and sought-after writer. The volume of her production—900 hand-written manuscript pages for *Uncle Tom's Cabin* alone—and the time that such output required also leads one to doubt her claim.

In March, 1852, Stowe published *Uncle Tom's Cabin* to immense critical and financial success. While she received only $300 for the serialization of the novel in *National Era* magazine, Stowe earned approximately $10,000 in royalties in the first three months of sales, "the largest sum of money ever received by any author, either American or European, from the sale of a single work in so short a period of time," according to a report in the *New York Daily Times* in September, 1852.[16] The same year, Calvin Stowe received a professorship in religion at the Andover Theological Seminary in Andover, Massachusetts, and implored his wife to move there. At first Stowe opposed the idea of leaving Maine: she was comfortable in the large white house whose starkness evoked purity and order; she liked her neighbors and the sea air, and felt the proximity to the ocean had done her family good. More importantly, she thought the change would be a poor career choice for Calvin, who had, only a year-and-a-half earlier, accepted his post at Bowdoin College. Once she saw the house that Calvin had procured, however, she had a change of heart.

Owned by the Seminary, the large, bulky, fieldstone house (originally constructed in 1828 as a workshop and gymnasium for its students) required a complete renovation to accommodate the Stowe family. Throughout 1852, the house was remodeled as a residence and now featured a central front hall and staircase flanked by two rooms on each side, and a kitchen off the rear parlor. On the second floor were four family bedrooms, and in the attic, two small rooms, one for the family's Irish servant.[17] Stowe oversaw the costly renovation, and requested that a portico and a semi-polygonal front porch be added to the front of the house to lend it a more genteel appearance. After the project was complete, the *Andover Advertiser* extolled the virtues of the building's transformation: "A very pretty piazza of Italian architecture, with a fence of unique appearance surrounding the front yard, completes the outside changes of this now commodious residence."[18] Though in reality the house did not resemble "Italian architecture" except perhaps for the fact that it was made of stone, it did provide the large family with enough room to dwell comfortably under one roof; by 1853, all seven of the Stowe children had been born.

The Stone Cabin provided the newly famous author with the means of experimenting with decorating ideas culled from her 1853 tour of Europe, an important step on Stowe's way to creating her personal Xanadu at Oakholm. She had been invited to England after the publication of *Uncle Tom's Cabin* in that country that year, and while there, she traveled across the channel to tour France, Switzerland, and Germany, where she marveled at the art and architecture and purchased various types of *objets d'art* not available in New England. Stowe made these journeys with her husband and only one or two other family members; thus, they were instrumental in offering her feelings of independence and freedom that she had not known in the United States. There was no shortage of fans and other luminaries who met up with her along the way; these fostered Stowe's celebrity. Visits to palaces of culture like the Louvre and Versailles also offered her an education in classical European taste. In the book she wrote based upon her travels, *Sunny Memories of Foreign Lands* (1854), Stowe praises the cultural environment she found in Europe: "There is no scene like this, as I gaze upward and downward, comprehending, in a glance, the immense panorama of art and architecture—life, motion, enterprise, pleasure, pomp, and power."[19] Just as such journeys overseas would be invaluable to Howells, James, and Wharton, Stowe's tours opened her eyes to realms that had thus far been closed to her and, in her memoir, Stowe writes forthrightly about what she considered her cultural starvation at home, made all the more obvious after she experienced the artistic wonders of France and Germany.[20] Overwhelmed, the modest New Englander "resigned herself" to the countless invitations and the sumptuous environment.[21]

Stowe was proud of her new sense of culture and taste and of her numerous European purchases, which included bronzes, plaster casts, paintings, books, and innumerable articles of fashionable clothing, ribbons, and lace. Upon her return to Andover, she gloated to family members of her acquisitions and included pencil sketches to show where she prominently displayed them.[22] The provenance of Stowe's belongings awed her neighbors, as did Stowe's new manner of decorating. A certain Agnes Park reported: "It was of [the parlor] that Mrs. Stowe made a fairy palace. Gathering here her many treasures from foreign lands, and gifts of admirers from every nation, arranging them with rare taste and skill, adding flowers and plants as her fancy prompted, it became [...] an enchanting room."[23] Stowe also began hosting evenings of *tableaux vivants*—the European entertainment in which guests pose as subjects of famous paintings—a fashionable pastime observed on her travels, which became immortalized by Lily Bart in Edith Wharton's 1905 novel *The House of Mirth*. Soon Stowe stood out and was recognized in Andover for her acquired sense of beauty and for the decorating motifs she brought to her home.

Travel abroad had become more popular in the United States after General Napoleon's defeat in 1814, but by the 1850s, only a small percentage of Americans were able to travel to Europe for pleasure, let alone purchase goods to be transported back across the Atlantic. There were primarily two types who could make the transatlantic journey: the independently wealthy such as the parents of Henry James and Edith Wharton who traveled abroad in the 1840s, 1850s, and 1860s for pleasure, leisure, and acculturation; and the art-makers and scholars, namely artists and writers who went to Europe to promote or publish their work. In his book, *The Dream of Arcadia: American Writers and Artists in Italy, 1760–1915*, Van Wyck Brooks presents a compelling history of the many American writers, from Fenimore Cooper to Longfellow, Margaret Fuller, and Hawthorne, who traveled to Italy in the nineteenth century, offering up only this question to explain its appeal: "To those who asked for nothing, what did Rome not give?"[24] Stowe was as inspired by England and France as she was by Italy, where she also voyaged when she returned to Europe twice more: in 1857 to secure a copyright for *Dred* (1856) and in 1859 to promote *The*

Minister's Wooing (1859). Her travels accounted for the publication of one of the earliest international novels, *Agnes of Sorrento* (1862), though that honor is usually bestowed upon Henry James for *The American* (1877) and his short novel, *Daisy Miller* (1878), published a decade and a half later. For the neighbors in the small towns in which she lived, such as Andover and Brunswick, and especially for the Beecher family from which she hailed, Stowe was a trendsetter and culture-maker of the highest order.

While Stowe's newfound wealth and celebrity enhanced her life dramatically—*Dred* was also immensely successful; 100,000 copies sold in four weeks in England alone[25]—her success smeared the lens of rural innocence through which she had always looked. When *Uncle Tom's Cabin* was published, Stowe's children ranged in age from two to sixteen; thus, her younger children (Charles and Georgiana) grew up amidst the household's new sense of financial freedom. Stowe's two eldest daughters (twins Hattie and Eliza) entered adulthood with luxury that had until now been unknown to them. With her success Stowe, too, changed from a modest (though disorganized and thus spendthrift) housewife, to someone who enjoyed conspicuous consumption. She had left Europe with twice as many trunks as she had arrived with, and could hardly believe the "whole gleanings of [her] continental tour" when compared to the original "entire stock of china for parlor and kitchen" that she had bought for eleven dollars when she was married.[26] The success of Stowe's novels, and her subsequent enjoyment of worldly pleasures, may have had something to do with her failure to raise her daughters to be conscientious, successful housekeepers.[27] In spite of lackadaisical family members, the enterprise of setting up a home to her liking empowered Stowe, and from this point forward she threw herself into the design and decoration of her future residences.

Stowe's years in Andover, which lasted through the outbreak of the Civil War, were monumental in many ways: during this decade, Stowe secured her reputation as an author; she experienced Europe and refined her aesthetic taste; she met many influential writers including John Ruskin and Frederick Douglass, who broadened her view of art in the former case and abolition in the latter; she had her last child in 1850, and with her children growing up, had time to focus on her own wants. Yet throughout these years—from 1854 to 1862— she was still living in a rented house that was owned by her husband's employer. By 1861, the fifty-year-old woman wanted more than ever to create her own home: one that truly reflected who she was and all that she had become. The construction of Oakholm in Hartford, Connecticut, from 1862 to 1864, fulfilled this dream.

Oakholm: The Realization of a Dream House

Together, Stowe's literary and financial success in the 1850s, her newly acquired European artistic sensibility, her husband's imminent retirement, and her fiftieth birthday, led her to desire a house of her own making. Knowing that her husband was almost sixty years old and ready to retire, Stowe contracted Messieurs Trask and Rust, Hartford builders, and Octavius Jordan, a local, English-trained architect, to design and build her dream house, Oakholm, so named because of its picturesque location amidst a grove of oak trees. At Harriet's urging, Calvin had purchased five acres of land along the Park River in October 1857 for $2,000. The land sat vacant for five years until 1862, when Stowe solidified plans to build a new house. In 1864, when the house was completed, Calvin Stowe formally retired from the Andover Theological Seminary and the family moved from Andover to Hartford.

Stowe was drawn to Hartford for a number of reasons: as a young girl she had attended the Hartford Female Academy, founded by her sister Catharine in 1824, and had fond memories of living with her at the time. She had dreamed as a child of building a house in Hartford "when she was rich."[28] She also had a half-sister, Isabella Beecher Hooker, who lived in the area around the Park River known as Nook Farm with her husband John Hooker; they built the first house there in 1853, using the architect, Jordan, whom Stowe employed.[29] In addition to a personal history with the city, Hartford was an important literary and cultural center in the mid-nineteenth century, and had a long legacy of philanthropy, publishing, and the arts. The city boasted the nation's first charitable society founded in 1792 and the first asylum for the deaf founded in 1817, as well as the nation's oldest public art museum, the Wadsworth Athenaeum, founded in 1842.[30] Stowe was pleased with her decision to build in Hartford, writing to her friend, Annie Fields, wife of publisher James T. Fields, "Stocks [are] higher than ever, business plenty—everything tranquil as possible."[31]

Without consulting Calvin, Stowe hired her brother-in-law's architect to begin work, once again taking on dual roles of business manager and homemaker; she paid for the house and took total control of its evolution. Throughout the two years that Stowe moved back and forth between Andover and Hartford, Calvin remained in Andover with the children. In this way, Stowe and her husband swapped traditional gender roles: she decided how to spend the money and took charge of business transactions, while Calvin oversaw the children. As frenetic as she was, Stowe invited no one to join her as the plans were finalized; she thoroughly enjoyed running the show. The endeavor also kept her from focusing on larger, far more distressing concerns, such as the war raging between North and South, about which Stowe felt completely helpless. Like Wharton after her, she seemed to thrive upon the stress of overseeing the building of a new house, and she poured a great deal of money and time into the enterprise. The strain of a new place was exacerbated by the fact that beginning in 1863, when Calvin left his job in Andover, he would no longer be contributing his two-thousand dollar yearly salary to the family's income—but even this fact did not mitigate Stowe's enthusiasm.

When it came time to design and decorate her new country manse, Stowe tapped into her early education in the subjects of art, architecture, and domestic science. Like other female readers, Stowe had been exposed to the domestic writings of her sister, Catharine, whose *Treatise on Domestic Economy* (1841) was reprinted throughout the century with house plans in subsequent editions, and the work of Sarah Josepha Hale, editor of *Godey's Lady's Book*—both widely-read publications for their novel ideas regarding household management, female education, art, and architecture. In 1846, Hale began publishing plans for model cottages in her magazine in order to educate readers in the art of beautiful architecture and the optimal settings for domesticity.[32] Stowe grew up under the tutelage of her older sister and came of age on Catharine's and Hale's ideas; as noted earlier, she also contributed her own pieces to Hale's magazine. Male readers, and women like Stowe, who gained exposure to ideas and authors through her sister, were similarly familiar with the writings of Andrew Jackson Downing, who published *Cottage Residences* in 1842 and *The Architecture of Country Houses* in 1850, and who began editing the garden design magazine, the *Horticulturist*, the year it was founded in 1846. As its subtitle reveals, the magazine was devoted to "Rural Art and Rural Taste," and sought from its inception to reform American country residences and landscapes.

Beecher's, Hale's, and Downing's pivotal work in the 1830s and 1840s argued for women's primacy in the household; Beecher promoted the home as a "glorious temple" in her 1841 book while Downing felt the house's most "graceful and charming elements" owed their existence to female hands. He never failed to recognize that women were his strongest allies in his crusade to improve American taste. In an 1850 issue of the *Horticulturist*, Downing asserted, "In all countries, it is the taste of the mother, the wife, the daughter, which educates and approves, and fixes, the tastes and habits of the people."[33] Hale considered the domestic environment so important that she also published appropriate designs for furniture along with the latest fashions in women's clothing in her magazine.[34]

Beecher's ideas for household management and Downing's for house and garden design and setting strongly resonate with Stowe's plans for Oakholm, by far the most significant of her properties to her. Envisioning a picturesque country house, Stowe worked with her team for two years, overseeing the design and construction of a stone and brick, eight-gable, Gothic Revival residence, which, she jested, would surpass Hawthorne's fictional seven-gabled home.[35] Stowe watched eagerly as Jordan added stylish ornamentation to the steeply-pitched gables, bow windows, and balustrades, including battlemented chimneys, crosses, hood moldings, brackets, and barge-board cut-outs—the same features that grace Downing's houses. Overall, the house's exterior bore many ecclesiastical associations, particularly its cross gables and diamond-paned windows—fitting for the religious Stowe (Figure 1.2).[36] Downing, like Stowe, believed that individuals should dwell in houses that reflected their true selves; he advocated "truthfulness in architecture," writing "Domestic architecture is only perfect when it is composed so as to express the utmost beauty and truth in the life of the individual."[37] From its long, winding driveway through a dense grove of oak trees, to its innumerable gables, Oakholm was in every way a grand departure from each of the Stowe family's previous residences; it was also the perfect embodiment of feminine taste as upheld by Downing and the now wealthy and trendsetting Stowe.

Once inside, a majestic entrance hall, measuring twenty-four by forty-eight feet with winding stairs to the upper floors, greeted the visitor. While no floor plans for Oakholm exist (the house was demolished early in the twentieth century), its elevation suggests a minimum of four large ground-floor rooms including two parlors, a dining room, and a library; a number of second story rooms, possibly as many as six, for Stowe wanted individual rooms for herself, Calvin, her twins, daughter Georgiana who lived at the house until her marriage in 1865, and son Charles who was fourteen when the family moved in; as well as an amply-sized, gabled third floor.[38] The first floor verandah and second story balconies also contributed to the living space and were used frequently by the family. Drawing on her knowledge of "indoor gardens"—or greenhouses—from her travels in England, where she saw the Crystal Palace in London's Hyde Park, Stowe incorporated a two-story glass conservatory in the center of the south side of the house, an element that William Dean Howells credited Stowe with inventing and bringing to the neighborhood.[39] Other Nook Farm residents including Mark Twain, Mary Beecher Perkins (Stowe's sister), and Franklin Chamberlin would soon incorporate hothouses in their nearby mansions.

Stowe's interior decoration of Oakholm may have included elements similar to those promulgated in *The American Woman's Home*, which she wrote with her sister throughout the first years at Oakholm, and which they published in 1869. Oakholm offers a large version of the type of "Christian House" that Stowe and her sister promoted in the book. In their work, essentially a revised and expanded version of Catharine's 1841 *Treatise on Domestic Economy*, Stowe and Beecher advocate the use of light muslin instead of heavy fabric curtains, "educating works of art" such as statuettes of Jesus and Mary, proximity to nature through the use of balconies and verandahs, easy-to-clean matting for the floor, delicate and organic bamboo furniture that evoked nature, and an open fireplace (53–57, 71–84, 308–317). These same features appear in Stowe's fiction, in the houses of her morally good characters, no matter how poor. In *Uncle Tom's Cabin*, Stowe supplied readers with her notions of "taste, beauty, and peace" in her rendering of Little Eva's bedroom, which, like those at Oakholm, opened on to a broad verandah and bore other similarities to the recommendations in the treatise. It is likely that Stowe furnished her own bedroom in a fashion similar to Eva's, where:

> The windows were hung with curtains of rose-colored and white muslin, the floor was spread with a matting which had been ordered in Paris [...] The bedstead, chairs, and lounges, were of bamboo, wrought in peculiarly graceful and fanciful patterns [...] There was a fireplace in the room, and on the marble mantle above stood a beautifully wrought statuette of Jesus.[40]

Even if Stowe's decoration of the bedrooms at Oakholm departed from this description, Eva's bedroom offers a picture of Stowe's archetype; its furnishings and its decorative details resonate with those in *The American Woman's Home*. In their treatise, Stowe and her sister praise the "influence of white-muslin curtains" for "giving an air of grace and elegance to a room." They write, "[The effect] is astonishing. White curtains really create a room out of nothing. No matter how coarse the muslin, so it be white and hang in graceful folds, there is a charm in it that supplies the want of multitudes of other things" (55).

Stowe spared no expense on the inside of the house, whether for plumbing or pretty curtains, yet all the while, she and Catharine were writing a manual in which they extolled frugality for women, inducing them to have "a heart that is humble" (75). In contrast to the manner in which Stowe was arranging her own rooms, the sisters outfit a small parlor for $61.75 in their book (75). Clearly Stowe saw herself as a taste-maker—even as a financial advisor—for white, middle-class women, like she herself once was. She was, however, no longer a part of that group. Her fame and financial success, as well as her status as a professional writer, moved her outside of, and above, that class.

One element that Oakholm curiously lacked was a study for Stowe, who long ago had requested a room of her own so that she could write in quiet.[41] Instead, Stowe procured a library for her husband. Rather than focus on her own space—a desire which may have been out of keeping with her role as a homemaker—Stowe turned her attention to her conservatory: "You must certainly come and help me arrange *my* conservatory and see if you can make a cascade in it."[42] It is reasonable to assume that Stowe viewed her indoor garden as an appropriate female workplace—a unique type of study—aligned as the cultivation of plants and flowers was in her mind with God.

Overseeing the building of Oakholm exhausted Stowe and depleted her financial resources, but though she complained, she was not willing to relinquish responsibility for the project. Throughout the two years of construction, Stowe wrote repeated letters to her daughters and husband seeking comfort and gratitude for her efforts. Stowe's stress was augmented by the expense of the mansion, and therefore, by the simultaneous need for her family to economize and for her to publish as frequently as possible. "Let me tell you first how heavy is the weight that lies upon me. To build and prepare the house and grounds we are to go to, in all its parts and details, one would think enough for one woman," she wrote to her daughters in 1863.[43] Stowe worried about money also because Calvin and her daughters depended upon her financially (neither Hattie nor Eliza married or had children). By all accounts, including those written by Stowe's son, Charles, and grandson, Lyman, Calvin Stowe was of no help during this trying time.[44] Stowe's dreams for the outcome of the house and for the peaceful domesticity she envisioned kept her going—"Mrs. Stowe spun her way out of her pecuniary troubles by the creations of her own brain"—but, her son and grandson continued, "Her ideas of finance might work among angels, but they were not adapted to New England."[45]

Stowe's central and invaluable position in her family empowered her but also left her anxious. Just as life in Brunswick and Andover was characterized by non-stop writing and housework, Oakholm kept her working relentlessly. In spite of tireless efforts to keep and train servants and her daughters, life at the Gothic Revival mansion never amounted to the New England ideal Stowe sought and promoted in her work. In *Uncle Tom's Cabin*, for example, Stowe evokes the ideal setting of a large New England farmhouse: "the air of order and stillness, of perpetuity and unchanging repose [...] seemed to breathe over the whole place. Nothing lost, or out of order; not a picket loose in the fence, not a particle of litter in the turfy yard" (135). She calls to mind the "wide, clean rooms [...] where everything is once and forever rigidly in place, and where all household arrangements move with the punctual exactness of the old clock in the corner" (135). In contrast to the home-life of the St. Clare's in New Orleans, in the New England home, where one such as Miss Ophelia would dwell, "the old kitchen floor never seems stained or spotted; the tables, the chairs, and the various cooking utensils, never seem deranged or disordered" (135–136). Stowe used her fiction the same way she did her non-fiction: to encourage household values that she aspired to but did not in fact achieve.

In order to finance the growing bill for Oakholm, Stowe sold material from her journals and letters for serialization in the *Independent* and the *Atlantic Monthly*. These articles resulted in two novels in 1862—*The Pearl of Orr's Island*, based on her Maine experiences, and *Agnes of Sorrento*, on her travels in Italy. Stowe was a confident and aggressive peddler of her wares and had no qualms writing to her editors, asking for work to be published or for an advance. Often she made decisions for her editors, as a letter to James Fields, editor of the *Atlantic Monthly* from 1861 to 1871, suggests: "I shall want about a hundred dollars a number for them and we will talk about a book after."[46] Stowe's letters to Fields sound almost dictatorial, revealing another of her numerous voices. Her assertive and professional tone belies her earlier claim that writing was the least of her concerns and underscores how seriously Stowe took her work and her need for remuneration.

Figure 1.1. **Harriet Beecher Stowe in the 1850s, around the time of her writing *Uncle Tom's Cabin*.** Stowe-Day Foundation, Hartford, CT.

Figure 1.2. **Stowe's custom-built eight-gabled mansion, Oakholm, in Hartford, CT, c. 1866.** Stowe-Day Foundation.

The next series of articles that Stowe proposed to Fields stemmed directly from experience, as most of Stowe's writing did—in this case, the building of Oakholm. Published as *House and Home Papers* in 1864, the book illustrates Stowe's attempt to order houses across the nation, a logical outgrowth of her recent chaotic house-building experiment. However, when she recommended the subject to her editor, she praised the topic's lightness, urging that a nation at war would need, as she did, "a little gentle household merriment and talk of common things": "[I have in mind] a sort of spicy, sprightly writing that I feel I need to write in these days to keep from thinking of things that make me dizzy and blind and fill my eyes with tears so that I can't see the paper," she wrote Fields. "It is not wise that all our literature should [...] cut through our hearts."[47] Whether Stowe was once again predicting national taste or alleviating her own great burden, the book's timing and subject matter effectively took the reader's mind off of the Civil War and brought it back to the home, where Stowe felt it belonged.

In *House and Home Papers*, Stowe uses the male pseudonym, Christopher Crowfield, which would appear on several of her future books, including *Little Foxes* (1865) and *The Chimney Corner* (1866). (Stowe would also use the pseudonym, "Horace Holyoke," on future works such as *Oldtown Folks* [1869]). Stowe's readers knew she was the author of the book because her name appeared opposite the title page, yet Stowe was compelled to put on a narrative mask and gain an authoritative male voice in the stories.[48] The decision was perplexing, for the scenarios in these works are based upon Stowe's life. Christopher Crowfield, the narrator, praises a home with an "old and worn-out" look, something a woman such as Stowe could not do, given her association with saintly household management and the Beecher name. Also noteworthy is the manner in which Crowfield disparages extravagance—even new furniture—and upholds antiquated, homey domesticity: "Our parlor has always been a sort of log-cabin—library, study, nursery, greenhouse, all combined. We have never had things like other people." He cautions his daughters: "You [are] not to expect to live like richer people, not to begin to try, not to think or inquire about certain rates or expenditures."[49] At the time of this writing, Stowe had moved into Oakholm, which boasted individual rooms for each person's needs. She had elevated her family's status both through the size and location of her house and the numerous European artifacts on display. In a chapter entitled "Economy," Stowe uses Crowfield to justify the high cost of building a house like Oakholm. The narrator explains that a "profusion of bathing accommodations," as the house had, was acceptable.[50] Because the numerous bathrooms are good for the family's health, Crowfield suggests, it is unobjectionable to spend a great deal of money on the plumbing that they required. In the chapter entitled "Our House," Crowfield highlights the benefits of bow windows for sunlight and verandahs for taking fresh air—both architectural features that Stowe incorporated at Oakholm. By adopting a male persona who questions extravagance and waste, Stowe was able to convey messages of frugality and morality. However, because she herself did not always abide by the advice she gave, the use of a male name allowed her some editorial distance from the reality of her home-life.

Another compelling reason for the use of a male narrator in *House and Home Papers* is offered by Joan Hedrick in her 1994 biography of the author. Hedrick asserts that speaking in a male voice was the "price of admission" to the elite club of *Atlantic Monthly* readers and writers. As Hedrick points out, Stowe's Crowfield sounds uncannily like Oliver Wendell Holmes in *The Autocrat of the Breakfast Table* (1858), which had appeared in the *Atlantic* to great acclaim a few years before Stowe's serialization of *House and Home Papers*. By becoming a highly valued contributor to the *Atlantic* early in its history—the magazine was founded in Boston in 1857—Stowe was able to attach herself to one of the "most highly refined cultural productions" of the time, thereby solidifying her place in America's literary history.[51]

In *House and Home Papers*, Stowe's narrator also introduces the notion of the "undress rehearsal," claiming that "[it] is better than the bad dress-rehearsal." She rationalizes disorderly or disorganized conduct: "If it becomes apparent in these entirely undressed rehearsals that your children are sometimes disorderly, and that your cook sometimes overdoes the meat, and that your second girl sometimes is awkward in waiting [...] your friend [...] shall feel easy with you."[52] Through her narrator, Stowe once again excuses the behavior of her children, whom she had a difficult time controlling, and whom, in reality, she often had to reprimand; in *House and Home Papers*, a child's flaws in essence are praised for putting other parents at ease. One cannot help but imagine that Stowe was making these types of assertions to justify the increasing domestic disarray and misbehavior within her own home.

Numerous other connections to and contradictions with Stowe's life appear in the book. While we now know that Stowe enjoyed shopping while in Europe, Crowfield disapproves of overspending, whether for clothing or European goods, particularly when American products can be had at a much lower price: "'The fact is, American women and girls must learn to economize,'" the narrator expounds. "'It isn't merely restricting oneself to American goods, it is general economy that is required.'"[53] In this instance, Stowe employs her male narrator not to justify her daughters' or her own misbehavior, but to denounce it. Stowe's account book, though erratically maintained and scratchily written, reveals that she and her daughters bought bonnets that ranged in price from nine to seventeen dollars, far more than the three dollars advocated in the book. And while Stowe could afford to be liberal in her spending, her personal writings reveal a preoccupation with frugality. Like her other non-fiction, *House and Home Papers* allowed Stowe to try out—or "try on"—different modes of living, in the same way that Stowe's life functioned as a "rehearsal." In a very real sense, Stowe's entire life was a rehearsal for the ultimate performance: her meeting with God in the hereafter.

Stowe Pioneers the Winter Home

As if building Oakholm and moving her family there in 1864 was not enough stimulation for the energetic writer, Stowe purchased a winter home in Mandarin, Florida, in 1867. With the acquisition of a second house, Stowe was capitalizing on her wealth and living the life of a conspicuous consumer by the end of the Civil War. That Stowe was about to own two very individualized homes highlights her success and crystallizes her notion of herself as an accomplished and deserving woman; now in her late fifties, she did not refrain from acquiring exactly what she wanted. Her behavior, though atypical for a Beecher, was in keeping with the times—the post-Civil War era of great economic growth—and as a result, a heightened degree of consumerism. Shopping for pleasure and the concept of display—or what Thorstein Veblen would refer to as "conspicuous consumption"— came into vogue at this time, though Stowe practiced her own art of acquisition in the late fifties and early sixties, at least a half-decade before the fads had enveloped most middle-class Americans. Authors as wide-ranging as Jan Cohn and Alan Trachtenberg have elucidated that houses in the late nineteenth century, like one's clothing, came to be seen as testaments to one's success in life, and even as projections of one's identity.[54] With a custom-built house in the literary community of Nook Farm in Hartford and a winter refuge in Florida, Stowe conveyed to the public her status as a successful woman writer. She also maintained a socially responsible image by offering an explanation for each house. While Oakholm suited the entire family due to its convenient location and size, the outpost in Florida enabled Stowe to educate and Christianize freed slaves.

In 1866, Stowe made her first trip to Florida, hoping to establish in business her son Frederick, who was unemployed after the Civil War. She advanced him $10,000 to rent a cotton plantation on the banks of the St. John's River, which she hoped would provide a work opportunity for Fred and freed slaves. The plantation was a failure, but throughout the year, on her visits to check on him, Stowe fell in love with the region's warm climate, beautiful flora, and sweet smells of jasmine and orange blossoms. In 1867, she spotted, and then hastily purchased, a 30-acre plot of land on the opposite side of the river in a small town named Mandarin, about 12 miles south of Jacksonville. The $5,000 parcel included 115 orange trees, five date palms, an olive tree in full bearing, and a small cottage.[55] Once again, Stowe made a significant financial and lifestyle decision without first consulting her husband. Her letter signaled that the decision to purchase was firm, just as it had been with the Oakholm property: "I want you to send the $5,000 at once—either by selling any of our stock—or borrowing on our house—or placing our Panama stock as collateral in Geo[rge] Bissels' hands," she ordered Calvin, "Only send it."[56] In a letter to her brother Charles, Stowe justifies the purchase of a second home, and asserts that the decision is not a materialistic one: "My plan of going to Florida [...] is not in any sense a mere worldly enterprise," she wrote. "I have for many years had a longing to be more immediately doing Christ's work on earth."[57] Though Stowe opened a school and church for former slaves, she also wished to escape harsh New England winters. She was one of the first famous Northerners to buy a property in Florida for the primary purpose of enjoying sunny weather and slower days, and her presence there aroused interest in the state. Walt Whitman would follow her south in the next decade.

Stowe reveled in the "easy, undress, picnic kind of a life far from the world and its cares" that she found in Mandarin, and in her correspondence she appears much more content and relaxed than in the North. "When I get here I enter another life," she wrote her son. "The world recedes; I am out of it."[58] Stowe seems to have needed several months a year to be "out of the world," for in the North she was a celebrity and resided in the public's gaze. It is even possible that life in the South relaxed the burden Stowe felt of having to live up to the ideals set forth in her fiction. The slower pace agreed with Stowe and enabled her to write more easily—she felt the cold New England weather numbed her brain. From Florida, she wrote more letters to friends than from anywhere else, yet was happy that mail came only twice a week so that she was not overwhelmed by daily letters.[59]

The house in Florida afforded the author a second opportunity to design and create a home, and once again Stowe spent a great deal of time and energy overseeing its expansion and its gardens. Its original configuration was small enough that Stowe found many ways to enhance the property. One way she did so was to integrate an enormous oak tree on the front lawn into a long, broad verandah that encircled it. She also added a large parlor, a conservatory, and an upstairs balcony. When completed, the house remained one and a half stories, but offered several small bedrooms, numerous gables, and looked like a smaller, more rustic version of Oakholm.[60] Each gable featured dripping bargeboard cutouts that mirrored the cutouts of the porch's posts, contributing to its unusual, gingerbread house-like appearance.

Stowe threw herself into the cultivation of her gardens, a favorite hobby, and the family passed many hours each day sitting on the expansive front verandah, looking across the five-mile-wide river, listening to the birds that hung in cages, and playing croquet. And Stowe continued to write, drawing upon life around her for her material. In *Palmetto Leaves*, a series of stories about life in Florida (published in 1873, five years after purchasing the southern getaway), she details: "The great charm [...] of this life is its outdoorness. To be able to spend your winter out of doors [...] to be able to sit with windows open; to hear birds daily; to eat fruit from trees, and pick flowers from hedges all winter long,—is about the whole of the story."[61] The Stowes brought many friends and family members to Florida with them, including Eunice Beecher, wife of Stowe's well-known brother Henry Ward Beecher.[62]

Palmetto Leaves, like Stowe's earlier collections from the 1860s that detailed her experiences in Maine and in Europe, can be interpreted as an early realist text, precursor to the work soon to be published by William Dean Howells. Based on Stowe's experiences in Florida, but like the realist novels produced by Howells in the 1870s and 1880s, and the local color work by Sarah Orne Jewett later in the century, the stories feature realistic depictions of everyday life, devoid of sugary sentiment or idealized romance. The book is filled with unsentimental characterizations of life in the southern state, such as this one: "It is not to be denied that full half of the tourists and travelers that come to

Florida return intensely disappointed, and even disgusted. Why? Evidently because Florida, like a piece of embroidery, has two sides to it,—one side all tag-rag and thrums, without order or position; and the other side showing flowers and arabesques and brilliant coloring. Both these sides exist."[63] It is striking that Stowe debunks the myth of Florida as the perfect winter escape as early as 1872, providing an eye-opener that has stayed with us today.

Palmetto Leaves like *The Pearl of Orr's Island* before it might be viewed as an early work of "local color" or regionalism. It makes sense that Stowe would turn to writing realistic portrayals of life around her in the 1860s when the duress of the Civil War was too much for her to contemplate; instead of writing about the war, she illuminated country life, family scenes, and different regional and foreign cultures. *The Pearl of Orr's Island* and *Agnes of Sorrento* were remarkably fresh in their content in the 1860s—the former predates the not-too-dissimilar *The Country of Pointed Firs* (1896) by more than three decades—and once again highlights Stowe's ability to tap into the reading public's latent interests. All three works introduced readers to regionally remote (Maine, Florida) or foreign (Italian) customs and climes at just the time, the dawn of the Gilded Age, when different Americans were looking for distinct types of experiences. The American nouveaux riches were eagerly looking toward a European Grand Tour to solidify their new class position; Stowe's breezy accounts of life in Europe provided such a tour. Another demographic, America's middle-class refugees from overcrowded and increasingly squalid cities, were looking to rural life for renewal and redemption; works that vividly illustrated country life in remote pockets, such as *The Pearl of Orr's Island* and *Palmetto Leaves,* offered much needed respite from the ills of city life in an immigrant-packed, tenement-populated postwar era. It remains remarkable that Stowe has been given little credit for her part in the advancement of a new literary genre—whether we call it local color or realism—during and after the Civil War, for that is precisely what she achieved.[64] Joan Hedrick, author of a Pulitzer prize-winning biography of Stowe, has underscored Stowe's contributions at this later stage in her career, asserting that Stowe's Italian stories in *Agnes of Sorrento*, like Hawthorne's *The Marble Faun*, set the stage for the international novel that Henry James turned into an art form a decade later.[65] Hedrick asserts a similar connection to James with respect to Stowe's work, *Oldtown Folks*, published three years before *Palmetto Leaves*. The use of a passive male narrator, a mere "observer and reporter," as he is called, "Horace Holyoke" anticipates the objective and omniscient narrative voice of the late nineteenth century.[66] Hedrick is the rare scholar who has aligned Stowe with the realist giants of the late nineteenth century, the subjects of the next three chapters of this book.

Throughout her years in Hartford and Florida—from 1862 when she designed Oakholm, to 1873 when she moved into her final home—Stowe determined to earn as much money as she could. She became a relentless marketer of her work; indeed, one reason for the success of *Oldtown Folks* was her promotion of the book. She considered her good health "gold" so that nothing would interfere with the desire to sell books. To her daughters she wrote: "In short you see that my health just now is gold for my family. I can make $10,000 a year with all ease if I can only keep my health, and if we can manage to live on $5,000, we can soon lay up a pretty sum to retire on."[67] With an annual income of $10,000 a year in 1869 (approximately $154,000 in today's dollars), Stowe was securely established in the upper middle class of her time. Her forthright declarations establish Stowe as a keen consumer, just as my analyses of Stowe at home in Andover and Oakholm do.

In the early 1870s, Stowe continued to produce realist works, most of them drawn directly from her life or from her observations of others'. While in Florida, Stowe worked on the aforementioned *Palmetto Leaves* and *Oldtown Folks*, as well as a trilogy of "society novels" (she also wrote chapters of them in Hartford): *Pink and White Tyranny* (1871), *My Wife and I* (1871), and *We and Our Neighbors* (1873). That Stowe chose to write about society at this time—particularly the wealthy, materialistic society that was the subject of her trilogy—was significant for two reasons: first, she desired to produce something new and subtly educational for the postwar years, just as she had with *House and Home Papers* in 1864 and *Little Foxes* in 1865. Secondly, Stowe had grown dismayed by her own spending and the lavish habits of her twin daughters, unmarried women who continued to enjoy shopping and gossip. Stowe found her daughters' attitudes and behavior tiresome and disappointing; now thirty-three years old, the women failed to show the discipline, hard work, and religious zeal that Stowe was known for.[68] On the contrary, in every way, Stowe's daughters failed to fulfill their mother's expectations of them, just as the protagonists in Stowe's trilogy of society novels fail those around them.

Tyrannized by Things

In *Pink and White Tyranny*, Stowe tells the story of "the celebrated, the divine" Lillie Ellis, a "petted creature," who, in her desire for money and comfort, is "vulgar and selfish." Lillie uses her beauty and wiles to seduce the benevolent capitalist Mr. John Seymour of the "well-known, respected Seymour house," and ends by bankrupting him when she decorates his house in "the French taste."[69] While the details differ from those of Stowe's daughters, who remained unmarried, the message is the same: the pursuit of extravagance and ostentation and other worldly concerns leads to ruin. Stowe seems to have enjoyed the spoils of wealth as much as Lillie and her daughters did—she even decorated the Andover house and Oakholm with some elements of "French taste"—but there was one key difference: Stowe earned her money, while Lillie married it and Stowe's daughters inherited it.

Pink and White Tyranny is striking in its contemporaneity, and once again, it highlights Stowe's almost preternatural ability to predict trends and concerns of her fellow countrymen and women. Indeed, Stowe was the woman who wrote forthrightly to her editor James Fields, "Whoever can write on home and family matters, on what people think of and are anxious about, and what to hear from, has an immense advantage."[70] She was right. Though published in 1871, long before Thorstein Veblen introduced Americans to the concepts of conspicuous consumption and invidious comparison in *The Theory of the Leisure Class* (1899), and over three decades before Wharton familiarized readers with the practice of these concepts through her character Lily Bart in *The House of Mirth* (1905), the book's main character, Lillie, and her actions, foretell these works. With the exception of being married, Lillie, like Lily, takes the greatest pleasure in indulging her love of beauty and spending money, and is most happy when luxuriously ensconced at a grand Newport mansion: "Behold, now, our Lillie at the height of her heart's desire, installed in fashionable apartments at Newport," Stowe encourages her readers, "All the dash and flash and furbelow of upper-tendom were there; and Lillie now felt the full power and glory of being a rich, pretty, young married woman, with oceans of money to spend, and nothing on earth to do but follow the fancies of the passing hour. This was Lillie's highest ideal of happiness" (112).

No matter where Lillie finds herself, however, she—again like Lily Bart—falls prey to envying what those around her have or do.

Richly settled in at her kind husband's Seymour House, Lillie is overcome by tears because, while their rooms are lovely, "'they aren't modern and cheerful, like those [Lillie] has been accustomed to.'" Imploring her husband to make some changes, Lillie continues: "'Well, then, John, don't you think it would be lovely to have [the rooms] frescoed? Did you ever see the Follingsbees' rooms in New York? They were so lovely!—one was all in blue, and the other in crimson, opening into each other; with carved furniture, and those marquetrie [sic] tables, and all sorts of little French things. They had such a gay and cheerful look'" (106). Despite having a patient and generous husband, Lillie's myopic pursuit of material comfort and one-upsmanship with her neighbors prevents her from valuing him and what he offers her. Stowe suggests that Lillie's desire for extravagant living disrupts the possibility of domestic harmony, while a different type of consumption—one that is tasteful and economical, such as perhaps Stowe saw her own materialism—signified high moral character.[71] The correlation between one's interior decoration and one's character—the same relationship that Wharton underlined several decades later—could not be more apparent; it is striking that Stowe articulated these themes in *Pink and White Tyranny* nearly three decades before Wharton much more systematically laid them bare in *The Decoration of Houses* (1897) and in *The House of Mirth*.

Stowe's final scene, not unlike Wharton's in 1905, offers her heroine redemption; on her deathbed, Lillie awakens to her spiritual depravation and begs for her husband's forgiveness, but her remorse comes too late. The saving grace comes in the form of "another Lillie," the couple's first child, named after her mother but wholly different from her. She grows to be much "fairer and sweeter" than her mother—"the tender confidant, the trusted friend of her father," making his suffering, in the end, entirely worthwhile (330).

Life in Florida, which continued until Calvin Stowe fell ill in 1884 and the house was sold, offered the family respite from the fast-paced, mercenary world of the North; however, it was not without its trials or its indulgences. One of its major inconveniences was its distance from Hartford. The trip, which required taking the boat, train, and carriage, was long and costly, especially since Stowe almost always traveled with her husband, daughters Hattie and Eliza, two servants, and a collection of animals (including six birds and two dogs). By the time of the purchase of the Mandarin house, Calvin Stowe had been retired for five years; the Stowes' yearly income was derived primarily from Stowe's writing, which yielded a great deal in the 1860s— anywhere from $2,000 to $10,000 a year, depending on how prolific she was. But still Stowe fretted about her expenditures and carefully noted in her small, cursive hand the cost of travel in her account book. The total expense of the eight-day journey amounted to $180.58, or about $3,000 in today's dollars.[72] Considering that Stowe and her entourage made the journey twice a year, the amount was significant. But while Stowe disliked the upheaval necessary to her semi-annual relocation, the benefits outweighed the expense and the inconvenience.

"Within My Means": Forest Street, 1873–1896

Like Howells and Wharton after her, Stowe left what seemed to have been her dream house prematurely. Oakholm proved too expensive to maintain; its plumbing systems posed continual problems, and Stowe bemoaned the "duress of the domestic trials of backwoods life."[73] She was forced to sell the house in 1870 after living there only six years, a devastating loss for the woman who had waited so long for her first real home. The blow was made worse by two transient years in which the family spent winters in Florida and camped at the houses of friends the rest of the year. At nearly sixty years of age, Stowe was loathe to be a "scattered wanderer," as she put it, but when she found her next—and last—home in early 1873, her travails were forgotten.[74]

Stowe's final home, a small house on Forest Street in Hartford, was located further away from the Park River than Oakholm, in the heart of the Nook Farm neighborhood that she loved. As was her nature, Stowe took charge of the purchase: "I have about concluded to buy [Franklin] Chamberlin's house," she wrote to her daughters. "It is a lovely, beautiful house and the terms are quite within my means."[75] In April 1873, Stowe closed the deal on the house in which she and Calvin would die: Calvin in 1886 and Stowe, ten years later, in 1896.

When the family moved in, the Samuel Clemenses were in the midst of building their house on the plot of land behind theirs; the Charles Dudley Warners, the Hookers, and the Gillettes lived close by. The Forest Street neighborhood was bustling, and reflected the growth and transformation of Hartford over the previous decade. The city was an early publishing capital, but by mid century, became better known for its philanthropies and insurance and manufacturing businesses.[76] A trolley line ran up and down Farmington Avenue, and the Stowe house sat amidst a veritable construction site for a decade while the Clemenses built their mansion from 1871 to 1874 and Chamberlin built his on the north side of her house from 1880 to 1881. Two large commercial greenhouses were located near the property, one in the backyard and one on the corner of Forest and Farmington.[77] The neighborhood was lively and mixed: the Stowes employed two African-American servants while their immediate neighbors employed two Irish servants and housed several boarders. At any given time, a passerby on Forest Street could encounter a world-famous author and her husband, sixty-two and seventy-one years old respectively; a wealthy lawyer and real estate speculator; a black girl aged twenty; a young widow with two small children; or a group of Irish teenagers.[78]

The house was far more modest than Oakholm, and was one of a series of speculation houses built in 1871 on Forest Street by Franklin Chamberlin, a wealthy Hartford lawyer and developer. The painted brick houses were similar in style and size and were built for $10,000 each. In 1873, the Stowes paid $15,000 for their house, which included a plot of land that measured seventy-five by one-hundred-and-fifty feet, gas fixtures, and the right to use the shared driveway.[79] Stowe was relieved that the smaller house would be easier to maintain than Oakholm: "It will not be an expensive place to keep like my other," she wrote to the twins. "We have a pretty yard in front and space for a little flower garden in back."[80] Because the house was fairly small at 5,000 square feet (relative to Oakholm and some of the neighbors' houses, such as Mark Twain's, which reached 13,000 square feet) and newly built, Stowe did little to it upon taking ownership; the alterations she effected entailed bringing the outdoors in: she added a portico to the front of the house, a trellis on the rear (south) side of the house, and small porches on the east and west sides. Beyond these structural elements, her main work consisted of decorating the interior and cultivating numerous gardens around the house.[81]

Though less picturesque and ornate than Oakholm, Stowe was drawn to the house's setting and its several bay windows on the north and west sides—both brought much sunlight into the house. It also contained many Gothic Revival details, including decorative cast-iron scrollwork on the balconies, barge-board cutouts on the two dormers, dormer scrolls at their bases, and decorative chimney pots. A thoroughly modern house, coal-burning fireplaces figured in the coldest rooms—those on the north and east sides of the house, such as the front and back parlors. The dining room in the southwest corner of the house and the bedroom above it did not have fireplaces.

Upon entering the Forest Street house (the only one of Stowe's properties to survive as a house museum today) the visitor arrived in a spacious front hall and found a commodious and comfortable interior with front and rear parlors on the north side of the house and a large dining room and kitchen on the south side. Upstairs a similar floor plan contained four bedrooms and one bathing-room. Stowe took care to showcase her values in the decoration of her interior space. In the front hall, for example, she kept lancet-arched bookcases filled with anti-slavery tracts—a sign to visitors of her political beliefs.[82] A lover of the principles of Charles Eastlake, whose *Hints on Household Taste in Furniture, Upholstery, and Other Details* was published in the United States in 1869, Stowe espoused many high Victorian decorating principles—the type with which Wharton came of age and abhorred as an adult. Like Wharton's mother, Stowe covered her walls with elaborate wallpaper, layered carpets on the floors, upholstered furniture with dark velvet, and displayed a great deal of bric-a-brac, such as gifts from England, small marble and bronze statues, and numerous books and photographs. Her walls were also adorned with artwork of her own production—paintings of flowers, birds, or nature scenes—or with paintings of the Madonna and Child from Europe and works by affordable regional landscape artists.[83] Each of these decorating choices evoked the trends that emerged in the late-nineteenth century and that high Victorianism became so well known for; her preferences also helped reveal who Stowe had become as a successful and enterprising woman.

Most middle-class homeowners in the 1870s and 1880s embraced the clutter that made the high Victorian aesthetic famous; an abundance of artifacts, books, curios, paintings, and the like, signified the wealth and aspirations of the homeowner. The more things one possessed, the more successfully one could showcase one's attributes. Briefly put, in the postwar era of mechanization and technological development, people (both middle and working classes) had more money and more time to purchase more goods, which were mass-produced more cheaply and advertised more widely than ever before. Simultaneously, the variety and amount of goods increased. Department stores and mail-order catalogs turned local markets into national ones and the proliferation of chain and franchise stores (as well as the increase in the number of women's magazines and the proliferation of gendered advertising) gradually brought about the shift from a society of producers to a society of consumers. As Thomas Schlereth has written, "The 'good life' came to mean the 'goods life.'"[84] Likewise, belongings came to signify "belonging." When Stowe was moving into the Forest Street house, however, "the tyranny of things" that took hold of Lillie Seymour in *Pink and White Tyranny* and that William Dean Howells would inveigh against in the 1890s was just beginning to take hold of the country's consumers. Stowe exemplified a somewhat tamer version of the voracious shoppers who would emerge in the late 1880s and 1890s.

Stowe was not inured to the pleasures of materialism and the development of one's aesthetic taste (recall that she had refined her own sensibilities during her three trips to Europe in the 1850s), and though her new Forest Street house was smaller and simpler than Oakholm, she took pride in displaying a great deal of bric-a-brac in her first floor parlors. Each item in the public rooms of Stowe's Forest Street house held a different key to understanding the author's many achievements: her variety of books showcased her love of learning; family photos highlighted her love of family and sentiment; plants underscored her interest in new sciences such as botany and taxidermy; exotic artifacts and sculptures emphasized her past travels abroad and interest in foreign cultures; her own artwork revealed her lack of "idle hands" and her artistic sensibility; finally, opulent fabrics in her two parlors on the floors, furniture, and walls, as well as the display of china and silver in glass-front cabinets, exposed the family's status and wealth.

In the front parlor, against the backdrop of heavily-patterned walls and carpets, Stowe placed little sofas, black ottomans, and a large, drop-leaf table that she may have used for writing. Into the dining room, she moved a glass bookcase—the type Eastlake popularized—and "five or six mahogany chairs" from Oakholm. Upstairs, Stowe added furniture from previous homes, including "the mahogany bedstead with mahogany bureau and table that used to be in Papa's room" for the second floor front bedroom and "the old dining room chairs [which] can be used in different rooms as needed."[85] The artistic, industrious Stowe also painted furniture that needed a bit of refreshing, such as a pine bedroom set. As much as Stowe embraced Victorian decoration and Charles Eastlake, she eschewed some typical elements of the style such as heavy drapery, preferring instead to let the sun shine through lightweight muslin curtains, as she had allowed in Little Eva's room some twenty years earlier. Overall, the furnishing of the house was considered "altogether simple, as suits with its character, and with the moderate circumstances of its occupants." Simple perhaps, but not without its charm, as Joseph Twitchell continued: "Yet it is a thoroughly attractive and charming home; for it bears throughout, in every detail of arrangement, the signature of that refined taste which has the art and secret of giving an air of grace to whatever it touches."[86]

Stowe and her sister Catharine dramatized the importance of aesthetic display and the "correctness of taste" in *The American Woman's Home*. In chapter six of the book, entitled "Home Decoration," the sisters instruct, "[The aesthetic element] holds a place of great significance among the influences which make home happy and attractive, which give it a constant and wholesome power over the young, and contributes much to the education of the entire household in refinement, intellectual development, and moral sensibility" (71). They further teach that by surrounding oneself and one's children with objects of beauty and "reminders of history and art," children would be "constantly trained to correctness of taste and refinement of thought" (78).

Written as the sisters' attempt to revive a nation dismayed by the recent war and to offer a point of stability amid the great geographic and social upheaval of the 1860s, the broad theme of the book was to garner appreciation and respect for women's duties at home and to stress that women's tasks were as important as the male professions. Beecher and Stowe argued that a healthful, Christian home would produce healthful, Christian citizens, which in turn would create a united, Christian nation.[87] A woman's work included the "sacred and important" duties of supervising "the care and nursing of the body in the critical periods of infancy and sickness," "the training of the human mind in the most impressible period of childhood," and "the government and economies of the family state" (19). While the book became the era's standard domestic handbook, it contains an intriguing irony: like Stowe's earlier work, *House and Home Papers*, its primary message—the need for women to create well-run, secure homes—was promulgated by two women who failed to achieve this goal in their own lives. As Nicole Tonkovich has pointed out, Catharine too was an unlikely author for the book, for she neither married nor ever owned a home.[88] Yet in the first chapter of the book, the authors note the incontestable importance for a woman to secure and run a well-ordered home: "The best end for a woman to seek is the training of God's children for their eternal home [...] she will aim to secure a house so planned that it will provide in the best manner for health, industry, and economy, those cardinal requisites of domestic enjoyment and success" (23–24).

The Beecher sisters dwelled in worlds divergent from those of their middle-class readers. From the beginning of their lives, they were different, destined to greatness because of the large and influential evangelical family from which they came. They enjoyed the added benefit of being supported in their efforts by their father—not something most women of the early nineteenth century could claim. They grew up to become educators, reformers, trendsetters, and outspoken leaders for women's roles in society. That did not mean they had to live by the standards they set for the general reading public; in fact, because they accomplished so much in their lives, it seems reasonable that they would not adhere to those ideals. While Catharine kept her life clear of a husband and child so she could focus on her larger purpose in life—elevating women's work in the home to a domestic science—Stowe struggled with each of the potential pitfalls the authors call attention to in the book: her children's ill-health, their lack of industry, and their spendthrift ways.

The account book that Stowe kept for Hartford and Florida illuminates the manner in which Stowe and her daughters lived, and underscores the lavishness of their lifestyle. Stowe paid each of her two servants and gardener about five dollars a week and employed a retinue of carpenters and other household laborers, such as women who washed and ironed.[89] Stowe did not refrain from buying expensive accoutrements for herself or her twin daughters; routine purchases included bonnets and ribbon, cambric and embroidery, parasols and veils. The Stowes also enjoyed a rich and expensive diet, regularly consuming brandy, butter, ice cream and candy, oysters, and many different types of meat such as hen, turkey, venison, mutton, and sausage.[90] Stowe's notations, though haphazard, underscore her financial concerns and her efforts to keep track of her finances; they also illustrate a degree of luxury that may have prevented Hattie, Eliza, and Georgiana from taking household duties seriously. It is hard to know if Stowe required much hired help because her daughters failed in their household responsibilities or if she chose to hire the help first, and as a result, bred extravagant daughters. What we do know is that, like other contradictions in Stowe's life, the author employed servants as early as 1840 when she was a young mother living in Cincinnati, while, in her writing, she advocates the servant-less home.

Until the end of her long life, Harriet Beecher Stowe remained prolific and active, writing letters to family and friends, corresponding with editors, visiting with her grandchildren by Georgiana and Charles, and painting still lifes until her death in 1896. She was fond of wandering around Nook Farm picking flowers, and was known for trampling across Mark Twain's lawn to do so.[91] After the death of Calvin Stowe in 1886, a great deal of Stowe's burden was lifted; she had been his full-time nurse during the last two years of his life. For the remaining decade, until her death, Stowe lived solely at Forest Street with her twin daughters and enjoyed visits from family and friends.[92]

~ ~ ~

When Harriet Beecher Stowe wrote *House and Home Papers* in the midst of the Civil War in 1864, she was an established and confident writer of 53 years, who beseeched young wives and mothers to embrace the home for its immense importance. In the book, Stowe asserted: "There are many women who know how to keep a house, but there are but few that know how to keep a home."[93] At the time, Stowe was trying to inspire herself as much as her readers. She set the challenge for herself to create not houses, but homes. Did Stowe achieve this goal?

Looking back over Stowe's long life and at her varied endeavors at Andover, Oakholm, Mandarin, and Forest Street, one remembers her fatigue and the monumentality of the tasks that she set for herself (and that usually she insisted on performing alone). She was a brilliant, driven woman who never stopped writing, plotting, building, designing, and decorating. In spite of her perfectionist tendencies, Stowe moved in many directions, leaving much in disarray. The interiors of her houses—her domestic life, in general—resembled "undress rehearsals," as she so accurately put it. The final place where Stowe dwelled—and where she died—in the house on Forest Street, was the simplest of her many domestic experiments: she did not design the house or oversee its construction; she did not write as prolifically here as at any other home; she had fewer people to manage; and for twelve years, it was the only house she owned. The dwelling was one of her smallest and by far the easiest to run; it included only a modest-sized plot of land and was located in a dynamic and convenient neighborhood. But Stowe's years on Forest Street were her happiest; when she died there at age eighty-five, she could rest peacefully, for, finally, the performance was over.

CHAPTER TWO

William Dean Howells:
Realism in Transit

"No man living always at home was ever so little under his own roof."
—William Dean Howells, *A Modern Instance* (1882)

In 1918, when William Dean Howells was eighty-one years old, he wrote to his sister Aurelia: "I have told you about my frequent dreaming of the dead, the earlier and the later; and last night I had a long dream about going to housekeeping with Elinor in a new Cambridge house. It is always in some new place."[1] After his wife Elinor died in 1910, Howells dreamt of her if not every day, at least once a week. Very often, his dreams, like the one recounted here, entailed housekeeping or house-hunting. In reality, Howells spent decades searching for the perfect home, and moved so often that one cannot help but wonder what was behind his and his wife's relentless itineration. Only in the last two decades of his life did Howells have a place he could call his own: the cottage in Kittery Point, Maine, from which this letter was written. This was the only house that Howells lived in consistently for many years, and tellingly, it is the only one that stayed in the Howells family long after the author died.[2]

Throughout his long life, Howells, a beloved and compassionate family man, relinquished countless homes to satisfy the needs of someone else, whether his wife Elinor, his daughters Winny and Pilla, or his son John. But he also had his own reasons for moving with such constancy: Howells was at the forefront of American realism in the late nineteenth century, and as an influential writer and editor, he was always looking for new material. That Howells never forgot the frequent changes he made on the home-front is attested to by his recurring dreams of housekeeping and by letters of his later years in which he revisits (spiritually or physically) the house in Cambridge that he and his wife had planned to "live in always." As far as Howells's search for a home was concerned, there was no "always"; there were only a few years at most.

What were the reasons for Howells's unusual history of continually changing residences? As suggested above, his moves provided endless sources of material for his writing; Howells was a dedicated and influential writer, and he often noted that each locale supplied excellent fodder for new observations. Howells also epitomized the late-nineteenth-century American middle-class citizen who sought the best that his money could buy and thus he felt the need to improve his home. As he purchased larger and more elegant houses, Howells grew more uncomfortable with his wealth and conspicuous consumption, and then chose to downsize. Perhaps his wife, Elinor, was the restless one with whom he complied, or perhaps Howells himself could not tolerate staying in one place too long—for friends and visitors stopped by often and wearied him. Many reasons lie behind Howells's search for the perfect dwelling; studying his moves and motives offers a unique, three-dimensional means of getting to know a great American author in a way other than through his writing.

Though Howells, Henry James, and Edith Wharton—the subjects who follow him in chapters three and four respectively—are often grouped together as three of America's greatest realists, their lives and concerns were profoundly different. Unlike Henry James, a close friend for over fifty years and a lifelong bachelor, Howells was a married man with three children when he began writing novels in the early 1870s. Unlike Edith Wharton, whom many consider his literary successor and who was independently wealthy, he had to work for his living. Because Howells had no early claim to any type of elite culture—as James and Wharton did—he broke into the literary world on his own and spent most of his adult life working at a full-time editorial job so that he could pay his bills. In his relentless hard work and lifelong concern about not having enough money, he most resembles his literary and chronological predecessor, Stowe, who was born a quarter of a century before him. Even when Howells was in his seventies, he continued to write a monthly "Easy Chair" column for *Harper's Monthly*, assuring him a fixed income of $5,000 per year. In spite of his rural, poor, Ohioan background, Howells became one of the nation's most respected and well-known authors and editors; his rise in status and wealth exemplifies that of the self-made man of late-nineteenth-century America.

Yet Howells's success, like Stowe's, did not come without its costs. Reading his fifty-year correspondence with family members, friends, and colleagues reveals a man for whom the living was not easy. Like many in his time, he was caught in the wheels of a country moving at a breakneck pace, and as a result, often his life changed too quickly even for him to keep up with it. Torn between the simplicity of his humble past and the comfort of his successful present, Howells lived in a state of almost continual conflict. His letters home reveal a number of ongoing tensions: his desire to be financially secure combined with his distaste for money (and for capitalism and consumerism in general); his debate over living in the country versus in the city; his conflict between working in journalism and writing literature; and his ambivalence about living the good life or embracing the simple life.

Each of these challenges is reflected in the number of houses, neighborhoods, and cities in which Howells and his family dwelled. Dubbed the "most addressless man I know" by Henry James and "singularly migratory" by friend and protégé Hamlin Garland, Howells changed residences so often that the number is matched only by that of his fictional characters, Mr. and Mrs. Basil March, whose search for a home Howells chronicled in *A Hazard of New Fortunes* (1890). These dislocations suggest his ambivalence towards home-ownership and upward mobility, spotlighting the same concerns felt by Americans in general in the late nineteenth century. While Howells quickly ascended to editor of the *Atlantic Monthly* and purchased a Beacon Street town house by the time he was forty-five, he detested the social inequality he saw around him in the post-Civil War world. At fifty, he sold his prominent home, embraced socialist doctrines fervently, wrote less romantic novels, and inhabited smaller and increasingly simple houses, spending his final years in a cottage in Maine and occasionally in his New York City apartment. While conflicted, not many Americans at this time—especially those who had achieved a similar level of success and fame like Stowe before him and Wharton after—relinquished so much for so little. In his ultimate abdication of large houses and superfluous things, Howells joined key socialists of the era: Edward Bellamy, Laurence Gronlund, and Richard T. Ely.

The themes of house hunting, home-making, and the conflict between upward mobility and social inequality are paramount in Howells's novels, particularly those written in the 1880s after he gave up the editorship of the *Atlantic Monthly* to focus exclusively on writing literature. For example, *A Modern Instance* (1882) follows newlyweds Bartley Hubbard and Marcia Gaylord as they seek to establish their first home in Boston; *The Rise of Silas Lapham* (1885) traces Vermonter Silas Lapham's migration east, subsequent mobility within Boston, and his ultimate purchase of a custom-built house in Boston's Back Bay; and *A Hazard of New Fortunes* documents the Marches' move from Boston to New York and the ensuing journey to find the perfect place of residence. Howells's novels generally, and the novels from the 1880s in particular, treat issues that the author was confronting in his own life—marriage, journalism, house-hunting, social mobility and social inequality—and, like the author's own houses, provide useful lenses through which to examine his domestic and philosophical preoccupations.

~ ~ ~

William Dean Howells was born in 1837 and grew up in a large, close-knit family in the small town of Jefferson, Ohio, the second child and second son of printer William Cooper Howells and Mary Dean Howells. Howells's father was a Free-Soiler and Swedenborgian who edited an Ohioan newspaper and published a Swedenborgian one on the side, and once took his family to live in a log cabin for a year as an experiment in utopian living. Howells's parents raised their eight children in a fashion that was liberal, experimental, and idealistic. When his formal education ended at the age of ten, the young Howells, or Will, as he was known, went to assist his father in the printing office; soon thereafter his father began publishing his son's poems in local magazines; the first one appeared in the *Ohio State Journal* in 1852 when Howells was fifteen.

In his numerous letters—published and unpublished—Howells's closeness to his many siblings and parents becomes readily apparent. For over fifty years, he diligently wrote a letter home every Sunday, and when this was not possible, he expressed his apologies at the top of the next missive. He offered literary guidance to many friends and family members including his father, his daughters, his sister Annie, and friends like Henry James and Mark Twain; and he provided financial assistance to less successful family members, like his brothers Sam, Joe, and Henry (who was developmentally delayed).

In spite of popularity, success, and kindliness—traits highlighted in the biographies—Howells's life was wracked with personal turmoil. "Dear heaven! The way is *so* rough and hard!" he lamented in a letter to his father early in his career.[3] For over five decades, Howells complained about a lack of money, time, energy, and good health, and yearned for "a little respectable commonplace"[4]—a simple path without the daily struggles to which he felt subjected. Only when Howells was in his seventies did his fear of not having enough money begin to subside. At this time, a new Howells emerges, one who has become much less restless and who can now focus exclusively on two pursuits: writing and joining his wife in heaven—his final home.

James's depiction of Howells as "a most addressless man" was no exaggeration. Between 1866 when Howells returned from a post as consul to the United States in Venice, and 1902 when he purchased the cottage in Kittery Point, Maine, Howells did not live in a single residence for more than four years.[5] Over these thirty-six years, he lived in three houses in Cambridge; one in Belmont, Massachusetts; four apartments in Boston; more than a dozen apartments, hotels, and boarding houses in New York City; and countless summer rentals along the east coast, to which he and his family would escape when the city was too hot or crowded.[6]

The Early Years: Cambridge, Massachusetts, 1866–1878

In 1866, back from four years in Italy, Howells moved with his wife, Elinor Mead Howells, and daughter, Winifred ("Winny"), to Cambridge, Massachusetts, and began work at the *Atlantic* in Boston. Howells elected to leave his first stateside position at the *Nation* in New York City after only a few months for the career possibilities promised by James T. Fields, editor of the *Atlantic*: Howells could likely succeed him within five years. As far as setting up a home was concerned, Howells and his wife chose to live in Cambridge instead of Boston (where the couple briefly rented an apartment on Bulfinch Street) for a number of practical reasons: relief from the city, lower housing costs, and proximity to his friend, mentor, and *North American Review* editor, Charles Eliot Norton, who lived nearby in an 1807 mansion set on thirty-four acres. Unlike Norton, who inherited "Shady Hill," as his property was called, Howells bought a relatively new, unremarkable "carpenter's box" at 41 Sacramento Street—a "high-perched little wooden house set back from the street with gardens, fruit trees, and grass all around it." About a mile from Harvard University and the Cambridge Common on one side and Porter Station on the other, Howells described the neighborhood in *Suburban Sketches* as "a frontier between city and country."[7] The young family was delighted with their first home, which they were able to purchase with the financial help of Elinor's father and Norton's co-signature on the mortgage.[8]

In the beginning, the modest clapboard house, which is still standing, provided a pleasant existence for Howells, Elinor, and Winny, who had been born in Venice in 1863. A second child, son John, was born at the Sacramento Street house in 1868. The family employed two live-in servants (a cook and a nanny) and, after the birth of John, a wet nurse.[9] Winny and John loved playing in the surrounding fields and with the cows and chickens across the road, and Howells liked being able to call upon his intellectual mentors Charles Eliot Norton, Henry Longfellow, and James Russell Lowell, who all lived in capacious, aristocratic houses relatively close by. Elinor spent her days accompanying Howells on his social calls, paying visits of her own, shopping, or sewing (though she loved to shop, she made almost all of the children's clothing and much of her own). The family's most regular guests were Howells or Mead family members and friends like the Samuel Clemenses who lived in Hartford, Connecticut, and came to stay for a few days at a time. On the surface, everyone seemed happy, as Howells summed up in a letter to Norton:

> We are safely housed here in 'Cottage Quiet,' and have commenced the long-deferred process of feeling at home, and of growing old. There is a fine sense of landed proprietorship about the present experiment which is as novel as it is agreeable, and which pleases me almost as much as the security and peace in which we live.[10]

"Cottage Quiet," as Howells referred to it, lay far enough beyond the hustle and bustle of Harvard Station to offer tranquility and, because of its modest size and appointments, was not large or extravagant enough to be overwhelming. At first glance, it seems that Howells and his family were eager to settle down and make Sacramento Street their home for many years—a place where they could "grow old." However, Howells's letter raises perplexing contradictions. He refers to his present situation as an "experiment"—hinting at its impermanence in spite of his praise for the situation. His language also recalls his own father's "experiment" when he took the family to live in a log cabin for a year. The apparent conflict between "experimenting" and "settling down" signals a certain remote, writerly approach to life, as well as a perhaps unconscious wanderlust. In this letter, Howells seems to take the stance of a writer looking down on his life, considering it from enough remove to see it as material. It is possible that he viewed each station in his life in the same way he did the circumstances invented in his fiction—as impermanent or illusory.

Howells's subtle ambivalence toward Sacramento Street belies the way in which the house met the family's needs. A straightforward box—thus the name "carpenter's box"—the house was comprised of four main rooms on the first floor, a kitchen behind them, and four on the second, as well as two small rooms for the staff in the attic. The rooms were snugly furnished according to Howells, their chief adornments carpets, books, and family mementos. Most of the furniture was passed down from the Howells or Mead families, except for a new study-chair, which Howells proudly purchased in late 1868. On the walls hung family portraits drawn by Elinor and small photographs, which the family liked to display. Also on view were "a few poor relics" of Howells's mother who died in 1869, and plants, including pots of ivy and a scarlet geranium that Howells felt "furnish[ed] the whole room."[11] The overall atmosphere was homey, comfortable, and relaxed—not unlike the place where the author grew up.

The "process of feeling at home" came intermittently at best, however, for interposed with this harmonious existence were Howells's immensely long hours of work: by day, assisting James Fields at the office of the *Atlantic* with soliciting, editing, and rejecting manuscripts, and by night, at his own desk, writing. The magazine was not yet ten years old when Howells was hired, and thus, he was soon welcomed as a regular contributor to the magazine in edition to being the editor's assistant. Juggling the two proved to be an exhausting task, and Howells complained frequently of "broken wrists" in his letters home. Yet he refused to abandon literary writing for editorial work, telling his father in 1866: "My object in life [is] to write books, and not to edit magazines."[12]

Howells's first published works, *Venetian Life* (1866) and *Italian Journeys* (1867), detailed his life in Italy from 1861 to 1865, where, it was said, he spent the Civil War in a "Venetian gondola." Many other works sprang from his walks around Cambridge. For example, his collection *Suburban Sketches* (1871), featured a piece called "Doorstep Acquaintance," which tells of organ grinders and beggars whom Howells saw on Sacramento Street, while another in the collection, "Pedestrian Tour," was his attempt to "interest people in a stroll I take from Sacramento Street up through the Brickyards and the Irish village of Dublin near by, and so down through North Avenue."[13] His first novel, *Their Wedding Journey*, was not published until 1871, and also drew upon material from Howells's life: his wedding journey in France and Italy after he married Elinor in 1862.

From the outset, Howells's work was grounded in reality and based upon his observations of daily life, which is not to say that the endeavor was easy. Explaining his subject matter and style to the young Henry James, whom he greatly admired and with whom he became friends, Howells wrote:

I have in type "A Romance of Real Life" which records a droll and curious experience of mine. In some ways these things seem rather small business to me; but I fell naturally into doing them; I persuaded myself (too fondly, perhaps) that they're a new kind of study of our life, and I have an impression that they're to lead me to some higher sort of performance. They're not easy to do, but cost me a great deal of work. They seem to be pretty well liked, and I'm told are looked for by readers."[14]

This letter reveals Howells's many reasons for working in the style that would come to be called realism: writing directly from life came naturally to him. The style was original and fresh, and his readers enjoyed his voice. Most importantly, the letter underscores the novelty of a style that owes its popularity directly to Howells. Howells was writing "a new kind of study of our life," and, as the eventual editor of a highly regarded magazine, he would influence an entire generation of writers who followed him, including Stephen Crane, Theodore Dreiser, Edith Wharton, Paul Laurence Dunbar, and W. E. B. DuBois. He continued to write about the world around him for the rest of his life in non-fictional essays and novels.

In spite of his quick success and public displays of happiness, financial insecurity and stress from overwork prevailed privately. In a letter to his father from this period, Howells questions his career choice and evinces a remarkable loss of innocence:

When I reflect upon this life which I have desired to live, and now live, I do not think it is by any means an easy one. I work almost ceaselessly, and never stop except from exhaustion; I am full of cares and anxieties, and I gain just enough money to live on. In literature it costs just as much to make a failure as a success.[15]

In his early thirties when he wrote this letter, Howells confronts head on his decision to be a writer and an editor. Not only does he face the reality of his chosen field—that even failure is expensive— but also the fact that no matter how hard he works, neither success nor money is guaranteed. Howells's uncertainty over the time spent on editing instead of writing recalls a similar dilemma faced by Bartley Hubbard in *A Modern Instance* (1882), who struggles with whether to become a journalist or a lawyer. While Bartley is torn between journalism and law, rather than fiction writing and editorial work like Howells, the voice of Bartley's future mother-in-law nevertheless resonates with that in Howells's head: "'He'd better give up his paper and go into the law. He's done well in the paper, and he's a smart writer; but editing a newspaper aint any work for a man. It's all well enough as long as he's single, but when he's got a wife to look after, he'd better get down to *work*."[16] Just as Bartley's prospective mother-in-law reveals, husbands are expected to choose a profession that earns them money, rather than one that they enjoy. Bartley's future mother-in-law thus gives expression to precisely the dilemma faced by Howells, who is afraid of not making enough money in one career (fiction writing) but is uneager to gain his livelihood solely from another (editorial work). The result is an uneasy balance of the two.

Howells's discontent with the arduousness of his chosen profession and the echo of this theme in his novel offer clues to the sources of tension in Howells's life. He disliked working primarily as an editor and secondarily as a novelist; he faced an uphill battle as a public figure trying to introduce a new style of writing to American readers; and, he was clearly concerned about the financial prospects of his chosen field. His private journals from the 1860s and 1870s are punctuated with fits of accounting in which he notes expenditures for small items like books and envelopes (he bought an extraordinary number of envelopes because he was such a prolific letter writer) and records each purchase to the cent. But because, like Stowe's, these notations never continue for more than a few days at a time, they also reveal the sporadic nature of such economies.[17] Part idealistic socialist, part realist businessman, Howells could not decide if he wanted to make a lot of money in his lifetime or not. In spite of financial stress, he regularly inveighed against having an excess of money—against excess of any kind—writing his father in 1869, "I feel so deeply the idleness of the worldly success I most strive for."[18] Late in his life, when his financial health was secure, his frugality remains, as if Howells could not by nature embrace profligacy.[19]

The peacefulness of the setting at Sacramento Street was short-lived also due to the changing demographics of the neighborhood; a great influx of Irish immigrants made Howells and his wife feel like outsiders. In late 1869, after living for only three years in the neighborhood, Howells wrote Charles Eliot Norton, "Our Sacramento Street has lately become much less desirable than it was. Irish have moved in."[20] Like many urban and suburban dwellers in the early 1870s, Howells was forced to reconfigure his idea of domesticity due to the changing environment around him, and, tired of hearing the "clamor of Irish children about us all day," he decided to move.[21]

In 1871, Howells was made the third editor of the *Atlantic*, following James Russell Lowell (1857–1861) and James T. Fields (1861–1871). The promotion brought not only greater visibility but also a much higher salary—the $3,500 a year he made as assistant editor rose to $10,000.[22] For the first time, the family could contemplate purchasing a property on their own, without the help of family or friends. For the time being, however, they were satisfied to rent a property at 3 Berkeley Street, which had recently become available. This house offered two features that the couple sought: extra space for guests and, most importantly, good neighbors. These factors—good location, ample space for entertaining, and prominent neighbors—were important as Howells gained renown as a Boston editor. He could not entertain guests in a neighborhood that, as he put it, had become undesirable. Pleased with the size of their new abode, Elinor crowed in a letter to her sister-in-law, Victoria Howells, "We have two guest chambers in this house so you see we are more ready for you than ever." She also cited the "good neighbors"—among them Longfellow and Richard Henry Dana.[23]

When Howells and his wife learned, after living there for two years, that the Berkeley Street house was ultimately not for sale, the "daring family" embarked on another "experiment," as Howells referred to his search for a home, and decided to buy a plot of land and build a house on a neighboring street, Concord Avenue. The plot of land for the new home, bought for $3,750, was located on the desirable side of Massachusetts Avenue and was closer to the Cambridge Common, assuring the Howellses a fine address.[24] For an additional $6,000, Elinor worked with a carpenter to design the two-story, wood-frame, mansard-roofed house.

While the house on Concord Avenue was not as grand or formal as the 18th and 19th century houses on Berkeley and Brattle Streets, it was well located: down the hill from the Harvard Observatory. It was a practical house with four bedrooms on the second floor—enough for the growing family (a third and final child, daughter Mildred, or "Pilla", as she was known, was born at Berkeley Street in 1872)—five more on the attic floor, a good location, plenty of sunlight, several open fireplaces, and a furnace. Family friend John Fiske deemed the house built "with an express view to economical management," rather than to aesthetic beauty, but at least the star editor, thirty-five when he moved in, could now entertain his friends and colleagues at home. Howells also had a more spacious study, which Fiske noted was "finished in chestnut with a frescoed ceiling."[25] Elinor added a number of artistic touches to several rooms as well, including her husband's monogram on either side of the fireplace mantel in his library.[26]

Though, on some levels, the decision to build and buy a home made sense for the rising star and his family, it also aroused dis-ease. In an 1872 letter to James, Howells refers to his family in the third person and terms the plan an adventure, just as he had called Sacramento Street "an experiment": "We take a very great interest in the new house which this daring family has begun to build."[27] Howells's position as an outsider looking in suggests that he may have been largely an observer to a move instigated primarily by Elinor. Though by all accounts, the Howellses had a close and companionate marriage for nearly fifty years, they differed greatly on two subjects: money and social status. Both were important to Elinor. She came from a large, patrician East Coast family and was not used to, and did not like, economizing; Howells, by contrast, was frugal by nature. Elinor enjoyed living comfortably, if not extravagantly, while Howells was content to live modestly. A minute example of their differences lies in their stationery: Elinor used engraved, embossed paper with her address at the top of each page, while Howells used plain white, thin paper. Unlike her husband, Elinor comes across in her correspondence as concerned with keeping up with the neighbors and knowing the right people, two prime factors in the move to Concord Avenue. Howells's enthusiasm was muted by the problem of money yet the fact that Howells could own a home, even design and build one to his liking, attests to his wealth.

In spite of good fortune and monetary success, Howells's financial insecurity is understandable. He was well aware of his position as a "working man" who had to "earn his bread," in contrast to the rarefied Bostonians with whom he socialized, most of them East Coast college graduates with ancestral estates. Like many of his fictional characters, Howells was a relative newcomer among established elites. He never fails, in his fiction and non-fiction, to register the irony of his acceptance by this set. Howells worked hard to fit in like his character Bartley Hubbard about whom he wrote: "He heard a great deal of talk that he did not understand, but he eagerly treasured every impression, and pieced it out by question or furtive observation into an image often shrewdly true [. . .] He civilized himself as rapidly as his light permitted."[28] In public, Howells assumed a posture of surprise and humility, which, in the case of James, for instance, probably made Howells's growing financial and professional successes easier to accept.

In 1872, Howells and his family were securely installed in their home at 37 Concord Avenue. Howells, now forty-five, had managed to accomplish all that he set out to when he came east: he had a wife, three children, a home, and a soaring career (Figure 2.1). Still, contentment escaped him. In many ways Howells was like his handwriting: small, tame, and constrained. He was somehow incapable of embracing his accomplishments. With one eye on his station in life and another focused on the outside world, Howells often dwelled upon the circumstances of his friends, balancing his wares against theirs. A classic victim of what Thorstein Veblen would label "invidious comparison," in which a relentlessly comparative mindset leads inevitably to discontent, he envied the lifestyles of his two closest friends, Henry James and Mark Twain, whom he met in the 1860s.[29] For Howells, Twain embodied ease, wealth, and community, while James epitomized writerly solitude with geographic and artistic freedom. Expressing his envy of James's lot and dissatisfaction with his own, Howells wrote to James in 1870: "I think longingly of the places you look on," adding that he found the current literary world at home "generally very dull."[30] Clearly, Howells saw his life from the vantage point of someone trying desperately to put the myriad pieces together.

By comparison, James enjoyed the freedom that only a single man can: living in various European capitals, relying on wealthy friends for lodging and food, and settling down in England, far from the ties that bind. At the other end of the spectrum, Twain enjoyed a small and secure community, living among a circle of friends at Nook Farm in Hartford, Connecticut, that included the writer Charles Dudley Warner and his wife, Susan Lee Warner, Harriet Beecher Stowe and her husband Calvin Stowe, and other Beecher, Stowe, and Hooker family members. While Twain did not come from money, he seems to have been much less conflicted about accumulating and spending it—which he did famously—especially when it came to building his mansion in Hartford from 1871 to 1874, in what amounted to Stowe's backyard.

Even though Howells and his wife were, on one level, deeply suspicious of consumerism and ostentation, they took note of other houses being built contemporaneously, for example, the "most-exalted fairy-palace" that Twain constructed in Hartford during the same period. They couldn't help but note that the Concord Avenue house, though larger than their two previous houses in Cambridge, and featuring Howells's favorite French mansard roof with dormers, hardly compared to nearby mansions.[31] These included the colonial Longfellow and Ruggles mansions, both built in the mid-eighteenth century on Brattle Street; Lowell's Elmwood built in 1767; and the immense Second Empire houses on Craigie and Buckingham Streets, one and two blocks away from Concord Avenue. Howells's narrow home with its simple front door, clapboard siding, and slate mansard roof made it a very modest variation on the elaborate Victorian dwellings of its era. Hamlin Garland, fellow literary critic, writer, and friend, called the Concord Avenue house Howells's "first poor home," noting that it "suffered the dusty side of the road" and approximated Sacramento Street in its "bleakness and humility."[32] In her letters, Mrs. Howells sized up Concord Avenue to the Warner's house in Hartford, echoing Marcia Gaylord in *A Modern Instance*, who finds her new house "too little for [her] happiness."[33] Like Marcia, Elinor takes comfort in the prospect of another, larger house on the horizon: the "Belmont chalet."[34]

Working relentlessly between 1872 and 1877, Howells became an ever-brighter spot on the literary map, so bright in fact that the house on Concord Avenue, with perhaps too good a location, was soon besieged with visitors. Howells bemoaned the amount of time and energy wasted on socializing for his editorial work: "Our lives are devoured by people we don't care for," he complained to his father in 1877, adding that the parties always "leave a bad taste in the mouth."[35] After four and a half years on Concord Avenue, he decided to sell the house and put some distance between himself and his work. Opting for Belmont, a town five miles from Cambridge that was serviced by a train that ran directly to Harvard Station and Boston, Howells hoped the new location would enable him to focus more on writing and less on receiving guests.

Howells's numerous moves in and around Cambridge and Boston might best be understood as attempts to have it all—the creative solitude of James's life and the ease and community of Twain's—yet in attempting to have it all, Howells ended up feeling like he had little, and in spite of his success and kindness, he remained out of reach to others. Edith Wharton, the subject of chapter four, recalled in her autobiography the extent of Howells's elusiveness:

> [He] was [. . .] another irreducible recluse, and though I was in a way accredited to him by my friendship with his two old friends, Charles Norton and Henry James, I seldom met him. I always regretted this, for I had a great admiration for *A Modern Instance* and *Silas Lapham*, and should have liked to talk with their author about the art in which he stood so nearly among the first; and he himself, whenever we met, was full of quiet friendliness [. . .] Though I felt he was amicably disposed, he remained inaccessible.[36]

What kept Howells "inaccessible"? Perhaps his distance was intentional, a manner of self-protection; he was enormously influential and was overwhelmed with requests for favors. But his aloofness may have been due to insecurity—the realization that no matter how much he achieved, he would never be born to privilege as so many of his friends had been.

"Redtop": The Belmont Chalet, 1878–1882

The Howells's move to the country setting of Belmont mirrored a widespread trend in the late-nineteenth-century United States. After the Civil War, the American home—and particularly the suburban home—was viewed increasingly as a refuge from the heterogeneous city. Just as the move across Massachusetts Avenue a few years earlier protected the Howellses from overrun streets, so too the move to Belmont was intended as a refuge from the city. As Gwendolyn Wright asserts in *Building the Dream*, "Those who moved to the new suburbs were assured of an escape from the problems of poor health, social unrest, and vice associated with urban life."[37] While the move to Belmont promised fresh air and expansive fields where Howells's children could play (his three children were now fifteen, ten, and six years old), as well as relief from the dirt, dust, and immigrants of the city, it also offered the author the possibility of seclusion and quietude that he sought for writing. For Howells, the move equally involved prioritizing his imaginative ambitions (writing) and his intimates (family) over the demands of his urban editorial career. Set atop a hill with wide views of Boston and the harbor, the new house was surrounded by gardens, farms, and fields, a far cry from the dusty, noisy streets of Cambridge.

Located far up Somerset Street, a country lane leading from the village's main road (Pleasant Street), the plot upon which the house was built was surrounded by cattle, horse, and garden farms. Outlying areas were populated with magnificent summer estates built in the 1850s and 1860s, while year-round residents lived mainly along Pleasant Street near the Wellington Hill train station. As small as the village of Belmont was (it had approximately 2,000 residents in the late 1870s), the neighborhood consisted of a mix of wealthy businessmen, artists, and writers, and thus, the family could enjoy the company of artists and entrepreneurs alike even though they were removed from the intellectual community of Harvard and the cultural offerings of Cambridge. Charles Fairchild, the man who leased the family the property upon which Redtop was built, was a Boston banker who lived in the city but owned a number of farms on Somerset Street. When he learned that Howells was looking for a house in the country, he offered to lease Howells part of his thirty-three acres, on which Howells could build a house. Fairchild also paid for the construction of the house, which originally was conceived to be a "plain and cheap," "five thousand dollar" house but ended up costing nearly twice as much. According to their agreement, Howells was to pay rent to live at Redtop until he could buy it from Fairchild after he sold his house on Concord Avenue, but because Howells did not sell the Concord Avenue house before he left Redtop, he rented the property the entire time he lived there.[38]

Like each of their previous homes, Redtop, so-called because of its red-shingled roof, embodies the era in which it was built.[39] From the outside, the picturesque site planning and natural building materials evoked the values set forth in a deluge of post-Civil War magazines and books: individuality, craftsmanship, and wholesomeness.[40] The work of the New York firm, McKim, Mead, and Bigelow (which became McKim, Mead, & White, the premier firm of the Gilded Age, one year later in 1879), Redtop embodies the "shingle style," fulfilling its penchant for eclecticism and naturalism. A blend of textures and colors—red shingles, copper drains, dark green "sticks," or, trim work—with porches, gables, and other protrusions, the house exemplified the heterogeneity that distinguished innovative architecture in the late-Victorian era (Figure 2.2). Both Howells and his wife, Elinor, were closely involved with the design of the house, and they chose the firm they did because Elinor's younger brother, William Rutherford Mead, was one of its partners.[41] Husband and wife wrote numerous letters to Mead highlighting their wishes, which at times changed from day to day; given their demands, it is not surprising that the correspondence often became contentious.[42] Despite arguments about the placement of certain rooms, they all agreed that the house should face east, towards Boston and the harbor, to maximize the view. While Elinor originally wished that the dining room and library sit on the east side of the house, in its final configuration the library was moved to the southwest corner.

Entering the house from its eastern side, one arrives in a small vestibule sandwiched between the large inner and outer doors, and then in the center hall. Around the square, oak-paneled hall lay all of the first floor's main rooms: the library in the southwest corner, the parlor in the southeast, the dining room in the northeast, and the

Figure 2.1. **William Dean Howells with his wife Elinor and their three children, c. 1860s**. Herrick Memorial Library, Alfred University.

Figure 2.2. **Howells's "dream house," Redtop, designed by his wife and the architectural firm, McKim, Mead, & White, c. 1876–1877**. Author's collection.

kitchen and pantry in the northwest. The parlor, considered Elinor's reception room, was flooded with morning light, while Howells's library (in effect, his reception room) had windows on its south side and a bank of bookcases on its west. Howells may have elected to use the southwest room for his study and put the parlor in the southeast location because it was the larger room. When one enters the house, the study is the first room one sees; from here, Howells could survey the activity on the first floor of his house. Surrounding the upstairs hall, three of the five bedrooms faced east towards Boston and the ocean. Howells and his wife shared the master bedroom; each child had his or her own room, though Pilla's was extremely small; and there was an extra room designated "Mark Twain's," perhaps in deference to the fact that Twain had conceived a spare bedroom for the Howellses at his Hartford mansion. On the third floor, two rooms were finished for the cook and housemaid.

The largest and most whimsical home that Howells would ever enjoy, Redtop was full of personal accents and custom-designed, handcrafted details. Intricate design work in the front hall wall panels and on the oak staircase met the visitor's eye upon entering the house. Each fireplace featured a different mantel. Howells's library had sunbursts carved in the ceiling panels and hand-painted quotations in a Gothic-like script on the walls above the bookcases. One of these—Longfellow's "Home-keeping Hearts are Happiest"— proved sadly ironic.[43] Given its handcrafted detail, uniqueness of style, and pristine setting, one cannot help but wonder how it was possible that the family lived here for only four years. It was to have been their dream house, but turned out to have been just a dream.

While the rural setting of Redtop presumably afforded health and domestic harmony, its remove from town meant that travel to the city was an exertion, and, though there were some neighbors, the children were often lonely and bored. It also meant that when sickness did come, it was hard to find doctors. Because the house was uniquely designed and represented a highly coveted style, it became, in effect, a "show house," and the family was again besieged by visitors. Many in fact came to see the script of the library's quotations, which Elinor designed and painted. The house was also a financial burden. Since Howells could afford neither such an extravagant house nor an architect to design it, the couple were indebted to their wealthy friend, Charles Fairchild, who leased the land to Howells and financed the building; and to Elinor's brother, William, who helped design it.

The collaboration with Elinor's brother and his architectural partners produced its share of familial disputes over design and decoration, the more so because Elinor had very explicit likes and dislikes. When Charles McKim, the firm's head architect, suggested that the library be painted white to lighten the room, she insisted, "The library we really do not want white." Two weeks later, she made a complete about-face, writing McKim, "The vellum suggestion seemed to throw light. White it shall be." As Ginette de B. Merrill has revealed in her study of Redtop, Mrs. Howells changed her mind quickly and often throughout the planning of the house, to the utter exasperation of McKim and her brother.[44]

Though the first year at Redtop was filled with gaiety and visiting friends, by the second year, both Elinor and Winny were continually exhausted from the heat or physical exertion. Winny, though only fifteen years old when the family moved to Redtop, spent more and more time in bed with mysterious symptoms that were never diagnosed. She would never recover. In the end, Redtop proved yet another home that failed to bring the Howells family the stability and comfort they sought.

While the children complained of isolation and Elinor of fatigue, Howells wrote at a feverish pace during his four years at Redtop: he completed *The Lady of the Aroostook* (1879), *The Undiscovered Country* (1880), *A Fearful Responsibility* (1881), and *Dr. Breen's Practice* (1881), and wrote most of *A Modern Instance* (1882)—considered by many to be his best work. The literary output combined with the subject matter of *A Modern Instance*—one of the first American novels to deal with divorce—tell us something about the author: perhaps he hid from his wife's and daughter's frequent illnesses in his work. Biographers Susan Goodman and Carl Dawson reveal in their 2005 biography of Howells that in the 1880s, while the author was growing more and more productive (and heavy-set), his wife and daughter became increasingly weak and thin. In the early 1880s, for example, Winny weighed around 60 pounds, having never weighed more than 90, and in 1889, she died weighing about 80 pounds.[45]

Throughout the years in Belmont, Howells also continued to serve as editor of the *Atlantic Monthly*; but by early 1881, he had wearied of editorial work and wished to devote himself to his own writing. In spite of the fruitfulness of his time in the countryside, Howells, like Elinor, began to suffer from a weak heart and the long climb up the hill from the train station grew intolerable. Further, he had not been able to sell his Cambridge house and his finances were tight; he could not afford to keep the two horses that normally transported family members to and from the station. All of these stresses combined to derail the family's plans of staying at Redtop for the rest of their years.

Whether expenses, emotions, or the desire for excitement were the cause of yet another move, Howells and his wife seemed destined to live in a peripatetic state. Howells grew up moving frequently in Ohio, while Elinor was a restless, daring sort who craved constant stimulation. In abandoning house after house, the couple pursued the familiar condition of displacement and distraction. Often dismayed by their helplessness with respect to Winny's sickness and numerous deaths in their large families, the Howellses may have relished the temporary feeling of control that each new move gave them. The fresh country air had not cured Winny as hoped, and by December 1881, Howells decided to forsake the home to be closer to his daughter's Boston doctors. He wrote Fairchild: "I shall have to give up Redtop and economize for Winny's expensive invalidism ahead of me— economize in every way."[46] Howells's words sound resigned, even repentant, as if he had to sacrifice the family home and economize more than necessary to make up for Winny's ill-health, but at least he was in control. That same year, in late 1881, Howells relinquished his post as editor of the *Atlantic*.

A Crowning Achievement:
302 Beacon Street, 1884–1887

The Howellses traveled the Northeast and Europe for two years before buying a house on Beacon Street in Boston—one of the city's most expensive addresses. For a hardworking, self-made man like Howells, the purchase of a dignified row house on Beacon Street was the ultimate accomplishment, just as the purchase of a house on the same "water side of Beacon Street" was for Silas Lapham in Howells's novel, *The Rise of Silas Lapham*.

In the 1880s, owning a house on Beacon Street was the surest way to assert one's status and success—the street was arguably one of America's finest. One critic could not understand how it could be so much more attractive than similar streets in New York City: "So much handsomer, neater, more homelike and engaging than our shabby Fifth Avenue," he praised. "Beacon Street is stately; so is Marlborough Street, that runs next parallel it; and even more so is Commonwealth Avenue—with its lines of trees down the center, like a Paris boulevard."[47] Like many of the residential streets in the Back Bay, Beacon Street was lined with rows of impressive brick or brownstone mansions—attached houses that were either made out of or had a façade of brick or reddish brown sandstone called brownstone.[48] Except for corner buildings, the houses had windows on only their narrow ends—the front and back—and were typically twenty-feet wide, in rare cases, twenty-five.

Then, like now, the Back Bay's streets project an air of taste and elegance; yet, many of the neighborhood's houses were constructed quickly in the 1870s and 1880s by speculators who realized the value of the land. One such man by the name of H. Whitwell built the adjacent brick buildings at 300 and 302 Beacon Street; the latter would be inhabited by two great American authors: George Santayana and William Dean Howells. In 1869, when the structures were built, little was done to render them charming. The philosopher and critic, George Santayana, who lived in number 302 as a young boy, offers a compelling snapshot of the place and of the mindset of the speculators in his autobiography, *Persons and Places*:

> Ours was one of two houses exactly alike; yet as they were only two, we could distinguish ours without looking at the number displayed in large figures on the semicircular glass panel over the front door: for ours was the house to the left, not the one to the right. The pair were a product of that 'producer's economy,' then beginning to prevail in America, which first creates articles and then attempts to create a demand for them [. . .] Our twin houses had been designed to attract the buyer, who might sell his bargain again at a profit if he didn't find it satisfactory.[49]

In 1872, when Santayana lived there, many vacant lots surrounded the house, but by 1884, when Howells arrived, the area was far more developed. Aside from the occasional Gothic or Queen Anne style house, the architecture followed a strict pattern: no house of more than five stories, no apartment houses, no fanciful architectural styles.[50] In spite of its prestigious address, Howells's abode at 302 Beacon Street neither "savor[ed] of the architect, nor of the mansion."[51] The narrow, straightforward house featured a reception room and dining room on the ground (or first) floor, front and back parlors on the second floor, two large bedrooms above those, and four small bedrooms on the attic (or fourth) floor; at the time the house was built, there was one bathroom.[52] In the same way he had at Concord Avenue and Redtop, Howells secured a prominent room in the house for his study, using the rear parlor on the second floor for this purpose.

According to Santayana, the redeeming feature of the structure was its "unmistakably impressive" unobstructed view of the Charles River.[53] Paradoxically, though townhouses such as the one that Santayana and Howells lived in were quickly and inexpensively built by profit-conscious speculators, they were also highly desirable and fashionable. Santayana confirms that even in 1872, "The advantages of our house were in the first place social or snobbish, that it was in Beacon Street and on the better or fashionable waterside of that street; which also rendered every room initially attractive, since it had either the sun if in the front, or the view if in the rear."[54]

Silas Lapham, who builds his house on Beacon Street in Howells's eponymous novel, expounds similarly on the street's attributes:

> It's about the sightliest view I know of. I always did like the water side of Beacon. Long before I owned property here, or ever expected to, m'wife and I used to ride down this way, and stop the buggy to get this view over the water . . Commonwealth Avenue don't hold a candle to the water side of Beacon [. . .] No, sir! When you come to the Back Bay at all, give me the water side of Beacon.[55]

Like Lapham, Howells reveled in his accomplishment as he wrote to James: "Sometimes I feel it an extraordinary thing that I should have been able to buy a house on Beacon Street." It was extraordinary. For a self-made man from rural Ohio, who had climbed the ladder of success for the last two decades, there was no point higher than Beacon Street if one lived in Boston—and all before the age of fifty, the age when Harriet Beecher Stowe was building her very first home. Pleased as he was, Howells was reluctant to assign much value to an address because, at least on the outside, he did not want to appear to care too much about such things. In the letter to James, Howells rehearses the details of how he will pay for the home and further justifies the purchase on the basis of its literary utility, as if to counter an assumption that he has become wealthy and self-indulgent; he tells James that he is "writing a story in which the chief personage builds a house 'on the water side of Beacon'" and notes that "I shall be able to use all my experiences down to the quick." Then he adds that the honorable task of writing about the domicile may in fact "pay for the house."[56] Howells's resemblance to Stowe in this regard is telling of the two authors' mutual distrust of consumerism, and even, of success. Unlike James and Wharton who came from wealthy families, Howells and Stowe seem intent upon projecting an image of modesty and frugality, regardless of how they lived and spent in actuality.

The letter to James reveals how quickly Howells shifts from the pleasure of his new home to matters of conscience, as if he must resist too much enjoyment of the material sort for fear of corruption. Howells felt ambivalent about his residence on Beacon Street—a status symbol enabled by a contract with *Harper's Monthly* signed in 1885 for $13,000 a year. Even though he had the income to live on Beacon Street, he was not one of the people who typically dwelled in the neighborhood. As Bainbridge Bunting points out in his history of the Back Bay, the area was made up of conservative Bostonians of comfortable wealth; within this broad category, there were several implied classes depending upon one's address: "The old rich on Beacon Street, the old poor on Marlborough, the new rich on Commonwealth Avenue, and the new poor on Newbury. Within this hierarchy an even loftier rank was conferred on the 'water side' of Beacon Street or the 'sunny side' of Commonwealth Avenue."[57] Howells was an outsider, a newly wealthy individual from the Midwest, yet the location of his townhouse suggested old money and even more—all because he dwelled on the waterside of Beacon Street.

The tension between new and old money—Howells was of the former group while types like Norton and Lowell (and later, James and Wharton) were of the latter—plagued Howells throughout his life, and seemed to be evident from the moment he entered the right neighborhood in Cambridge when he moved to Berkeley Street. Each house, including the one-of-a-kind bucolic retreat in Belmont and the Beacon Street residence, in its comfort and novelty, contrasted with the modest world of Howells's upbringing. These homes were mixed blessings: on the one hand, signs of accomplishment; on the other, reminders of the family and background he left behind. The impulse to abandon each grand home was there from the moment he moved in. While Howells enjoyed the fruits of his hard work, he could never ignore that back in Ohio, his father and siblings were struggling to make ends meet. Nor could he forget the four-room stone house that his father built with his own hands and in which he and his family of ten grew up. His childhood, though poor, was happy, and as a result, Howells had suspicions of wealth and materialism. Even though, as a young man, he was eager to leave Ohio, see the world, and make his own way, he remained close to his parents and siblings, none of whom achieved the type of success and fame that Howells did. For most of his adult life, he sent money home to help care for his unmarried sisters and his jobless brothers Henry and Sam.

The dis-ease associated with wealth, abundance, and consumption, a disease that Howells struggled to avoid, was a topic making its way into the magazines of the day in the late nineteenth and early twentieth centuries. Howells's own, the *Atlantic* and *Harper's*, were among the journals that published articles on the risk of losing "health of spirit" to excess. One piece, "The Tyranny of Things," published in the *Atlantic* in 1906, expounded: "The passion for accumulation is upon us [. . .] houses are filled with an undigested mass of things [. . .] But to some of us a day comes when we begin to grow weary of things. We realize that we do not possess them; they possess us."[58] Howells too expressed his amazement at the amount of stuff that crept into his own home and bemoaned the "thousand distractions that ambush me."[59] The Beacon Street house was decorated with all the Victorian embellishment in which Edith Wharton would come of age and soon despise: ornately patterned wallpaper and drapery, heavily carpeted floors, thickly upholstered furniture. In Howells's study alone, six carpets lay overlapped on the floor. Fireplace mantels and walls were crammed with family pictures, Elinor's sketches, and knick-knacks.[60] In spite of his own crowded interiors, Howells advised family members to keep their belongings to a minimum, writing to his sister Annie: "[Sell] all your possessions, or any of them [. . .] Don't let them become *ob*sessions."[61] Howells had felt the effects of his twenty-year career and of the hard work and ambition that resulted in his success. As his literary celebrity grew during his time on Beacon Street, the chasm between his circumstances and those of the poor increasingly troubled him, yet he seemed unable to renounce the comforts that he had earned. He referred ironically to himself, his wife, Mark Twain, and Twain's wife as "theoretical socialists" and "practical aristocrats," adding in a letter to his father, "But it is a comfort to be right theoretically and to be ashamed of oneself practically."[62]

Always an avid walker, Howells could not help but notice the unfortunate who inhabited peripheral Back Bay streets and the area closer to the Boston Common, a hub of transportation. What he saw in his neighborhood troubled him, as he wrote his father in the summer of 1884: "There are miles of empty houses all around me. How unequally things are divided in this world. While these beautiful, airy, wholesome houses are uninhabited, thousands of poor creatures are stifling in wretched barracks in the city here, whole families in one room. I wonder that men are so patient with society as they are."[63] These words appeared in slightly different form one year later in a dialogue in *The Rise of Silas Lapham*. Over a sumptuous dinner, Mr. Bromfield Corey and Miss Kingsbury discuss her charity work: "'I have often thought of our great, cool houses standing useless here, and the thousands of poor creatures stifling in their holes and dens, and the little children dying for wholesome shelter. How cruelly selfish we are!"(171). While Howells notes that the world is "unequal" but its citizens "patient" when he writes his father, in the novel, he confirms the "cruel selfishness" of the wealthy—a group to which he now belonged. Further in the novel, Howells states this message once again: "It is the curse of prosperity that it takes work away from us, and shuts that door to hope and health of spirit" (204). By the end of the novel, Mrs. Lapham realizes how little happiness her family's newfound wealth has brought her; rather, their affluence has only made her realize her misery. The narrator tells us: "In this house, where everything had come to be done for her, she had no tasks to interpose between her and her despair" (204). Perhaps Howells felt the same way in the late 1880s: he had over $100,000 in assets—did he even need to work anymore? But his beloved daughter was dead at the age of twenty-five and his wife was routinely bedridden. Life had become increasingly hard for him to enjoy. His misgivings about wealth, materialism, and those less fortunate, as well as his sadness over the death of his father, daughter, and sister, set the stage for a near-religious conversion. Howells was about to change from a man of wealth and status to a man of few needs (family and writing) and ardent political views (socialism).

At the start of the new decade, the 1890s, Howells yearned to be "settled somewhere humbly and simply," but he arrived in New York City, and instead, fictionalized an ideal world in his utopian novel, *A Traveler From Altruria* (1892–1893). In this work, Howells presents Aristedes Homos, a morally idealistic young man from the utopian Altruria, who arrives in America to shed light on and offer solutions to the nation's current problems. Through Mr. Homos, Howells reveals the American love of money, desire for individuality, and accepted inequality among people. Mr. Homos critiques a number of senseless customs in which Howells himself partook, but of which he privately disapproved, such as leaving the city for several months during the summer to go to another home; wanting to work in business rather than at a creative pursuit in order to make money; and hiring servants to do one's housework. Mr. Homos, like Howells, is shocked by the greed and materialism of Americans, and by the way in which the very poor and the very rich live side by side with nary a word spoken between them. Only on a visit to a farmhouse in the country does Mr. Homos find a home that approximates the ideal world in Altruria, where "[All are] assured of enough, and are forbidden any and every sort of superfluity."[64]

Like the simple, peaceful, and clean Quaker house where Eliza and baby Harry take shelter at the midpoint of *Uncle Tom's Cabin*, this house lacks excess, and thus "brings man into the closest relations to the deity, through a grateful sense of the divine bounty." The farmer who lives here is equally exalted for he is endeared to "that piece of soil which he tills, and so strengthens his love of home." The owners of the modest, homey property, Mr. and Mrs. Camp, embody all of Howells's ideals for a simple, natural, satisfying life, and also recall the Lapham's retreat to Vermont for a more wholesome lifestyle. Though the room is bare, "a great many things might have happened [in it]," suggesting the power and enlightenment that come with simplicity.[65]

While Howells was conceiving the idealistic Altrurian world where people "live for one another instead of each for himself," he was preparing to sell his Beacon Street townhouse (which he did in 1887), after living there for only three years. The sale of the house signaled the end of Howells's house-life in Boston and any future attachment to a status-symbol home. Even though the author often expressed his desire to "go back there to live, or at least to die," he spent just two more years in Boston after Winifred's death—an event which left him increasingly alone.[66] In the aftermath of this tragedy, his wife became "a shadow" of her former self. Howells was left with his daughter Pilla and son John. When the latter married in 1906, Pilla became her father's caretaker until his death in 1920.

"A Wild Goose Chase": Apartment Hunting in New York City, 1891–1909

In spite of once stating that he would never live in New York, Howells justified his family's move to the city in 1891 in a letter to his father: "New York is a prodigious field of material for me [. . .] There is more for me to see and learn there."[67] The practical reason for the move was, as Howells termed it, "the money basis": a job at *Cosmopolitan* magazine that Howells accepted and began in November 1891.[68] Howells remained only six months in the job, however; in 1892, at age fifty-five, he finally fulfilled his dream of becoming a full-time writer.

From December 1891, when the family arrived in New York, to January 1909, when they purchased an apartment at 130 West 57th

Street, the family made at least fifteen moves within the city, sometimes as many as six in a year. Their search for a city apartment, a "wild goose chase," as Howells called it, surpassed even the Marches' in *A Hazard of New Fortunes*—the novel he published in 1890 before he and his family relocated to New York.[69] There was one significant hiatus from February 1904 to April 1905 when the family lived in Europe. In today's modern world, it is difficult to imagine the trials of such an itinerant lifestyle, but in an era that predated storage facilities and large trucks, the mental and physical anguish of such upheaval was extreme. Countless porters, workers, horses, and carriages had to be hired to pack, load, and move belongings, and for weeks on end, the Howellses would live amid a mess of boxes and out of suitcases. Most of their belongings remained in boxes or in the basements and attics of friends and family members until 1909, but each move still required packing all the clothes and books that were not stored. Howells, his wife, and daughter were exhausted and often sick; Elinor spent many days at a time lying in bed, leaving Howells to attend dinners with Pilla. In spite of the turmoil that their restlessness invoked, the family enjoyed many of the novel conveniences of hotel and apartment living, such as prepared meals (if they wanted them) and elevators.[70]

The family's lifestyle in New York is perplexing given Howells's desire to be settled permanently and his view of himself as a domestic man. Howells was domestic in the sense that there was no place he would rather have been than in his study at home with his family nearby; yet, the pursuit of the house in which this domesticity was to take place seemed forever elusive. Within a few years—from 1891 to 1897—Howells and his family made several moves between East 17th Street and West 59th Street, each time to a different apartment building or hotel. Sometimes they stayed one week (as they did at the now demolished Oxford Hotel); sometimes they leased an apartment for two or three years (as they did at 40 West 50th Street); once, they purchased an apartment (located at 38 East 73rd Street) only to sell it six months later. In their constant movement, the Howellses experienced numerous New York City neighborhoods; perhaps they were trying to determine the best one in which to buy; or, Howells and his wife may have been still too traumatized by the loss of their daughter to remain in one location. Being on the move freed the couple from thinking about and experiencing their loss. Another possibility speaks to Howells as a writer and to his wife as an endlessly curious woman: the constant change provided a regular feast for their eyes and minds.

In the 1890s, apartment living for the upper class was still a relatively new concept. In an earlier age, during the Civil War, for example, an itinerant family like the Howellses would have had to stay in an upscale boarding house, hotel, or stand-alone house. But beginning in 1870, the face of temporary housing was changing significantly: New York's population was nearly one million and plans for large-scale residential development of the city were underway. These plans took the form of the earliest apartment buildings, which were called "French" or "Parisian flats" and looked much like the city's hotels. By 1890, the population had grown to one and a half million and the modes of entertainment and methods of transportation had increased dramatically: the elevated railroad was completed in 1878 and there were 135 miles of horse-car lines, as well as 1,500 cabs and hacks. Newly-constructed streets had opened up whole new territories to the west and north of Central Park.[71] For a writer such as Howells, who drew upon life around him for his work, there was quite simply no more stimulating or exciting place to be than New York City in the 1890s.

Large apartment buildings of eight, nine, or ten stories erected in the 1880s were unfamiliar mammoths to a couple like the Howellses who had always dwelled in their own homes. At first, they were appalled by them—and by the impermanence that hotel-living suggested—just as the Marches are in *A Hazard of New Fortunes*, where Mr. March rails against apartment living: "'The flat means society life; that is, the pretense of society life. It's made to give artificial people a society basis on a little money—too much money, of course, for what they get.'" March goes on: "'The flat abolishes the family consciousness. It's confinement without coziness; it's cluttered without being snug.'"[72] Hotels did not simply jeopardize the family unit, as March fears they will; they also threatened cultural concerns about home ownership and property, as Betsy Klimasmith elucidates in *At Home in the City*.[73] Yet, once the Howellses settled into such a dwelling, where they found spaces of ten or twelve rooms that might have been larger than their previous free-standing houses, they delighted in the newness and the convenience of the apartment. Similarly, after the Marches move into the Grosvenor Green apartment in New York, the narrator tells us: "The flat developed [. . .] a roominess and coziness in it unsuspected before."[74] Roominess and coziness were not the only attributes of hotel living, either. It is quite possible that Howells and his wife relocated so frequently for the reason that Klimasmith puts forth: just as the hotel can "rebuild itself in a more profitable location," so, too, can its inhabitants. For Howells, at this later stage in his life and career, there were no more barriers to upward mobility, and, as soon as he found a more ideally situated or more comfortable dwelling place, he could move.[75]

When the Howellses bought an apartment on West 57th Street in 1909, they chose a commodious twelve-room layout. The new, grand apartment buildings were built with the upper-class urban dweller in mind and cost anywhere from $1,800 a year for ten rooms to $3,000 a year for fifteen rooms; these apartments ranged in size from 3,000 to 3,750 square feet or more.[76] With the price came many advantages: residents often shared the cost of centralized equipment such as heating, elevators, water, gas, and other utilities, and some buildings offered meals. The well-known (and still standing) Dakota Apartments at 72nd Street and Central Park West, for example, offered a restaurant and a private dining room. Because of their cost and location, these types of buildings attracted a wealthy clientele, people like Howells, his wife, and daughter, Pilla, who was now twenty years old. The buildings even had names—as Howells's beloved Redtop did—which lent them an air of exclusivity and individuality.[77] Dwelling in an upscale apartment building with an exotic name (like "Dakota") quickly became the preferred choice of discriminating urbanites like Howells and his wife; over the years, they sampled quite a few, among them the "Ramon," "the Oxford," and the "Burlington."[78]

"Our Rugged Little Nest": Life on the Maine Coast, 1902–1920

Many of the Howells's moves during the 1890s were instigated by the search for a summer residence as well, as Howells noted in a letter to his old friend, Charles Eliot Norton (who remained contentedly at Shady Hill in Cambridge and at his rural retreat in Ashfield, Massachusetts, until his death): "We are drifting from one place to another this summer, trying to discover some spot within a few hours of New York where we might pitch our ragged tent for the few summers that yet remain to us."[79] In this missive, Howells's tone is noticeably morose, which can be explained by the recent death of daughter Winny and by the fact that if Howells's proverbial tent was not by now in shreds, surely his spirit was.

After pitching their tent in regions as diverse as Magnolia, Massachusetts; Long Beach, Long Island; Bermuda; and St. Augustine, Florida, the Howellses purchased a summer house in Kittery Point, Maine, in October 1902, where the family could spend several peaceful months each year. Howells and Elinor, who were sixty-five and sixty-six respectively, were delighted to have "at last a home for our old age."[80] Howells fell in love with the modest Maine cottage set on two acres of oceanfront in part because of the nearby stable that he planned to move closer to the main house and convert to a study; he sighed to Mark Twain: "I ought to have had [the deed to this place] twenty five years ago."[81] Of the renovation of the stable, which Howells oversaw step by step, he wrote to William James, "To move a building was about all that remained for me to do; and it is such an American experience!"[82] Each morning he would awake to find a different laborer—a roofer, a plumber, a stone-cutter—and would marvel at the democracy of the project and at the good-nature of his workers. In Maine, Howells felt he inhabited an Altrurian world, where men seemed to work for each other rather than against each other. During his months on the coast, Howells remained very productive: he began the long, arduous process of compiling notes for a possible autobiography, and he wrote *The Kentons* (1902), *The Son of Royal Langbrith* (1904), *The Leatherwood God* (1916), and several books about England, including *London Films* (1906) and *Certain Delightful English Towns* (1906). Surely Howells was able to remain prolific because he was fulfilled: "My ideal has always been a study outside of the dwelling house, and now I am to have it," he wrote his sister Aurelia soon after acquiring the property.[83]

On the exterior, the Kittery Point house recalls the one with which Howells first fell in love—37 Concord Avenue. A relatively small, clapboard house with a mansard roof, the main house offers a seaside architectural counterpart to the Cambridge dwelling. Though it stood only two stories, the house featured several ample ground floor rooms: a large dining room with two corner cabinets and a bay window; two front parlors that looked out at the Atlantic Ocean; and a large kitchen. A charming porch covered the back of the structure, effectively doubling the size of the living space during the warm summer months. Upstairs there were four moderately-sized bedrooms and two smaller rooms that were used for servants. A key advantage of the house lay in its two additional buildings: a stable and barn. Howells converted the former into a study. Both boasted views of the lawn and of Portsmouth Harbor and Gerrish Island.[84] Period photographs of the study show a large first floor natural wood-paneled room with a writing table and bookcases; a small rocking chair sits in front of the fireplace; and several photographs of the Howells women (Elinor, Winny, and Pilla) adorn the walls and the mantel.[85] One can only imagine how happy

Howells must have felt here, in this ample space devoted solely to writing, surrounded by the solitude of nature and the sound of the sea. This type of environment—an immense, spacious study, quietude, and time—was precisely what Howells had found so elusive throughout his years in Boston and Cambridge. At the end of each summer season, Howells dreaded his return to the city, so much so that each year he extended his stay in Maine—from an initial sojourn from May to September, to one that lasted from April to November. In his letters to friends and family in the early 1900s, Howells eagerly anticipates "taking flight to our rugged little nest on the Maine coast."[86] The Maine cottage was the only one of his dozens of residences that Howells ever referred to as a nest, rather than as a tent or other temporary resting-spot.

~ ~ ~

As a man in his sixties and seventies, Howells loomed large: he weighed about fifty-pounds more than he did as a young man in his thirties, but maintained the quiet dignity for which he was known. With physical stature came an emotional groundedness which relieved him of his previous restlessness. During his last three decades, Howells pared down his life to his three loves: writing, family, and friends. As he aged and had more money than he knew what to do with, his life became more and more uncomplicated.[87] He admitted that the focus of his writing had changed as well, from "outer life" to "studies of the inner life." During the last decades of his life, Howells continued to be prolific but focused primarily on non-fiction, writing memoirs, remembrances of others, and imaginary interviews with past and present writers. The pace of his life slowed (if not necessarily by choice), and with the slower pace came a deep appreciation of the people who had been so long in his life. Having lost his favorite sister Victoria (in 1886), his daughter Winny (in 1889), his mentors James Russell Lowell (in 1891) and Charles Eliot Norton (in 1908), his mother and father (in 1894), and numerous other friends, Howells considered himself "of the generation next to death," yet he also marveled with each passing year that he was still alive.[88]

After Elinor died in 1910, Howells's life became still more peaceful even though he never stopped dreaming of his wife. At this point, content as he was to work, see friends, and spend time with his family, his house and belongings lost nearly all meaning. In his seventies and eighties, Howells moved slowly through life, awaiting the time when he would be reunited with Elinor in eternity. He missed his wife terribly, writing to one friend in 1914 that meeting her in 1860 was "the vastly most important thing in my whole life."[89] Many of his letters to friends and family in the last decade of his life confirm his yearning to be with Elinor again; he joined her on May 11, 1920.

PART TWO

Living to Write

CHAPTER THREE

Henry James:
Dwelling in the "House of Fiction"

"The house of fiction has in short not one window, but a million—a number of possible windows not to be reckoned; rather, every one of which has been pierced, or is still pierceable, in its vast front, by the need of the individual vision and by the pressure of the individual will."
—Henry James, Preface to *The Portrait of a Lady*
(New York Edition, 1908)

In 1897 when he was fifty-four years old, Henry James moved into the first house that he would ever own: Lamb House, located in the English coastal town of Rye, sixty-three miles from London.[1] For the previous quarter-century, the writer had lived in two apartments in London, one at 3 Bolton Street and the other at 34 De Vere Gardens. Why did it take James so long to buy his first home? Surely his bachelorhood had something to do with it—he did not need a secure residence in the way that William Dean Howells and Harriet Beecher Stowe, with their spouses and numerous children, did—but the decision not to own was more than a question of logistics or finances. Until he moved to Rye, James had lived in London for over twenty years (1876–1897); the city, he felt, was the place of necessity for the writer who wished to "suck the atmosphere of its intimations and edifications."[2] From the time he was a young man, James was intent upon becoming a writer of consequence, and aside from a sunlit room in which to write, he wanted to dwell in an atmosphere that was "full of impressions." Indeed, James began his career by "soaking up" and "inhaling" impressions.[3]

For most of his life, a home was not on James's mind. He did not want a large or luxurious place to live; he was not fond of spending money; he was not even particularly keen on receiving guests. In spite of his reputation as a frequent diner-out and socializer, his letters reveal someone who was essentially alone. He wrote his brother in 1877, "I go on seeing a great many people, and yet [...] I encounter no one of whom I hanker to see more." To Grace Norton the same year he explained, "I have formed no intimacies [...] to have become a cosmopolitan is to be a good deal alone."[4] Renting apartments in London enabled James to keep visitors to a minimum and provided him with the means to sublet the rooms quickly should he wish to spend several months on the Continent or elsewhere in England. His Bolton Street apartment had so little spare room that when his brother William or sister Alice came to visit, he would leave them the place while he stayed at a nearby hotel or gentlemen's club. Small apartments meant that James could live comfortably and afford a housemaid, but not spend a great deal of money—often a consideration. His furniture was minimal and cast-off from family members or friends. Though James was a master illustrator of houses and interiors and of the metaphoric "tall stone walls which fatally divide us,"[5] he was not concerned with having his own home; he built "houses of fiction"[6] instead of his own house.

James's detachment from his personal space reveals much about the type of man that he was, and the sort of writer as well. While Stowe, Howells, and Wharton emphasized the establishment of a comfortable home—and needed such a domicile for reasons as varied as family size, public image, or personal empowerment—James was unique in the way that he divested himself of the burden of home ownership. His lack of a home was similar to his lack of a wife or a steady lover—both were responsibilities that he chose not to assume. Throughout his life, James avoided anything or anyone who would "incapacitate or paralyze" him, and when he did choose to buy, in 1899 at age fifty-six, he kept possessions and accessories to a minimum.[7] In this way, James's home life mirrored his conception of the structure of a novel, apropos of which he said: "I would rather have too little architecture than too much—when there's danger of its interfering with my measure of the truth" (*Portrait*, 5). James's domestic choices—particularly his status as a renter unencumbered by family or belongings—enabled him to keep an eye on the truth; nothing was allowed to interfere with his writing. His life at home, in short, embodied the "severe taste of a scholar and private gentleman."[8]

While detached, James was in no way divorced from his environment; in fact, though he invested far less time in setting up or keeping house (to borrow Howells's phrase), he may have been more interested in the world around him than even Stowe, Howells, or Wharton. Today there is no question of James's ever-penetrating eye and of the way in which he absorbed his surroundings; his "vision" has been the subject of many studies.[9] In his everyday life, he sought, as he put it, to guess "the unseen from the seen;" he was "keen of eye, retentive of memory, interrogative of tongue, [and] copious of pen."[10] As attuned to their environment as Stowe, Howells, and Wharton were—and as their numerous houses, decorative choices, and fiction attest—James was almost supernaturally so. Everything he wrote— letters, notebooks, novels—reveals his attention to detail and his commitment to his unique vision. Of course, vision was a complex subject for the writer, and entailed far more than mere looking. As he wrote to his American friend, Sarah Butler Wister, when he was traveling in Italy, "But what's the use of writing at all, unless imaginatively? Unless one's vision can lend something to a thing, there's small reason in proceeding to proclaim one has seen it. Mere *looking* everyone can do for himself."[11]

James's consciousness of the environment is striking because of how young he was when he was able to articulate it. As a boy, the young Harry, as he was known, wanted first to be a painter and then, in an attempt to be practical, a lawyer, but he abandoned these possibilities for his love of letters. His parents, Henry James, Sr. and Mary Robertson Walsh, were, by all accounts, loving, supportive, and unconventional. While his father never held a traditional job—he inherited real estate that yielded him $10,000 a year (about $212,000 a year in today's dollars)[12]—he was a well-known and respected intellectual in New York and Cambridge who counted Thoreau, Emerson, and Hawthorne among his friends. From a young age, the five James children were inculcated with a love of learning, creativity, and culture.[13] Feeling that New York City was too provincial an environment in which to raise his children, the senior Henry moved his family to Europe in 1855 when Henry James was twelve; an itinerant lifestyle followed in which the James children studied with tutors in Paris, Geneva, London, Bologna, and Bonn. They returned to the United States after three years abroad and settled in Newport, Rhode Island—the first New England town in which they lived.[14] In Newport, James met two young men who would become his lifelong friends: painter John La Farge and writer/editor Thomas Sergeant Perry.[15] Two years later, in 1863, he moved to Cambridge to attend Harvard Law School, but dropped out after one semester and began to write short essays.

James was confident enough of his skill as a writer to submit some of his early work to Charles Eliot Norton and James Russell Lowell, editors of the *North American Review*, without a letter of introduction even though both editors knew James's father from the intellectual circles of Cambridge. James also took the initiative in submitting work to Edwin Lawrence Godkin, founding editor of the *Nation*, and to James T. Fields, then the editor of the *Atlantic Monthly*. He enjoyed success at each publication: the *North American Review* published James's earliest unsigned reviews in 1864 and 1865 and his first signed tale, "The Story of a Year," was published in the *Atlantic* in March 1865 when he was twenty-two.[16]

From youth, James was a consummate reader and observer; he absorbed the intellectual atmosphere of his childhood, listened in on conversations between his father and his philosopher friends, and determined to use his gifts of visual and verbal acuity to become a writer. In his early twenties, James wrote his friend Perry: "It is [...] by the wear and tear of living and talking and observing that works of art shape themselves into completeness."[17] When he discussed the art of fiction in his early forties, he advised young writers to do as he did, "to trace the implication of things, to judge the whole piece by the pattern."[18] Unlike Stowe, and his friends Howells and Wharton, James knew by the time he was twenty-four that he would become an important writer and determined early to find precisely the types of settings that were most conducive to his craft. His lifestyle furthered his cause: he did not marry or have children; he lived far away from his family; he chose not to become burdened by the responsibility of real estate. James's focus was on his vision and his craft: the world from which he culled the material for his novels and the manner in which to tell of what he saw.[19] In *The Art of Fiction*, James wrote, "The only reason for the existence of a novel is that it *does* compete with life."[20] In a very real sense, James's novels competed with his life; in his case, it becomes difficult to discern where he dwelled more comfortably or more often: in the "house of fiction" or the "house of life."[21]

London Literary Lairs, 1876–1886

While James enjoyed the fast-paced excitement of New York City for six months in 1875, he decided to move permanently to Europe on November 1, 1875, when he was thirty-two years old (Figure 3.1). In Europe, he figured, he could obtain a correspondence with an American paper or magazine, and provide sketches of people, places, and the art scene—pieces that would pay him much more than the ten to thirty-five dollars he received for book reviews for the *Nation*.[22] He had noticed that American readers liked this kind of thing, but believed the material was "rather flimsily and vulgarly supplied." James was certain that he could offer sketches of a "more intelligent and cultivated fashion," adding, "I think I know how to observe, and may claim that I should observe to good purpose and chronicle my observations agreeably."[23]

The young writer settled first in Paris for thirteen months before deciding that in London he could feel "nearer, geographically, to [his] field of operation at home," New York. Unlike Florence, Rome, and Paris—cities he loved and visited regularly throughout his life— London offered him the comfort of his language, access to magazines and publishers, affordable lodgings, and a number of American contacts. For practical and professional reasons, James decided it was the best European city in which to live, and he found it "interesting, inspiring, even exhilarating." "I feel very near New York," he wrote his mother soon after arriving.[24]

At the end of December 1876, James secured a small apartment on the second floor of a four-story Georgian house (now demolished) at 3 Bolton Street where he would reside for ten years. For about sixteen dollars a week, James had a sitting room with a balcony, a bedroom, and a small kitchen, as well as the services of Louisa, his housemaid.[25] He spent almost no time setting up his "little shabby furnished apartment" and was happy simply to have found two quiet, warm, and sunlit rooms.[26] Aside from those three features—sunlight, quietude, and warmth—his only other requirements for living were a central, downtown location and proximity to a park. The apartment on Bolton Street was situated ideally: just off of the main thoroughfare of Piccadilly and on the edge of London's fashionable Mayfair district, the sunny rooms lay directly across the street from Green Park (which James could see from his balcony) and less than half a mile from Hyde Park and Buckingham Palace. The building was a short walk from Pall Mall, the area known for its palatial clubs, and St. James's Park and Palace. Within a few minutes, then, James could spend time in three large parks, visit the shops of Piccadilly, the clubs on Pall Mall, or Victoria Station. Access to these places of culture, nature, and transport was an important consideration when James was deciding where to live; he walked a great deal, sometimes as much as six hours in a day, and enjoyed the visual stimulation that the city sites and parks provided.[27] Unlike the other authors of this study who were all married by the time they were thirty-two years old and settled into one of many houses they would own, in 1876, as James approached his thirty-third birthday, he was single, solitary, and an expatriate, but he was happy: "*Chez moi*, I am really very well off," he wrote home, "And it is a rare pleasure to feel warm, in my room, as I sit scribbling [...] I am extremely glad to have come here."[28]

Though London was superficially very ugly compared to Paris— "with its darkness, dirt, poverty and general unaesthetic cachet"— James was "much pleased with the economical character of [his] move."[29] He was certain that he would be able to be more productive and feel like less of an outsider in the city. In his journal, he noted: "London is on the whole the most possible form of life. I take it as an artist and a bachelor; as one who has the passion of observation and whose business is the study of human life [...] The human race is better represented here than anywhere else, and if you learn to know your London, you learn a great many things."[30] In a sense, the "lugubrious," "absolutely glutinous fog," and "the deadly darkness" of London aided James in his work, as he could "do nothing better than commune a bit" with family members and fictional characters through writing. He affirmed in letters to friends and family that he would "scribble better" in London, which, to him, was "everything."[31]

Rather than emphasize interior décor or comfort in setting up his first London apartment, as Stowe and Howells did in their homes on the other side of the Atlantic, James focused on settling into a workday routine. When he arrived in London in the winter of 1876, James had already serialized *Roderick Hudson* and *The American* in the *Atlantic Monthly*, thanks largely to the support of Howells. He had begun to think about his future works, *The Europeans* and *The Portrait of a Lady*, which he would publish in 1879 and 1881, respectively.[32] Thus, he wasted no time establishing a productive schedule, which entailed an early breakfast (tea, eggs, bacon, and "the exquisite English loaf"), followed by three hours of writing (from roughly nine o'clock to noon), a mid-afternoon dinner out, several hours of walking, a late-afternoon tea or dinner of "a chop and a pint" around five or six o'clock, and several hours of reading at home in front of the fire, where he usually fell asleep.[33] Most important to James in the early years of his career were the hours he spent walking around the city, for it was on his walks that he absorbed the countless impressions and observations that would inform his novels. He described his days to his brother: "Mornings and very often evenings in my room; afternoons in the streets, walking, strolling, *flânant*, prying, staring, lingering at bookstalls and shop-windows [...] Most of my social intercourse consists of looking at people in the streets, theaters and restaurants."[34] It was a solitary existence for the self-described "lone literary exile," one which enabled him "to do some quiet work."[35]

James resembled the "flâneur" that he alludes to in his letter to William—an identity which helps explain his lack of attachment to a residence. First defined by French poet Charles Baudelaire in 1850, the flâneur was the archetypal "man-about-town,"[36] for whom, as for James, the city was "now a landscape, now a room." In the twentieth century, Walter Benjamin described the flâneur in terms that also evoke James:

> The street becomes a dwelling for the flâneur; he is as much at home among the façades of houses as a citizen is in his four walls. To him the shiny, enameled signs of businesses are at least as good a wall ornament as an oil painting is to the bourgeois in his salon. The walls are the desk against which he presses his notebooks; news-stands are his libraries.[37]

Benjamin aptly reveals that for the flâneur the ornaments of city streets replaced the oil paintings of bourgeois interiors; for the man-about-town, as for James, the street offered far greater "interiors." By walking for several hours each day, he was able to soak up innumerable impressions of London life, as well as process—or "work off," to use his phrase—previously accumulated ones.[38] In his volumes of correspondence and notebooks, James makes no mention of acquiring works of art or other decorative objects until his late fifties. Throughout his years in Bolton Street—an apartment that came furnished—the only adornments he made to his walls were photographs or sketches sent from home.[39] Not until he moved to his second apartment at 34 De Vere Gardens in 1887, when he was forty-four, did James purchase furniture.

Within the Bolton Street flat, James again resembled the flâneur as he spent hours gazing out his front windows (which faced Piccadilly), noting to his father that he would only get some work done if he succeeded in "learning not to keep looking out of the window."[40] After a day on the city streets, James returned to his apartment to observe (from the window) "his household after his work [was] done."[41] In this sense, as Benjamin suggests, his home lay beyond his four walls, in the streets where he spent his days. When James determined to write, he forced himself to sit in the west corner of his apartment so that he would face an "ugly brick wall" and have no diversion but "the great smutty blank wall of Lord Ashburton's house."[42] In both scenarios, whether James looked out the window for material or faced a brick wall so that he could write, his apartment functioned more like a studio than a home. He used the place to work and sleep; the rest of his life took place outside.

Because James lived in a small apartment and was a writer, he needed—and actively sought—social interaction; though, as an observer and a loner by nature, he did not necessarily make close friends.[43] One of the first and most useful steps he took to extend both his social circle and the size of his apartment was to frequent and then join several gentlemen's clubs in London, including, in his early days, the Oxford and Cambridge Club, the Arts Club, the St. James, the Athenaeum, and the Rabelais Club.[44] By far the most important of these to James's life as a bachelor was the Reform Club, to which he was elected earlier than he expected, in May, 1878, at age thirty-five.[45]

The Reform Club, located in the Pall Mall near James's residence, was founded in 1836 and named for the Reform movement, which it promoted. It was known as the most liberal of London's elite clubs. It was also one of the only older clubs to provide bedrooms for its members—a convenience much appreciated by James since he did not have room in his apartment for guests. Designed by the architect Sir Charles Barry in 1832, who was instructed to build a clubhouse more splendid than any other in existence, the structure was modeled on an Italian palazzo and completed after four years of construction.[46] Its grand exterior was matched on the inside by a sky-lit entrance hall, vast library, and luxurious sitting rooms. James reveled in the number of books and the elaborate meals offered by the Club, and soon, he was dining regularly there.[47] He wrote to his father of the Club's necessity to his life: "It is a precious good thing for me— something of the kind had become indispensable—and makes me feel strangely and profoundly at home here."[48] However, James added, "There is no rose without its thorn," for he had to borrow the forty-two pounds for entrance dues from the elder Henry—something he did fairly often during his first few years in London.[49]

While James enjoyed the camaraderie and masculine atmosphere of the Club, he was perhaps most enticed by its very comfortable interiors. At the Reform Club, as at the Athenaeum, they were striking, and featured, on the main floor, large morning rooms with leather armchairs and writing tables and a forty-two-yards-long dining room, which overlooked terraced gardens. The second floor, reached by a grand Italian marble staircase, contained the billiards and card rooms and the library; on the top, or fourth, floor were twenty-eight bedrooms for members.[50] James enjoyed all of the public rooms, telling his father, "I am writing this [letter] in the big tranquil library [of the Reform Club], looking out upon the green gardens [...] and furnished with a store of English literature sufficiently large and delightful to last me a lifetime."[51]

The Reform Club provided social interaction, good food, and a rarified environment in which to read and write letters. For the most private task of writing novels, however, James remained at home on Bolton Street. Thus, while the city street and atmospheric clubs provided James with a sense of "home," his actual home continued to function as an office or a studio.

"Palaces of Art": The English Country House and the Italian Villa

Just as James was able to expand the parameters of his world by spending time at the Reform Club, he enlarged his feeling of being "at home" by frequenting the grand country houses of friends and acquaintances. These journeys too were invaluable in building his fund of impressions, and observations culled from them would make their way into his fiction. The country houses of wealthy English gentry and the Italian villas and palazzi of American friends functioned in a sense like the "palaces of art" of his youth—James's phrase for the cultural institutions (namely, museums) that he frequented with his family when living in Europe.[53]

While James arrived in England knowing a number of people from Cambridge who were living in Europe temporarily or permanently (such as James Russell Lowell who had a house in England; Charles Eliot Norton; and Francis Boott and his daughter Lizzie, who lived in Italy), he cultivated friendships with several British lords and ladies as well, including the Marchioness of Ailesbury (or "Lady A."), Lady Rose (the former Charlotte Temple), and Lord and Lady Rosebery. James was perhaps unrivaled among writers in his ability to meet and befriend individuals of exceptional wealth. He sought them out, dazzled them with his charm, intellect, and insight, and quickly made himself one of the most sought-after dinner guests (as well as one of the most eligible bachelors) in London. Quelling frequent rumors that he was about to be engaged, James instead became the choice companion for elderly widowed women or unmarried aristocratic ladies.[54] These friendships, like the clubs, introduced James to the luxurious, old-world surroundings and customs that he loved and that he would not have seen otherwise; therefore, they played a crucial role in his writing.

The most significant of James's friendships with landed and titled aristocrats was with Lord Rosebery, an Englishman who married the extremely wealthy Hannah de Rothschild and who was close friends with several other Rothschild family members, including Ferdinand de Rothschild, owner of the immense Renaissance-style château, Waddesdon Manor. James was genuinely fond of the Roseberys, who were his contemporaries, and he was irrepressibly drawn to the high life that his friendship with them afforded him. Though Lady Rosebery died of typhoid fever in 1890, James remained close friends with the Lord, who was considered one of the most widely read men of his time—a good match for the highly erudite James. The Lord also traveled extensively, raced horses, and became Prime Minister in 1894—activities in which James was happy to partake or assist.

James was also regularly invited to weekend-long gatherings hosted at Hannah de Rothschild's château, Mentmore, an English palace built by Joseph Paxton from 1851 to 1855, and Waddesdon, a newly constructed (1889) French château modeled on those of the Loire Valley. His letters home on the subject read like pages from the gossip columns: "There are several people here, but no one very important, save John Bright and Lord Northbrook, the last Liberal Viceroy of India [...] There are no ladies save a little Mrs. Godley [...] and a graceful Lady Emma Baring, daughter of Lord Northbrook, whose prettiness, as is so often the misfortune of the British damsel, is impaired by protruding teeth."[55] While James enjoyed the conversation of aristocrats and heads-of-state, and could not help being taken with the gorgeousness of the surroundings, he worked all the while, listening and observing. During a long weekend at Mentmore—"a huge modern palace, filled with wonderful objects"— James wrote to his mother: "I have retired from the glittering scene to meditate by my bedroom fire on the fleeting character of earthly possessions." Detailing the scene with unmistakable irony, James continued, "A supreme being in the shape of a dumb footman arrives, to ventilate my shirt and turn my stockings inside out [...] preparatory to my dressing for dinner." Finally, he concluded: "But, after all, there is much to say—more than can be said in a letter— about one's relations with these people."[56] James clearly saw himself as different from "these people"—whom he also referred to in the French as "ces gens ci"—and was able to stand back and take mental notes as he accumulated impressions. Later, from the quiet chamber on Bolton Street, he spun what he saw into his novels.

James enjoyed the exposure to incredible inherited wealth and the company of the Roseberys and other luminaries, and, in spite of seeing himself as different from them, was not above wishing his own family had "a little more of the Rothschild element in [its] existence."[57] Yet he felt more motivated to settle down and write after time spent in their company: "Tomorrow I return to London and to my personal occupation, always doubly valued after forty eight hours passed among *ces gens-ci,* whose chief effect upon me is to sharpen my desire to distinguish myself by personal achievement [...] It is the only answer one can make to their atrocious good fortune."[58]

The people more like James culturally were his many Boston or Cambridge friends who, like he, dwelled in Europe. These expatriates included the widower Francis Boott and his daughter, Lizzie, who lived in the Villa Castellani on the Bellosguardo in Florence; Mr. and Mrs. Daniel Sargent Curtis, who owned the Palazzo Barbaro in Venice;[59] Mrs. Isabella Stewart Gardner, who rented the Palazzo Barbaro during the summer from the Curtises; and Constance Fenimore Woolson, who leased the villa next door to the Boott's in Florence and whose great uncle, James Fenimore Cooper, had once lived on the Bellosguardo. On his trips to Italy throughout the last two decades of the nineteenth century, James regularly stayed with the Bootts in Florence and with Gardner or the Curtises in Venice. When, from 1886 to 1887, Woolson moved into the fourteen-room property adjoining the Boott house, Villa Brichieri-Colombi, James often stayed in one of her spare rooms. These dwellings reappear in James's fiction, sometimes years after his visits, most notably, the Palazzo Barbaro in *The Wings of the Dove* (1902) and the Boott's Villa Castellani in *The Portrait of a Lady* (1881), which is explored later in this chapter.

Just as James was captivated by the charm and extravagance of Lord Rosebery, his host at Mentmore and Waddesdon, he was equally seduced by Mrs. Isabella Stewart Gardner (or "Mrs. Jack," as James called her) and the Palazzo Barbaro.[60] The Palazzo was in fact one half of two adjacent buildings that face the Grand Canal of Venice; the one on the left, a Gothic palace dating from 1425, was acquired by the Curtis family in 1885; the one on the right, a Baroque addition that was built around 1700. The section belonging to the Curtises, who restored the building, has four stories, a mezzanine, and two loggias with four pointed arches on the two main floors. It was here that Mrs. Gardner held court for several summers, inviting writers and artists including James, John Singer Sargent, Robert Browning, and Vernon Lee (the writer who also used the name Violet Paget) to

converse on art and ideas. Though Gardner was but a temporary
resident at the Palazzo, she moved into her surroundings with
luxurious spoils acquired on her travels in Italy. James was not
inured to the gilded furniture, the 15th-century paintings by Filippo
Lippi, the canvases by Dante Gabriel Rossetti; nor to the pieces of
Gothic carving, panels, and tapestries that would eventually adorn
her palace in the Fenway in Boston. The overall environment was
extremely rarified.

When James arrived at the Palazzo, he was usually one of many
guests and was given a place to sleep in the large library, where, like
his heroine Milly Theale in *The Wings of the Dove*, he awoke each
morning to find himself staring at the medallions and arabesques on
the ceiling. The Italian servant, Tita, would enter his room on tiptoe,
bringing a pot of hot coffee. In the library, James was surrounded by
luxurious pink chairs, a lemon-colored sofa, and a cool tiled floor; he
reveled in the grandeur of his environment and of the beautiful views
of Venice's Grand Canal.[61] The Venetian life of Mrs. Gardner was as
different from James's life as a solitary writer in London as it could
be. Where the library at the Reform Club was dark, masculine, and
staid, and the overall club atmosphere, stuffy and smoky, the Palazzo
Barbaro enveloped James in sumptuously ornate Baroque furnishings
and paintings, the warm air of the Italian sirocco, and the high
energy of the greatly bejeweled Mrs. Jack. It was difficult for him to
leave the divine setting, but when he did, he was content to take his
many observations with him to London and add them to his notebooks
for future literary use.

Like the streets of London and his club memberships, stays at
Mentmore and the Palazzo Barbaro furthered James's work in three
ways: they provided him with "homes away from home" where he
could indulge his love of beauty, his passion for the high life, and his
need for conversation; aesthetic scenes that could (and would)
reappear in his fiction or non-fiction; and perhaps most important, the
longing to return to his small studio-like space to work. James was
committed to "total aestheticism," since for him all the arts were one;
thus, visits to the grand homes of his friends were as important to the
flâneur as walking the streets of Mayfair.[62] As William Gass so
eloquently put it, "His aim [was] to appreciate and to respect the
things of his experience and to set them, finally, free."[63]

Houses of Fiction

James used the world as the fodder for his fiction, as we have seen, but with his distance and detachment—his persona as a writer— where did he locate himself in that world? He was not particularly invested in his first London dwelling as his compatriots Stowe and Howells were in their Cambridge or Hartford homes, yet he was clearly preoccupied with exteriors and interiors—both metaphoric and actual—and his fiction often centered on significant elaborations of houses. As William Gass has written, James's awareness was so pervasive that "it invaded furniture and walls and ornamental gardens and perched upon the shoulders of his people a dove for spirit."[64] In James's work, houses or art objects function as main characters, such as Poynton Park in *The Spoils of Poynton* (1897), a novel originally entitled *The House Beautiful*,[65] and the eponymous object in *The Golden Bowl* (1904); or, they contribute greatly to scene and plot such as Gardencourt in *The Portrait of a Lady* (1881) and the Palazzo Barbaro in *The Wings of the Dove* (1902).

In 1878 and 1879, around the time that James met the Roseberys, he began conceiving his masterpiece, *The Portrait of a Lady*, the novel that, looking back, James felt to be his most "architecturally competent" (11). Having secured his reputation as a writer of the "international scene" with the successful novellas *Daisy Miller* (1878) and *An International Episode* (1878), James, now thirty-five, began work on an important novel; when writing of his plan, he referred to everything leading up to this novel as a series of "experiments of form," the first stage of a "step-by-step evolution."[66] As he ruminated on his idea for a woman who would become Isabel Archer, he wrote to his friend, Isabella Gardner, "Look out for my next big novel; it will immortalize me."[67] Fully conscious of his ambition, his potential, and his desire for greatness, James dotted his letters with similarly self-assured words.[68]

The first of his major works to earn him large sums of money and fame in London, Boston, and New York literary circles, *The Portrait of a Lady* encapsulates the types of domiciles and interiors that captivated James as an expatriate and in which he dwelled for both literary and social purposes. While the *Portrait* is first and foremost a psychological novel, a novel of "consciousness" as James insisted in his preface to the New York Edition, and enables us to see the inner life of the heroine, Isabel Archer, the reader finds him or herself in intensely external milieus, like the setting of the novel's opening

Figure 3.1. **Henry James c. 1905, in Northampton, MA,
when he was visiting the United States and was staying
with Edith Wharton at the Mount.** Sophia Smith Collection, Smith College.

Figure 3.2. **James's beloved Lamb House in Rye, England,
where he lived for the last twenty years of his life.** Author's collection.

scene.[69] Details of houses and their inhabitants reveal the way James looked through exteriors in his attempt to understand interiors, to, as he had put it, guess the unseen from the seen.

The Portrait of a Lady opens with the presentation of Gardencourt, an old English country house owned by an American banker, Mr. Touchett, and later bequeathed to his son, Ralph Touchett. Rising beyond the lawn, the mansion has "a long gabled front of red brick, with the complexion of which time and the weather had played all sorts of pictorial tricks, only, however, to improve and refine it" (18). Further eliciting our appreciation for the dignified manse, James tells us that the house has "a name and a history," having been built "under Edward the Sixth, [and having] offered a night's hospitality to the great Queen Elizabeth" (18). This house bears no likeness to the Rothschild châteaux—Waddesdon Manor, for example—which were often new creations inspired by old ones. Gardencourt was a typical English country house styled after those James saw when he traveled outside of London. After the turn of the century he had his photographer, Alvin Langdon Coburn, take a picture of one of these properties for the frontispiece to the novel, where it appeared in the New York Edition.

In spite of its antiquity and authenticity, James has mixed feelings about Gardencourt, and about the English country house in general. He was both attracted to and repelled by them: on one hand, he admired their history and sense of privacy and privilege; on the other, he bemoaned their ugliness, incommodity, and extravagance. Such houses, as biographer Leon Edel has noted, ministered to James's innate aristocratic sense and to his feelings for past and present, for the fruits of ripe civilization.[70] But they also opened his eyes to a degree of corruption that he was loath to see. In a letter to his friend Grace Norton (sister of Charles Eliot Norton) at this time, he regretted the "great total of labor and poverty on whose base all the luxury and leisure of English country houses [were] built up."[71] Like Howells back in Boston, James was sickened by the chasm dividing the rich and the poor.

The narrator's feelings (and, it seems, James's) for the Touchetts, who own and inhabit Gardencourt, are similarly mixed. The senior Mr. Touchett, the proprietor of the house, is a successful American businessman who came to England some thirty years before and enjoys relatively new wealth, though by no means on the scale of the Rothschilds. Everything about Mr. Touchett, as James intones, is placid, acute, clean, and shrewd. His son, Ralph Touchett, who inherits the house, is his opposite: "ugly," "sickly," "straggling," "shambling," and "wandering" are the adjectives used to describe him. While father exudes the spoils of wealth, son encompasses the weakness of ill health. The lovingly described house upon whose lawn the first chapter of the novel unfolds, then, can be seen as a concrete manifestation of both father and son: it is both stately and decrepit. Having withstood a certain number of years, the house, like the individuals, has been bruised, defaced, repaired, enlarged, remodeled, disfigured—all James's words—and, only now, after a good deal of time, has come to be appreciated for its aesthetic value. Without pushing the point too far, one might speculate that the Touchetts— and their representation through Gardencourt—function together as stand-ins for James, who saw himself as both powerful and enfeebled, particularly in respect to his literary production, but physically as well.[72] Through Mr. Touchett's appreciation for the house—"at the end of twenty years, [he] had become conscious of a real aesthetic passion for it" (18)—James implies that the longer something is treasured, the greater its value becomes, an appreciation no doubt sought from his readers.[73]

While James was enchanted by the English country house—its stateliness and potential for decay—he was equally fascinated by the Italian villa, another domain that appears in the *Portrait* in the form of Gilbert Osmond's dwelling. This residence too was based upon James's firsthand observations and was modeled on Francis Boott's fifteenth-century Villa Castellani in Florence. James was visiting Boott and his daughter Elizabeth ("Lizzie") in Florence just as he was completing the first installments of the novel in 1880 and had Boott in mind as a physical type when he conceived of Osmond. Three years earlier, James had described the Boott's Florentine villa in a travel sketch, which foreshadowed the setting he used for Osmond's villa.[74] While the Boott house provided James with "the setting of a massive old Tuscan residence [...] in the authenticated way, with its essential fund of truth," the inhabitants of the actual and fictional abodes do not resemble each other. While Boott and Osmond are both "addicted to the arts," Boott was a close friend of James's, and the author reassures us in his memoirs that his "admirable old friend [...] had no single note of character or temper, not a grain of the non-essential, in common with [his] Gilbert Osmond."[75]

Also unlike Francis Boott, Osmond bears a striking resemblance to his house. His palace, the Villa Roccanera, sits, like the Boott's, upon a Florentine hill, but aside from this proclamation, remains difficult to read. James writes of its façade: "This antique, solid, weather-worn, yet imposing front had a somewhat incommunicative character. It was the mask, not the face of the house" (195). The house's windows, like their owner's eyes (as we will see), "seemed less to offer communication with the world than to defy the world to look in [...] they were placed at such a height that curiosity, even on tiptoe, expired before it reached them" (196). Osmond's villa perfectly encapsulates his person. As readers of the novel know, Osmond is perhaps the shadiest, most villainous of James's characters.

Yet the house, like Osmond, has a charming side. James writes of its interior: "The room was less somber than our indications may have represented, for it had a wide, high door, which now stood open into the tangled garden behind; and tall iron lattices admitted on occasion more than enough of the Italian sunshine. It was moreover a seat of ease, indeed of luxury, telling of arrangements subtly studied and refinements frankly proclaimed" (196). Osmond's rooms resemble the type that James frequented, even the type that he wished one day to appropriate. Replete with damask hangings, tapestries, "chests and cabinets of carved and time-polished oak," "angular specimens of pictorial art in frames as pedantically primitive," "perverse-looking relics of medieval brass and pottery," books, magazines, and newspapers—all speak to Osmond's culture and refinement, however "lounging" he may be (196). James resembles Osmond in his ease, sense of luxury, and culture of refinement, as scholars have elucidated, but, unlike Osmond, James could not live in Italy; he found the environment too "relaxing" and thus not conducive to literary production.[76] Osmond's physical appearance calls to mind James's as well, including "his conscious, curious eyes [which are...] eyes at once vague and penetrating, intelligent and hard, expressive of the observer as well as of the dreamer" (197). Both James and Osmond, in their positions as detached observers, inhabit the "house of fiction" through which they view the world. As a writer, James locates himself in his characters and in their dwellings, and thus does not need to locate himself in his actual home.

Just as James dwelled primarily in his mind, building a metaphoric mansion therein, Isabel (also a character whom James resembles) inhabits Osmond's mind, a place as richly decorated as James's, but also a place of great "terror." When she realizes that her husband's mind, not the Villa Roccanera, appears to have become her habitation, she is incapacitated with fear: "She could live it over again, the incredulous terror with which she had taken the measure of her dwelling. It was the house of darkness, the house of dumbness, the house of suffocation" (360). It is not only Isabel who suffocates at home, for the reader, by this time, has been led through a seemingly endless house of mirrors in which characters resemble not only each other but their author as well. James's ornate, claustrophobic interiors, combined with the density of his prose, take possession of us so that we are left wishing for the same "light" and "air" that Isabel desperately desires.

James's portrayals of Osmond and Isabel and of their domiciles add to our understanding of James's solitary, monastic apartment-life; we can read his fear of marriage in Isabel's fate and his fear of himself in his depiction of Osmond. Like Osmond, James could be clever, good-natured, and amenable, cultured, knowledgeable, and often easy to be around; but also like Osmond, James could be egotistical and narcissistic. When writing on the subject of marriage, he sounds like Osmond in his chill objectivity and steely autonomy: "Sooner or later, I suppose, I shall take a house, but there is no hurry, and when I do, a conjugal Mrs. H. is not among the articles of furniture that I should put into it."[77]

Drama and De Vere Gardens, London, 1886–1897

Soon after the publication of *The Portrait of a Lady* in 1881, James's connection to the United States changed forever. Within six months of each other in 1882, both of his parents died. After the death of his mother early in the year, James returned to Cambridge, Massachusetts, to the family home at 20 Quincy Street to console his father and sister Alice. Unable to stand being in the large house without his wife, the elder James sold the family homestead; soon after, he died. James found himself at thirty-nine orphaned and adrift—without parents or a family home. Losing his mother dealt him a double blow: "It is impossible for me to say—to begin to say—all that has gone down into the grave with her," he wrote Grace Norton, "She was our life, she was the house, she was the keystone of the arch."[78] When James returned to England with unprecedented feelings of melancholy and loneliness, he threw himself into a frantic search for a new place to live; suddenly, his two small rooms on Bolton Street were not enough. His frenzied house hunt was indicative of his malaise, just as it was for Howells and would be for Wharton, and it took him three years to find the right place. In 1886, he settled upon a commodious apartment at 34 De Vere Gardens that he leased until he moved to Rye in 1897.

James's move to a larger apartment in a different part of London coincided with his increasingly introspective lifestyle brought on by the loss of his parents and, in the following year (1883), his younger brother, Wilkie, and his dear friend and inspiration, Ivan Turgenev. His fourth floor flat was located in the quiet literary neighborhood of Kensington, far from the bustling Mayfair district of his Bolton Street dwelling, and within walking distance of Kensington Gardens. James now preferred the quietness of his new neighborhood, which had been home to other writers such as Elizabeth Barrett and Robert Browning. He was especially pleased with amenities that his previous apartment lacked, including an elevator, servants' quarters (for a man and his wife), an abundance of sunlight (his main windows faced west), and good ventilation. Soon after he moved in, he wrote his friend Grace Norton: "My small home seems most pleasant [...] and my servants are as punctual as they are prim—which is saying much."[79] Though James had enough space to receive guests, an activity he enjoyed, he kept his membership at the Reform Club and usually lodged visitors there instead of at his home, as he had done at Bolton Street. He also varied his days by using the Club's library for reading and letter writing.

In spite of extra rooms—instead of the two that he had at Bolton Street, at De Vere Gardens he had five rooms for himself, not including the two for the servants—James continued to use his space primarily for work; he set up a study in the large sun-filled parlor, placing his desk in front of a long row of windows. He also had a library where he kept his books and a small sitting room that he used as the parlor. Writing to his brother of his new situation, James asserted, "I shall do far better work here than I have ever done before," and referred to the place as "chaste and secluded," "new-and-airy, conducive-to-work-and-quiet."[80] Ever budget-conscious, James took his time furnishing the place, looking for old pieces of furniture at small shops; he assured his friends that he would have "no treasures or spoils." On the walls he hung pictures of friends and family, telling Francis Boott, "I have no less than three Bootts on my wall [...] they furnish my apartment, simply—or rather, richly."[81]

The books that James wrote immediately following the deaths of his parents reflected his new preoccupations—loss and loneliness— and are highly personal works. *The Bostonians* (1884), for example, deals with his lost American home and *The Princess Casamassima*

(1885), which James described as "very long-winded," tells the story of an orphaned young man adrift in London.[82] In his subsequent novel, *The Tragic Muse* (1890), which he spent three years writing and which amounted to seventeen installments in the *Atlantic* (his longest serial), James treated English art and life. He provides a clear picture of London Bohemia and the dance between the classes through his portrayal of Miriam Rooth, an ambitious young girl who is half Jewish and half English and wants to be an actress, and Nick Dormer, an upper-class Englishman who wants to be an artist but is expected to be a politician and marry well.[83]

The years following the publication of *The Tragic Muse* were the most dramatic of James's life—in both the literary and emotional senses. In the early 1890s, James adapted his 1877 novel, *The American*, for the stage and wrote the play, *Guy Domville* (1894), fulfilling a longtime desire to write drama. He failed miserably in his attempt to stage his work; both plays received caustic reviews and poor attendances. James also had to swallow a substantial pay cut by his English publishers, Macmillan, who resigned themselves, finally, to the fact that James's work did not sell—a decision which prompted James to hire a literary agent for the first time in his life.[84] Further, in the 1890s, James endured the deaths of more loved ones, which led him to question his place in the world. His long-time friend James Russell Lowell died in 1891, followed by the death of his sister Alice in 1892, and the unexpected suicide of his friend Constance Fenimore Woolson in Venice in 1894. When James opened his play, *Guy Domville,* in London in January 1895, and was booed when he came on stage to take a bow, it is miraculous that he did not wish to die as well.

Instead of ending his misery by his own hand, James used his hand to express the disgust and dismay that consumed him following the disaster of *Guy Domville*, writing to one friend:

> I have no good news for you—for there has been since the New Year, none but the very worst possible for myself. The utter and complete failure of my play at the St. James's has completely sickened me with the theater and made me feel [...] like washing my hands of it forever [...] As I walked home, alone, after that first night, I swore to myself an oath never again to have anything to do with a business which lets one into such traps, abysses and heart-break. 'Never' is a long word, but I don't see beyond it yet.[85]

James was true to his word and never again attempted to stage a play for the London audience. Still, the degree to which he was humiliated threw him into a state of psychological introspection which caused him to reevaluate the subject and style of his writing. The era that began in the early 1890s, when James was fifty years old, and took him to Lamb House in Rye in 1897, resulted in the period of his greatest productivity and achievement. The two decades until his death in 1916, spent mostly in Rye, established James's reputation as "the Master."

Lamb House: "My Own Little Corner"

James's friendships with the landed gentry as well as with writers who owned houses in the country opened his eyes to beautiful milieus on the outskirts of London and beyond. In his peregrinations, one of the places he came to know was the county of Sussex, on the southeastern coast of England. In the summer of 1896, James had visited Playden, a hilltop town that looked across a valley to Rye, Sussex, a place he described as "a deliciously vacant and admirably blue-sea'd and densely verdured and lovely-viewed warm corner of England."[86] In the fall of 1896, James decided to prolong his stay in the area and rented the Old Vicarage in Rye, from which he first saw Lamb House. The next year, he was established in what would soon become his most fully inhabited home.

James's desire to live in Rye, a two-and-a-half hour ride by train from London, represented, most significantly, his hunger to be still more productive. Now fifty-four years old and no longer enamored of the glittering London social scene, James wished to write his family's memoirs and revisit his entire oeuvre. Unlike many writers who gradually slow down as they age, James became more prolific than ever in his final years. His removal from London was the major reason for this increased output, and though James originally intended to spend winters in rented rooms at the Reform Club, he put off doing so for several years so he could maximize the isolation of Lamb House. Only after 1910 did he secure a small, modest flat in Chelsea, where thereafter he relocated from November to March, and where he died on February 28, 1916.[87]

James's final two decades, while his most inspired, were also his saddest. During this period—from 1897 when he moved to Rye, to 1916 when he died—James lost his two remaining brothers, William and Bob (both in 1910), and became, as he put it, "the sole survivor of all my Father's house."[88] Toward the end of this period, he was beset with increasingly serious physical ailments, including the digestive and gastric problems of his younger days, angina, and weight gain. Finally, this era brought with it the First World War, an event that James saw as a "total descent into barbarism" and that provoked him to assert his loyalty to his adoptive country by applying for English citizenship, a status he achieved in September 1915, six months before he died.[89]

~ ~ ~

Soon after signing the papers to rent Lamb House (before the house was for sale), James wrote his friend Arthur Benson:

> I am just drawing a long breath from having signed [...] a most portentous parchment: the lease of a smallish, charming, cheap old house [...] for twenty-one years! (One would think I was your age!) But it is exactly what I want and secretly and hopelessly coveted without dreaming it would ever fall. But it has fallen.[90]

In another letter to the architect, Edward Warren, who had helped James find a home in Rye, James wrote that upon learning that Lamb House had suddenly become available to rent, he felt as if he had received "a blow in the stomach."[91] The next two years, however, would lead to a love affair that essentially resulted in marriage; James grew so fond of his "little corner," his "little backwater," that he professed to be "really domesticated."[92] When the property came up for sale in 1899, James plunged into the commitment of purchase. Defying his brother William's admonition that the house was over-priced, he bought it, writing Rudyard Kipling: "I am marching bravely to the altar—for that is what it seems like: the making an 'honest woman' of a trusting thing whom I had publicly taken up with. I don't regret it. She wears well—but I have to make some 'settlements.'"[93] For James, the purchase of a house was akin to marriage; it represented the highest level of promise he had made thus far. Evidently the arrangement suited him, for soon after the deal was finalized, he gained a dachshund, two servants (augmented to four within a few years), a bicycle, a typewriter and typist, and a garden, which he proclaimed to be "a pure and unmitigated blessing."[94] The once inveterate London flâneur had become, at fifty-six, truly settled.

James enjoyed the old-world feel of the small village and the early Georgian house, which was built circa 1720 by James Lamb. Between the Lamb family and James, the house had only one other owner, Francis Bellingham, who acquired the property from the Lamb family in 1864 and sold it to James in 1899. Owing to its long history with one family, when James bought the house it contained numerous original features, such as a kitchen with a wide open fireplace and supporting oak beams, a stone cellar below the kitchen, and a large brick wine vault.

Large in comparison to James's London apartments, the simple but elegant brick house (Figure 3.2) offered the writer what he needed to settle into years of unparalleled creativity: remoteness, quietude, sunlight, and space. The ground floor of the house featured a wide entrance hall and a staircase with an oak-paneled drawing room (now known as the Morning Room) immediately to the left, and a dining room beyond it also on the left; both rooms contained original tiled corner fireplaces. James enlisted Warren to add long French windows to both the drawing and dining rooms so that their views of the garden would be better enjoyed. To the right of the hall was a small sitting room that gave onto the cobblestone street and the church across the way. Upstairs lay three bedrooms and the Green Room, a sitting room so named for the color of its paneling, and that James used as his winter study.

When James first moved into the house, he used the Morning Room as a place for work; however, nine months after he moved in, the house caught fire, and, when renovating it, James commissioned Warren to turn the small building adjacent to the house into a "Garden Studio," which he used for work during the summer months.[95] James was happiest reading and writing in this small, sun-filled building, and he spent several hours there each day. Mrs. James T. Fields, widow of the publisher and long-time friend of Harriet Beecher Stowe, was one of the earliest visitors to the house, and wrote of the space:

> At an angle with the house is a building which [James] laughingly called the temple of the Muse. This is his own place par excellence. A good writing table and one for his secretary, a typewriter, books and a sketch by Du Maurier, with a few other pictures (rather mementoes than works of art), excellent windows with clear light—such is the temple! Evidently an admirable spot for his work.[96]

After the fire in 1898, and the completion of the Garden Studio several months later, James settled into his "temple" to begin the task of writing three great novels in three years: *The Wings of a Dove* (1902), *The Ambassadors* (serialized in the *North American Review* from January to December 1903 and published in December 1903),

and *The Golden Bowl* (1904). All (including *The Sacred Fount* [1901])
were written in the Garden Studio during the late spring and
summer, and in the Morning Room throughout the winter. Entranced
with his work—though still dismayed by his failure to sell—James
hardly found the time to keep up with his correspondence. Writing his
sister-in-law in early 1900, he admitted: "I have a pile of letters chin-
high before me—and am so working now, more and more, at fiction
that, after my mornings, I feel quite depleted for even the most trivial
forms of composition. And this grows as the fiction grows. So bear
with my meagerness."[97] As far as letter-writing was concerned,
James's "meagerness" might mean a letter of five hand-written pages
instead of his usual ten to twenty page reams.

James's routine resembled the workaday schedule he had set for
himself as a young man, but in the country, he felt better able to
concentrate. His first priority, as always, was his writing, so he kept
his engagements to a minimum, particularly from 1899 to 1904. When
he wasn't reading or writing, James no longer displayed the need to
"consume" impressions—in fact, he had had his fill of them—and
instead he kept fit by biking through the countryside, walking by the
sea, and tending his garden with the help of George Gammon (who
stayed on as gardener at Lamb House long after James's death).
James summed up his glorious new life in a letter to his friend
Henrietta Reubell: "The autumn and winter charm of the country is
the evenings—selfish and unsocial, with the firelight, lamplight, and
the book—always the same. It is rapture."[98] Once again, the author
had managed to find for himself exactly what he needed for his craft,
just as he had done at Bolton Street twenty years before.

James's health during his early years in Rye was particularly
strong, owing, in part, to regular biking and walking but also to a
revolutionary method of eating called "Fletcherizing," so called for the
popular food faddist Horace Fletcher, who recommended chewing one's
food into liquidity before swallowing it.[99] James began "Fletcherizing"
soon after the turn of the century because he had been told by his
doctor to lose weight—he had gained a considerable amount due to his
depression in the 1880s and 1890s—and found Fletcher's regime
invaluable for this purpose. He wrote his brother: "I continue to found
my life on Fletcher. He is immense—thanks to which I am getting
much less so."[100] Inspired by the results of the regime, James urged
friends to practice, writing Mrs. Humphrey Ward: "Fletcherize hard
[...] Am I a convert? You ask. A fanatic, I reply [...] It's none the less
supremely difficult—really to do it (and I really do it): all life and

conversation are so arrayed against it." When James describes in more detail how he eats, we begin to understand why his practice made socializing and conversation difficult, but James was pleased to have a good reason for declining dinner invitations: "Here I spend fifty minutes [...] over a cold partridge, a potato (three potatoes) and a baked apple—all with much bread [...] which means that I munch unsociably and in passionate silence, and that is making me both unsociable and inhospitable (without at the same time making me in the least ashamed of so being. I brazenly glory in it)."[101] James's adoption of the Fletcher mode of eating enhanced his life in a curious way: it forced him to remain seated—"a luxurious immobility"—and chew his food much longer than he normally would. As a result, it offered him another opportunity to "chew on" his ideas.[102] Residing two and a half hours away from the metropolis and spending most of his meals alone in deliberate mastication, James inhabited his mind more and more, and lived increasingly for his writing. When his brother William visited in 1908, James characterized himself as "a corpulent, slowly-circulating, slowly-masticating master."[103]

Measured and methodical as James was, he took advantage of technologies that in some ways made his life easier. These included the bicycle, the typewriter, the telephone, and the car—all of which James first warily accepted but then fully embraced. In 1896, when he was working on *What Maisie Knew*, James developed a severe cramp in his right hand, and in 1897, hired the first of his three amanuenses, William MacAlpine, who accompanied the author to Rye, and rented an apartment close by. Because it took MacAlpine—a shorthand reporter—a long time to transcribe his notes, James purchased a typewriter (a Remington) and began to dictate directly to his typist, a mode which became his permanent way of work.[104] Dictation—which James gave while pacing back and forth in the room—changed his life. While it enabled him to think freely without the distraction of putting thoughts to paper, it also pinned him down; he could not easily transport his typewriter and his typist wherever he wished to go. The Reform Club, for example, which James frequented when he was in London, did not allow him to bring a female amanuensis (which he had after MacAlpine) into the building. (As a result, James ended up renting a workspace near his typist so he could work while in the city). The consequence of his new mode of work was that he no longer traveled as frequently as he used to. Between 1896 and 1916, he made a yearlong trip to the United States from 1904 to 1905 (upon which *The American Scene* is based), another after the death of his brothers from 1910 to 1911, and an episodic visit to the Continent. After 1912, James was too weak to handwrite or type letters and began dictating these as well, though he hated the thought of the "impersonal machine" carrying his messages to his friends.[105]

While the typewriter kept James planted peacefully in Rye, the newly invented automobile liberated him. Though he never owned a car—he claimed he was too poor to buy one—James took great pleasure in the novel experience of touring the French, English, and American countryside by automobile. His new friend, Edith Wharton, whom he had met in 1902 through Paul Bourget, initiated him to the joy of "motoring" when he visited her in the United States in 1904.[106] James spent several weeks at the Mount, Wharton's mansion in Lenox, Massachusetts, and was won over: "The mountain-and-valley, lake-and-river beauty extends so far and goes so on and on," he wrote his friend Jessie Allen, "that even the longest spins do not take one out of it." While James was impressed with Wharton's lifestyle, he felt somewhat out of place in her vast country house: "The region, as I say, is lovely, and—or rather *but*—everyone is oppressively rich [...] and 'a million a year' seems to be the usual income."[107] Rather than delight in the "high life" of Wharton and her husband Teddy, as he once would have, James now expressed his dismay with the "death-dealing leisure" of his friends; such amusements distracted him from the one thing he most wanted to do: write. James described traveling with Wharton as "an expensive fairy-tale," and complained, "It is one's rich friends who cost one!"[108]

Just as the lifestyle of the Roseberys and other aristocrats had left James yearning for the quietude of his Bolton Street apartment, so too did the "riotous living" of the Whartons and their entourage, leave him aching for the "life-saving retreat" of Lamb House, "poor frowsy, tea-and-toasty Lamb House."[109] As James became better acquainted with Wharton—whose career he took interest in after her publication of *The House of Mirth* in 1905—and learned about her troubled marriage with Teddy and of her love affair with his friend Morton Fullerton, he seems to have become more and more convinced of the blessing of his own small "mouse-like existence."[110]

In February 1905, while still on his American tour, James visited George Washington Vanderbilt's Biltmore, in Asheville, North Carolina, and was once again troubled (rather than awed) by the "strange, colossal, heartbreaking house," which he said could contain "two or three Mentmores or Waddesdons."[111] He wrote to Wharton:

It has all been verily a strange experience...the extraordinary impenitent madness (of millions) which led to the erection [...] of so gigantic and elaborate a monument to all that *isn't* socially possible there. It's *in effect*, like a gorgeous practical joke—but at one's own expense, after all, if one has to live in solitude in these league-long marble halls and sit in alternate Gothic and Palladian cathedrals."[112]

Contrary to the pleasure he once found at being invited to such palaces, on this occasion, James was moved to conclude, "I would rather live a beggar at Lamb House—and it's to that I shall return."[113] The "gilded bondage" of enormous country houses had lost its luster and James vowed never again "to attempt, for more than the fleeting hour, to lead other people's [lives]."[114]

When James returned to Rye in July 1905, he was buoyed with an immense amount of energy just as he had been when he first moved there, and promptly set upon his greatest task yet: the *New York Edition*, published between 1907 and 1909. The *New York Edition* comprised twenty-four volumes of his best work. James revised each of these works and wrote a lengthy autobiographical preface for each one—something no other writer had done before or has done since. The process took an immense amount of time and labor, and in a sense, can be seen as James's final effort to "touch up" or "renovate" his houses of fiction for eternal dwelling. As Leon Edel has written, the *New York Edition* was James's "final canon," over which he exercised total control.[115] Rather than write new fiction, which he wanted less and less to do, James returned to—moved back into—his early "houses," and decorated them too. For each revised work, James agreed to include an illustration that represented the type of setting he had meant to create. He sent Alvin Langdon Coburn, a young American photographer, throughout Europe, England, and America to find appropriate sites for each of the twenty-four frontispieces that eventually graced the revised works.[116]

James's publication of the final volumes of the *New York Edition* in 1909 was followed by the death of William, the family member with whom James had been closest. James returned to the United States for one year to "cleave intensely together" with William's wife Alice and their four grown children. When he returned to England in the summer of 1911, he declared the era of "Rye hibernations" over and procured a small apartment in Chelsea on Cheyne Walk for the winter months.[117] He took refuge in his art and in his past through the autobiographical volumes *A Small Boy and Others* (1913) and *Notes of a Son and Brother* (1914). As the bona fide master of his craft, he counseled younger writers such as Edith Wharton, Morton Fullerton, and Paul Bourget to believe in "Art" and in their craft, and reassured himself of his own conviction. To Paul Bourget, he wrote:

> I'm very glad to hear you have opened the door again to the fairy Invention. She always passes and repasses a few times before she comes in, but come in she at last *does* if you only keep the threshold swept and put a chair to keep the door back. I am sure indeed that by this time she is comfortably seated with you. For myself, more than ever, our famous 'Art' is the one refuge and sanatorium.[118]

Nearly a decade later, James reiterated his unwavering faith in art: "The life of art [...] religiously invoked and handsomely understood [...] *never* fails the sincere invoker," he wrote Morton Fullerton, "She has seen *me* through everything, and that was a large order too."[119] The meticulous, disciplined James had kept his door open and his threshold swept, and, to the end, his art saw him through his life.

CHAPTER FOUR

Edith Wharton:
"A Beautiful Construction"

"No one fully knows our Edith who has not seen her in the act of creating a habitation for herself."

—Henry James

A visit to Edith Wharton's estate in Lenox, Massachusetts, reveals contradictions as profound as those of the author herself. Approaching the house from a long, wooded drive, one passes a gatehouse, stables, and caretakers' lodging, and finally, after bending to the left and the right, one sees the mansion standing partially obscured by a ten-foot-high wall that circles the front of the house like a moat. Entering the gravel "forecourt" as it is called, one faces another nondescript door, leaving the visitor to wonder if he or she is in the wrong place: at the servants' entrance or on the wrong side of the structure. Such are the complications of penetrating Edith Wharton's famous abode, the Mount, which stands on the hilly terrain of the Berkshires in Western Massachusetts.

The inconsistencies of Wharton's home continue beyond the small front door: once inside the entrance hall, there is no sign of a staircase. Typically when one approaches a grand country mansion—the type that dotted Lenox at the time Wharton was constructing the Mount— one enters through an equally impressive front door and is welcomed by a dominant staircase. Not so at the Wharton home. One stands in a room that is dark and largely unadorned, like a cave or grotto. All details combine to produce a mysterious effect: a small fountain of dripping water, walls paneled with rippling stucco, a dark tiled floor. The overall atmosphere is dank and mystifying, hardly welcoming, but rather, a bit disturbing. At this point, one would be greeted by a servant and only then would learn that the stairs are intentionally hidden from view. They lie to the right behind a set of double doors, narrow and discreet enough to call to mind the type of back stairs used for staff.

Such a configuration provided Wharton with just what she wanted: "security from intrusion."[1] In fact, the author was so well insulated at her Berkshires home that she sometimes signed her letters "the hermit of Western Massachusetts, Edith Wharton."[2] One cannot help but wonder why, when constructing a grand country mansion, Wharton wanted such protection, particularly since the author could also be very sociable. The incongruities of the Mount and of the myriad other homes in which Wharton dwelled tap into lifelong tensions in her life—tensions between Wharton the aristocratic hostess and Wharton the novelist; between the socialite and the hermit; between the confident taste-maker and the insecure lover; and between the asexual Wharton whose childless marriage ended in divorce and the passionate, sensual Wharton who wrote "at a high pitch of creative joy."[3]

Writers, in general, and those of this study in particular, create oases where they can read and write in solitude, so in her pursuit of a country refuge, which the Mount was, Wharton was not unusual. Unlike her peers' homes, however, the Mount was not only difficult to get to, but off-putting upon arrival as well. Only when guests make their way to the second floor gallery do they feel welcome. It is as if the house is not intended for visitors at all—it does not encourage them—but remains open primarily to its owner, its creator, Edith Wharton. William Dean Howells's rural Belmont escape, Redtop, was also a challenge to find for even a Boston visitor, but was, upon arrival, amply hospitable. In ways typical of late-nineteenth-century eclectic architecture, the house offered a spacious central front hall, a broad staircase, and double doors leading to the library, parlor, and dining room. One has no trouble discerning where the front door lay. The same holds true for Harriet Beecher Stowe's beloved eight-gabled home, Oakholm, in Hartford, Connecticut, which featured an open entrance foyer and reception room not unlike those at Redtop.[4]

The Mount was different. From a distance it appears to be a straightforward country estate, sitting nobly upon a hill, gazing into the distant lakes and mountains. But if one were fortunate enough to be a guest there, one had to traverse numerous barriers to find the way to Wharton, who received guests on the main floor upstairs. Furthermore, in contrast to the enormity of the exterior of the house, there are few public spaces inside: only the dining and living rooms were conceived for formal entertaining. The other main floor rooms included Wharton's library, which was reserved for close friends of the authoress, and her husband Teddy's den.[5]

As writers and individuals, Wharton and her predecessors, Stowe, Howells, and James, share an intriguing combination of traits: each author mixes elusiveness and popularity, a desire for privacy and a yearning for success; these qualities manifest themselves in where and how they chose to live. Stowe struggled to find calm at home while she became increasingly famous and wealthy. Howells was endlessly popular and had to fight for his solitude. James had the opposite problem: he prioritized his writing, and begged for engagements, which would offer a reprieve from his solitude. Wharton too strove to balance her two lives—that of reclusive writer and that of celebrity author. Of the four, she was perhaps the most successful. She did not begin writing until mid life, had ample financial means, and was childless; these factors facilitated her pursuit of the perfect home.[6] More importantly, Wharton was extremely attuned to her physical environment and realized that architecture and decoration affected her state of mind. She spent years creating spaces that truly met her needs and was even considered "intolerably self-assured" in her principles of design and decoration, a quality that none of the other authors, including Stowe, boasted.[7] Thus, the dance between the public and the private spheres that marks the approach to and the layout of the Mount was part of a carefully realized plan, just as the diversity and complexity of her other homes was fully intentional. As her niece Beatrix Jones Farrand wrote to their mutual friend Gaillard Lapsley after Wharton's death, "She was a beautiful construction built around a great gift."[8] Wharton's gift was writing; the rest of her life was a beautiful construction.

Houses and their outlying landscapes were more than hobbies for Wharton; they were worlds into which she could throw herself completely. Like her fiction, they provided realms that she could utterly control. In her key residences—the Newport, Rhode Island, estate Land's End; the Mount in Lenox, Massachusetts; and Pavillon Colombe and Sainte-Claire le Château in France—Wharton went to great and expensive lengths to create harmonious, elegant rooms on the inside and to cultivate expansive formal and informal gardens on the outside.[9] The variety of spaces and of forms, inside and out—and the variation in the houses themselves—helped fulfill different aspects of Wharton's many personae. So much did she enjoy "creating a habitation for herself," as Henry James wrote of her, that she often bought and renovated a home when her personal life was in a state of disarray. Decorating and gardening offered Wharton cures, refuges from what she called the "usual endless petrifying drip of Little Things."[10] Wharton herself used the metaphor of the house as a antidote to life's travails in a letter to a friend: "I believe I know the only cure which is [...] to decorate one's inner house so richly that one is content there, glad to welcome anyone who wants to come and stay, but happy all the same when one is inevitably alone."[11]

In spite of her penchant for creating habitations, Wharton was a woman on the move. Frequent enough were her dislocations that James referred to Wharton as the "pendulum woman," constantly "wound up" and "ready for new worlds to conquer."[12] In his eyes, Wharton existed in a state of continual motion, never content with one locale or one abode. She was forward-moving, fast-paced, and energetic; her letters overflow with exclamation points and dashes; her words run together on the page. She crossed the Atlantic every year to sightsee and visit friends, and when living in France, traveled extensively in Morocco, Germany, Italy, England, and Scotland. Wharton's motto for life says it all: "Fish, cut bait, or get out of the boat."[13] When she needed a change of scenery, or things were not going well in one location, Wharton quickly found another.

It is curious, given Wharton's enormous energy, haste, and even impatience that she could write such meticulously crafted novels, where each word seems to count for so much. But this dichotomy, like her many others, is what makes her so complex. She wrote fast letters but slow novels; she loved to travel but yearned to return home; she enjoyed people but was most content alone in her gardens; she was phenomenally passionate and excitable, yet she married Teddy Wharton—by all accounts the least exciting of all the men she knew in her lifetime. In many ways, Wharton encompassed two people. As she herself said, she comprised both "the *netteté* [clearness, clarity], the line—in thinking and in conduct," but also the "'natural magic,' the *au-delà*, dream-side of things."[14] That she successfully married the two—the "line" and the "magic"—was perhaps her ultimate achievement.

Swinging Between Old and New

Born in 1862 in her parents' house in New York City, Wharton (Figure 4.1) was the last child and only daughter of independently wealthy New Yorkers George Frederic and Lucretia Stevens Jones ("Lu"), who were part of the set who "ruled New York society before the Civil War."[15] Wharton's numerous biographers have detailed the stifling, narrow-minded world in which she grew up, and Wharton herself noted in her autobiography: "When I was young it used to seem to me that the group in which I grew up was like an empty vessel into which no new wine would ever again be poured."[16] Her two brothers, Frederic Rhinelander ("Freddie") and Henry Edward ("Harry"), were sixteen and twelve years older than she, respectively, so the young Edith Jones, practically speaking, grew up as an only child. She had a famously chilly relationship with her mother, who cared more about keeping up with appearances than with the emotional wellbeing of her children. The Jones household on West 23rd Street near Fifth Avenue, by all accounts, was not a cheerful place. Wharton lived in dread of her mother's critical eye, and her father either buried his head in bills (Lucretia, a "born shopper," was a famous spender of his money) or hid himself in his library. Wharton soon followed his example, and owed to her father her love of reading and her introduction to works such as John Ruskin's *The Stones of Venice* and Walter Pater's *Renaissance Studies*.[17]

Wharton's first exposure to interior decoration and household management came, as might be expected, from her mother, the former Lucretia Stevens Rhinelander, who was a consummate hostess and entertainer. Mrs. Jones proudly upheld a high Victorian aesthetic and espoused all things elaborate and embellished. Photographs of the Wharton home reveal an avalanche of heavy velvet and brocade fabrics on the curtains, furniture, and walls. Wharton herself recalled "three layers of curtains" in every room, through which "no eye from the street could possibly penetrate."[18] The rooms featured expensive heavy walnut furniture or monumental pieces of Dutch marquetry but lacked delicacy and harmony. In the narrow, three-story brownstone, made up of many small square rooms, the overall effect was dizzying and claustrophobic, and young Edith hated it.[19]

To escape the stultifying and emotionless environment at home, Wharton threw herself into the world of her imagination, her "secret garden" as she called it, a place she could control as a means of escaping her mother's world.[20] While she once noted how "pitiful a provision was made for the life of the imagination behind those uniform brownstone facades [in which she came of age]," Wharton concluded that the creative mind "thrives best on a reduced diet."[21] Thus, as a result of her suffocation at home, Wharton developed a keen inner life. Controlling and embellishing her environment (imaginatively and physically) became her focus, and reading or writing books, designing houses, and planning gardens provided the perfect means to do so. Always attentive to details, Wharton was well prepared for her career as a realist writer and as a connoisseur of architecture. Of her gift for realism, she offered: "The truth is that I have always found it hard to explain that gradual absorption into my pores of a myriad details—

details of landscape, architecture, old furniture and eighteenth century portraits." Rather than studying these details with a book in mind, she continued, her writing is simply "saturated with the atmosphere I had so long lived in."[22]

The environment of New York City in the early 1870s added to Wharton's disgust with her youth. "One of the most depressing impressions of my childhood," she wrote, "is my recollection of the intolerable ugliness of New York, of its untended streets and the narrow houses so lacking in external dignity, so crammed with smug and suffocating upholstery."[23] While she and her parents were fortunate enough to live in Europe from 1866 to 1872 (Wharton was four when they left the States), a stay that imbued her young mind with its earliest notions of beauty, the transition back to New York was painful: "Out of doors, in the mean monotonous streets, without architecture, without great churches or palaces, or any visible memorials of an historic past, what could New York offer a child whose eyes had been filled with shapes of immortal beauty and immemorial significance?"[24] By contrast, the move from New York to Rome was blissfully easy, as Wharton noted: "The chief difference was that the things about me were now not ugly but incredibly beautiful."[25]

Wharton's six-year stay in Europe helped form her acute sensibility to classical lines and symmetry, what she would later refer to as "architectural fitness and proportion." She acknowledges her debt to Europe in her autobiography: "[It] gave me, for the rest of my life, that background of beauty and old-established order."[26] Because Wharton spent the formative years of ages four to ten in Europe, her eye was trained to a certain harmonious style that remained with her for life.

Gaston Bachelard, the French philosopher who wrote *The Poetics of Space* in 1958, asserts that everything we see or live with holds a spot—a poetic image—in our mind.[27] For Wharton as a child, there were images of Italian arches, porticoes, frescoes, walls, and windows that hummed with harmony and symmetry. These images reverberated in Wharton's mind and made her reentry to New York City extremely difficult. They also provided the aesthetic template for her future residences and her novels. When she began to decorate her own homes after her marriage, she chose a style antithetical to her mother's: European Renaissance models and the American Georgian, "a spirit of rediscovered classicism," as Richard Guy Wilson calls it.[28] In her novels, which she would begin writing regularly at the turn of the century, Wharton uses claustrophobic Victorian interiors like her mother's to illustrate characters who are mean-spirited and superficial such as Lily Bart's Aunt Peniston in *The House of Mirth*. Her work is curiously devoid of characters who dwell in the type of clean, classically-inspired residences that Wharton admired. The closest she comes to creating a morally upright character who can call home a somewhat architecturally honorable abode, for example, is Lawrence Selden who resides in the Benedict, a "pseudo-Georgian" apartment building in New York City. Yet, while Selden's apartment building, with its symmetrical and refined façade, speaks more positively for him than does Mrs. Peniston's garish Victorian dwelling for her, the Benedict remains emblematic of Selden's weak character because it is a *faux* Georgian building, not an authentic one.

On another visit to Italy many years later, Wharton vividly recalled the effect of architecture upon her—doorways, windows, walls—an effect of love, and then of heartbreak when she leaves the scene. She wrote to a friend: "I never weary of driving through the streets and looking at the doorways and windows and courtyards and walls and all the glimpses one gets—Oh, there is nothing like it in the world, and it breaks my heart every time I have to leave it."[29] These feelings make special sense when viewed in light of Bachelard's *The Poetics of Space*, where he writes, "Our soul is an abode." By remembering houses and rooms in particular, and architecture and space in general, he asserts, "we learn to 'abide' within ourselves."[30] Wharton made a similar point many years before Bachelard when she famously equated a woman's nature to a "great house full of rooms;" however, in her view, "in the innermost room, the holy of holies, the soul sits alone and waits for a footstep that never comes."[31] Wharton's words speak to a fundamental solitude that Bachelard's do not underscore. As Wharton moved through the various rooms that comprised her life, she sought to accept this essential aloneness, yet she remained indebted to rooms and to houses for the grounded sense of place they provided her. Indeed, as Wharton highlights in *The House of Mirth*, with respect to Lily Bart's ultimate homelessness, "the being to whom no four walls mean more than any others, is [...] expatriate everywhere."[32]

Wharton's visceral reactions to and detailed observations of her New York childhood, as well as her self-professed "photographic memory of rooms and houses—even those seen but briefly,"[33] set the stage for her achievement as a novelist. When she chronicles the New York of her childhood in *The House of Mirth* (1905), *The Age of Innocence* (1920), and *Old New York* (1924), she draws detailed scenes of the city and its houses. Her memories of brownstone townhouses, limestone mansions, carriages, thoroughfares, and operas to delineate different social strata and their customs, infiltrate the pages of her greatest works. Many of her characters spring from people in her life. Mrs. Manson Mingott in *The Age of Innocence*, for example, is based upon Wharton's wealthy, widowed aunt, Mary Mason Jones, who, like Mingott, "watch[es] calmly for life and fashion to flow northward to her solitary doors," far above Central Park.[34]

So great was Wharton's interest in her environment that her search for an aesthetically pleasing one was arguably more important to her than anything else, including her writing and her romantic life. One might posit that without an agreeable environment, Wharton could neither write nor love. When she traveled to Italy—her mind's apex of physical beauty—she breathed more easily, for, she said, "the very air is full of architecture."[35] She equated her houses with love affairs, as if they were substitutes for relationships with people. Upon seeing the home in the south of France to which she would retire in 1925, she declared to a friend: "I saw the house and fell in love with it [...] it has never failed me since."[36] For Wharton, architecture and decoration were life forces, or, as the case may be, lifelines.[37]

Perhaps houses were so important to Wharton for the very reason that she was not particularly successful in love. In the summer of 1881 as a young woman of nineteen, she was engaged to Harry Stevens but this relationship ended suddenly supposedly due to Wharton's "preponderance of intellectuality" and literary ambition.[38] Soon thereafter, Wharton's father died, leaving her devastated and alone with her mother. In the summer of 1883, Wharton met two men in Bar Harbor, Maine: Walter Van Rensselaer Berry and Edward "Teddy" Robbins Wharton. Berry, Wharton later recalled, was "the love of all my life," but fearing the "dreadful devouring quality in love,"[39] she chose instead to marry Teddy, an upper-class gentleman thirteen years her senior whom she knew through her brother Harry. Teddy came from a wealthy Boston family, but aside from their class and their taste for travel, they had little in common, though Wharton said she appreciated his sweetness of temper and boyish enjoyment of life.[40] Many years later, in the early 1900s, Wharton had a great love affair with Morton Fullerton, but even this relationship was short-lived and a source of much anguish for the author.[41]

Around the same time as her marriage to Teddy in 1885, Wharton met a group of intellectual men who would become friends or mentors. These men, among them Ogden Codman, Jr., Egerton Winthrop, and

Charles McKim, also frequented Newport like Teddy, but were unlike him in that they greatly enlarged Wharton's knowledge of art, architecture, and literature.[42] Winthrop, nearly twice her age and a widower, lived on East 33rd Street in Manhattan, and his cosmopolitan and elegantly furnished interiors were, for Wharton, a revelation. As she recalled in her autobiography, "Educated taste replaced stuffy upholstery and rubbishy 'ornaments' with objects of real beauty in a simply designed setting."[43] In each of her future homes, Wharton sought Winthrop's type of "educated taste"—the opposite of the aesthetics she found in her mother's houses in New York City and Newport. For the rest of her life, Wharton surrounded herself with cultivated intellectual males like those she met in the mid-1880s. Later, in France, for example, her circle included Henry James, Walter Berry, Bernard Berenson, and Percy Lubbock.[44] Only much later in life did Wharton embrace women as friends; memories of her mother's "icy disapproval" must have been too chilling for her to seek out female friendship.[45]

~   ~   ~

Wharton's progression through her various homes began modestly enough: after her marriage to Teddy Wharton in 1885 when she was twenty-three, she and her husband lived in a Newport, Rhode Island, cottage that belonged to her parents and which lay directly across the street from their much larger home. Within a decade, at the still-young age of thirty-three, Wharton decided that she needed a home of her own—one that did not sit so close by her mother's—and in quick gestures that are reminiscent of Harriet Beecher Stowe, she secured two properties, one in Newport and a set of brownstones in New York City. My study of Wharton at home begins with these residences. Ever on the move, the impatient Wharton relinquished both properties within a decade. At the turn of the century, when she was nearing forty, Wharton embarked on her largest and most extravagant venture: the design and construction of the Mount, from 1900 to 1902. This move too echoed Stowe's pursuit of a dream house when Stowe was fifty. And, just as Oakholm and Redtop proved unrealistic dwelling places for Stowe and Howells, Wharton could not keep the Mount after she decided to leave her husband; she was forced to sell her prized mansion after living there for only ten years. During the troubled years before and after her divorce, which was finalized in 1913, Wharton rented a spacious apartment on the Rue de Varenne in Paris,

France; in 1919 she bought Pavillon Colombe, a large villa ten miles north of the French capital. Shortly thereafter, in 1920, she cemented her status as a thoroughly aristocratic and privileged woman with the purchase of a château on the French Mediterranean. Wharton kept these two properties and divided her time between them until she died in bed at Pavillon Colombe on August 11, 1937.

Dignifying the "Incurably Ugly": Land's End, Newport, Rhode Island

Five years after receiving her inheritance, Wharton bought Land's End, a large $80,000 house on the other side of Newport, assuring her the much-wanted distance between herself and her mother.[46] As its name suggests, the property was made up of a large corner lot—approximately 200,000 square feet with stables—on a bluff overlooking the Atlantic, with views "straight across to the west coast of Ireland."[47] While the views were gorgeous, the house and gardens needed improvement. Originally designed for Samuel G. Ward in 1864 by John Hubbard Sturgis, Wharton found the exterior of the house "incurably ugly" with its bulging mansard roof and utter lack of proportion, and soon convinced her friend, architect and interior decorator Ogden Codman, Jr., to remodel the house.[48]

Together Wharton and Codman redecorated all of the rooms and simplified the outside, stripping away unnecessary ornament and adding trelliswork to lend dignity to the place. They also enhanced the approach to the house with a circular forecourt and high hedges which gave a sense of formality to the exterior and hid the view of the service wing—a design similar to that which Codman and Wharton would employ at the Mount. One of their most successful alterations was the conversion of an outdoor porch into a large glass-walled verandah, by all accounts, the most beautiful room in the house. Wharton and Codman enclosed the space and made it a second sitting room with wide views of the gardens and ocean.

The renovation and decoration of Land's End was Wharton's and Codman's first collaboration; their correspondence about the work at the house reveals much about Wharton's personality and her taste. She shows herself to be tough, determined, and, as claimed by her contemporaries, highly self-assured in matters of design and decoration. While in Europe in 1895, for example, Wharton purchased walnut and gilt panels for the glass verandah and beseeched Codman to have the new room ready by the time she and Teddy returned to

Newport in June: "I do hope you will be an angel and have the room ready and the paint dry when we arrive." Fearing his delay, she resorted to a bit of a bribe: "You ought to, for I am bringing you a lot of photographs of Mantua which will make you fall down and worship, and then tear your hair out to think you didn't go there." Before closing her letter, she made one final attempt: "I count on the glass verandah, remember! Do please have the paint dry!"[49] Wharton's habit of imploring Codman to do as she wished—and using a number of endearments, exclamations, and benign bribes to get what she wanted—would lead her into trouble with her friend. When it came time to design and decorate the Mount in Western Massachusetts, he had wearied of her relentless requests and concern over money, and backed out of the project.

The ceiling for the glass verandah in Newport would have to wait, however, for Wharton was not able to procure one in Rome as she had hoped. As her letters show, she was a consummate collector and spender; like her contemporaries, the exceedingly wealthy Vanderbilts, she did her "shopping" in Europe and had entire rooms— complete with ceilings and walls—shipped back to the United States. Her letters offer a rare opportunity to witness Wharton the decorator at work and reveal her similarity, in terms of acquisition and spending habits, to millionaires of the epoch. However, in her own eyes, Wharton was nothing like the robber barons whose taste and excessively large homes on nearby Bellevue Avenue, such as the Breakers and Rosecliff, she considered vulgar and overdone.

With the help of Codman, and in spite of its amorphous shell, the interior of Land's End evolved into a series of beautiful, elegant, and symmetrical rooms. Wharton and Codman borrowed extensively from eighteenth-century Italian and French influences to complement the pieces of art and furniture she purchased overseas. In the front hall, Wharton requested a French-inspired staircase with wrought-iron railing flanked by wood balusters (the same type of railing she would install at the Mount) and a dark stair carpet that was held in place by brass carpet rods. Strong architectural moldings and panels gave a sense of order and proportion to the hallway.

In the library, Wharton grouped comfortable chairs and a sofa around a marble fireplace (one of Wharton's favorite pastimes was sitting in a comfortable chair and reading aloud to friends in front of a fire). The walls were painted white and punctuated by scrollwork and architectural moldings, which Codman designed and hung with engravings of European cities and monuments. Everything—from the bookcases, to the pictures on the walls, to the sconces and candelabras on the fireplace mantel—was arranged neatly and symmetrically, in stark contrast to the exterior of the house.

The rooms at Land's End fulfilled Wharton's desire for classical, not Victorian, interiors, and within a few years, Wharton was able to promote this style of decoration in a book she co-authored with Codman, *The Decoration of Houses* (1897). One of the key tenets of the book is the architectural aspect of decoration, specifically that a building's decoration can (and must) come from its architecture. Wharton writes in the introduction: "Rooms may be decorated in two ways: by a superficial application of ornament totally independent of structure, or by means of those architectural features which are part of the organism of every house, inside as well as out."[50] These words underscore Wharton's abhorrence of the superficiality of Victorian architecture and decoration. Instead of embellishment, Wharton upholds "classic tradition, proportion, and the relation of voids to masses"—the linchpins of her homes, as witnessed in Land's End.[51] Working from the bones outward, Wharton achieved these effects at Land's End through arched symmetrical doorways, well-placed windows, verandahs, and built-in bookcases—the same elements she would employ at the Mount and in her French homes.

When Wharton discusses the qualities of writing that she most admired—she was just beginning to find her literary footing during her last years at Land's End—she uses the same terms as she does when referring to architecture, noting, for example, that with each book, she sought "a higher standard in economy of expression, in purity of language, in the avoidance of the hackneyed and the precious."[52] In a sense, Wharton's principles of design and decoration paved the way for the "design" of her literary works. In the same way she conceived domestic interiors, Wharton would first sketch the "bones" of a story and have in mind one or two main characters who would anchor the plot. After these essentials were in place, the rest—the embellishment—could be added. She explains the process of writing fiction in her autobiography: "In my own case, a situation sometimes occurs to me first, and sometimes a single figure suddenly walks into my mind. If the situation takes the lead, I leave it lying about, as it were, in a quiet place, and wait till the characters creep stealthily up and wriggle themselves into it."[53] While a situation would usually provide the foundation for a short story, a main character would ground each novel: Lily Bart in *The House of Mirth*;

Newland Archer in *The Age of Innocence*; and Undine Spragg in *The Custom of the Country*, to name a few.

From Shanty to Château:
Wharton's Park Avenue Pied à Terre

At roughly the same time she bought Land's End, Wharton continued to make use of her financial windfall and paid $20,000 for a narrow, four-story brownstone in New York, located, once again, at the opposite end of the city from her mother's abode on East 23rd Street. The apartment's site—on Park Avenue between 71st and 72nd Street—was so remote at the time that Wharton referred to the place as "far up in the suburbs" in a letter to her friend Sara Norton.[54] Until this point, the couple stayed with Mrs. Jones when they visited New York, thus the new apartment offered Wharton much-wanted independence from her mother. So hasty was Wharton's purchase of the fifteen-foot-wide building—the first and only property she would own in New York City—that she did not see it before making the purchase. From Venice, she wrote Codman a lengthy letter asking him to count and estimate the size of the rooms, as well as assess the practicality of various additions to the property:

> You may remember that I told you that I own a little shanty in Park Avenue, no. 884, I think, between 71st and 72nd Streets. I meant to go take a look at it before sailing for I thought it might be possible to use it as a *pied à terre* for a couple of months in the winter [...] However, I never carried out my intention of inspecting the house, and now I want you to take a look at it for me [...] I don't want a measured plan of the house, but should simply like you to tell me how many rooms there are, and about what their size is. Also, please take a look at the plumbing, and see whether you think it would be possible to build out a pantry and add an attic with servants' rooms, and whether the house is well enough built to warrant such additions.[55]

Wharton's letter highlights a number of noteworthy points, namely her competing personality traits of impatience and meticulousness. Her letter reveals that she did not see the Park Avenue brownstone before she bought it; she is not even sure where it is located. This oversight does not seem possible for the Wharton who was fully invested in her homes, but in contrast to the shocking degree of casualness when referring to the property, Wharton also evinces the meticulousness she brought to each of her renovation projects. She expects to turn the "shanty" into a beautiful home and, from across the ocean, fixes her eye on how she will achieve her goal.

Wharton's letter also exposes her conflicting attitude towards money: "Bear in mind that we only want a cheap *pied à terre*," she writes Codman. By the end of the letter, however, her tone changes; she refers no longer to the property as a shanty but as a château: "Now do take a careful observation of my Park Avenue château, for if it is *at all* possible I really think we'll occupy it."[56] On the other side of Wharton's casual impatience lies her sense of perfection, that part of her that wants to turn the "shanty" into a "château," something grand and worthy of her. Her alternation of these words underscores competing desires to at once diminish the property and embellish it. We can only imagine what was going through Wharton's mind when she dashed off this letter (her handwriting bears the quality of being rushed), but above all, her tone is hasty and beseeching, traits that grew all too familiar to Codman. In the end, Wharton threw her financial concerns aside, for she bought the adjoining property a few years later and housed her staff there. The two properties, which no longer stand, became 882 and 884 Park Avenue.[57]

Together Wharton and Codman set out plans for adding or eliminating doorways, creating a pantry, and furnishing and decorating the interiors of the New York townhouses. Some of their ideas, including the original intention of uniting the two buildings, were not carried out, but Wharton reveled nonetheless in her eight-room city home—there were two rooms on each of the four floors—which she appointed entirely to her taste.[58] She rarely entered the other building, though she housed a staff of anywhere from four to seven individuals there, including her head housekeeper Catherine Gross, whom Wharton employed for over fifty years.

Wharton communicated with Codman through letters from Europe, where she continued to spend the spring months (generally from March to May). While abroad, Wharton visited numerous châteaux and villas, picking up ideas here and there and indulging her love of "antique-ing" as she looked for pieces. She recounted her purchases to Codman so that he would know what type of interiors she had in mind for the brownstones. From Venice, Wharton writes: "I have got some nice furniture for the morning room, and such a nice XVIII century picture of a carnival scene! The 'pickings' here are very pleasant, for people who adore *simple* XVIII century Italian furniture, as I do more and more every day. It is still to be had for the asking, too. We are negotiating now for a beautiful armchair covered with old silk for 40 francs!"[59] One month later, in June 1892, Wharton wrote ecstatically about the "pickings" she had found in Italy:

> We have been having lots of fun since I last wrote you, picking up odds and ends of furniture. I never realized before the absurd cheapness of XVIII century furniture in Italy, and there is so much of it left. I suppose you will think me crazy when I say that I *infinitely* prefer it to French, but I think in time you will come round to my way of thinking, and so will others, and then the prices will go up.[60]

Wharton's words illuminate her confidence in herself as a trendsetter in interior decoration, for she asserts that not only Codman but also others will come soon to appreciate the furniture that she does. She resembles Stowe both in her confidence in her ideas and the haste with which she made decisions. It is almost as if Wharton knew that she would one day write *The Decoration of Houses*, so firmly did she believe in her ability to recognize a "find." Interestingly, when she and Codman wrote the book in 1897, Wharton admitted that the task of reforming American house decoration was for the upper-class, for people like herself: "It must be admitted that such reform [in house-decoration] can originate only with those whose means permit of any experiments which their taste may suggest. When the rich man demands good architecture his neighbors will get it too [...] Once the right precedent is established, it costs less to follow than to oppose it."[61] Wharton's assertion here plays interestingly with her comment about the price of XVIII furniture in Italy: the price of old things goes up with popularity; the price of new things goes down with popularity. As evidenced by her words in *The Decoration of Houses*, Wharton saw herself as one of the wealthy who could afford to set the right precedents, and she did; she also foresaw trends long before they took hold just as Stowe did.

In the letter to Codman written in 1895, Wharton also details the type and cost of the furniture she was buying in Italy, pieces whose style and provenance she would celebrate in *The Decoration of Houses*:

> Meanwhile, here are some of our purchases: 2 large armchairs white and gold, very late Louis XVI, very ornate, and in perfect condition, the pair for 80 lire! Late Louis XVI commode, white and gold, very much ornamented, marble top, 125 lire!! 6 Louis XVI armchairs, 100 lire!!! All I can say is, Wait until you see the morning room!!"[62]

These letters reveal qualities in Wharton that few people ever saw: the sheer exuberance and joy brought on by "the hunt," by the search for beautiful things. Such exclamations (she uses no fewer than eight exclamation points in four short sentences) provide a glimpse into Wharton's imagination; her excitement speaks to what Bachelard calls "the flare-up of being in the imagination," or, "the poetic act."[63] Such an outpouring of breathless rapture seems positively orgasmic, which, for Wharton, it was. Each article in her house held great psychic repercussions and each object she was able to see or acquire in Europe, as her letters illustrate, awakened new levels of joy in her. In this light, it becomes possible to understand how her houses and things functioned as surrogates for love and sexuality.

"My First Real Home": The Mount, 1902–1912

"I am in love with the place [...] climate, scenery, life and all [...] and when I have built a villa and have planted my gardens and laid out paths through my *bosco* [woods], I doubt if I will ever leave here."[64] So wrote an enamored Wharton to Codman when she first scouted out the land in Western Massachusetts upon which she would eventually construct the Mount. In 1901, the deal was finalized and for $40,600 (about one million dollars in 2009), Wharton purchased 113 acres of land from Georgiana Sargent, whose family owned several hundred acres in the area.

At the top of the list of Wharton's priorities for the Mount, named after her great-grandfather's estate in New York state, was a home that provided her ample space to entertain intellectuals such as Owen Wister, Daniel Chester French, and Charles Eliot Norton (who all owned country houses in the Berkshires), as well as solitude in which to write and garden. Wharton was only now, at the turn of the century, beginning to tap into her talent as a literary writer, and thus, at the Mount, was eager for room in which to probe this new dimension of herself. These goals resonate throughout the home in its combination of elegantly public and distinctly private spheres.

In the beginning, Wharton worked with Codman on the house's design, but she replaced him with another friend, architect Francis Hoppin of the firm Hoppin & Koen. Letters between Wharton and Codman at this time expose the strain in their partnership and the difficulty Codman had in dealing with Wharton's controlling and sometimes-parsimonious personality. They also reveal the extent to which Teddy was felt by some to be "in the way." Codman wrote a letter to his mother complaining of "what an idiot Teddy is,"[65] and that he could no longer stand the demands that both Whartons were making on him; this time, Wharton was asking Codman to drive from Newport, Rhode Island, to Lenox, Massachusetts (a distance of approximately 150 miles), to oversee progress at the mansion, something he had neither the time nor inclination to do.

Wharton resolved the situation by bringing in Hoppin, who had studied architecture at the Massachusetts Institute of Technology and at the Ecole des Beaux-Arts in Paris, and had worked at McKim, Mead, & White in New York, thus offering the classical training and beaux-arts method of design that Wharton sought. In 1894, he left McKim, Mead & White and founded his own partnership with his friend Terrence Koen, also a former employee of the McKim firm. Codman did not envy Hoppin his new client, writing to his mother that "[Hoppin] is having an awful time with the house...[Edith] telegraphs him every day or two and fusses terribly over every detail."[66] The imbroglio between Wharton and Codman was short-lived, however, for when Wharton was dissatisfied with the designs of a new interior decorator, she implored Codman to come back and do them, which he did willingly. "I am much pleased as [our reunion] will put a stop to all talk about our having quarreled," he explained to his mother.[67]

In the design of her spacious and dignified home, Wharton was both extravagant and practical: she blended her aforementioned clarity of thought (*la ligne*) with her ability to dream (*la nettété*). For example, although she preferred the style of Italian villas over French or English country houses (and states her preference in chapter one of *The Decoration of Houses*), she felt the latter would be more appropriate for an estate in New England:

> Charming as the Italian villa is, it can hardly be used in our Northern States without certain modifications, unless it is merely occupied for a few weeks in mid-summer; whereas the average French or English country house built after 1600 is perfectly suited to our climate and habits.[68]

Thus the Mount (Figure 4.2) was modeled after a seventeenth-century English country estate, Belton House, built from 1684–1686, and attributed to English architect Sir Christopher Wren. Its key difference from Belton House lies in its use of a circular, gravel forecourt—a feature Wharton added based upon the French *cours d'honneur* which she felt enhanced the sense of privacy and intimacy in one's approach to the mansion. The forecourt offers a logical separation of the principal entrance from that of the servants, which lay outside the wall to the right, and shields from the casual visitor all views of the formal gardens, grass terraces, pond, lake, and mountain that lay beyond the house. Another difference from Belton House was the material out of which the home was built, not stone or brick as Wharton had hoped, but a wooden frame covered with stucco, the less expensive option. Wharton added green shutters to the white house, thus creating a proper New England home of the Colonial Revival.

The out-of-doors was vast and multifaceted. A broad marble and brick terrace grows out of the house's dining and living rooms and stretches almost the entire length of the principal, or east, elevation. A grand Palladian staircase leads to a gravel walk below that links the house and terrace to the lower gardens. Here lay an expanse of formal box-hedge gardens, kitchen gardens from which to pick fresh herbs and vegetables, and row upon row of flower gardens with which to make beautiful bouquets. (Wharton adored the scent and look of fresh cut flowers in her rooms). Beyond the formal gardens extended the larger landscape of over 100 acres, which included pasture for the farm animals, fields, lakes, and mountains. In total, the landscape brought out in Wharton the "childish ecstasy" that she felt in nature, while the "country quiet stimulated her creative zeal."[69] The terrace and the gardens were Wharton's favorite features at the Mount and when she entertained throughout the summer, it was usually outdoors. Writing a letter to her friend, art critic Bernard Berenson, she recalled: "This place of ours is really beautiful, and the stillness, the greenness, the exuberance of my flowers, the perfume of my hemlock woods, and above all the moonlight nights on my big terrace, overlooking the lake, are a very satisfying change from six months of Paris."[70]

Wharton painstakingly planned the details of her gardens from layout to flower and shrub selection, only minimally seeking the help of her niece, landscape architect Beatrix Jones Farrand. Though she turned to eighteenth-century French and Italian models for her interiors and then published her ideas in *The Decoration of Houses*, Wharton used Italian gardens of the fifteenth to seventeenth centuries for inspiration on the outside of her mansion, and brought out a book on the subject a few years later, *Italian Villas and Their Gardens* (1905). Both the extensiveness and arrangement of the gardens at the Mount and Wharton's second treatise on design, *Italian Villas and Their Gardens*, go far in revealing the author's "secret sensitiveness" to the out of doors. Wharton carefully organized the land so that it unfolded gradually from systematic and formal near the house to wild and free the further one moved from the domestic realm. This

Figure 4.1. **Edith Wharton in a 1905 publicity photo taken at her home, The Mount, in Lenox, MA.** The Edith Wharton Collection, Beinecke Rare Book and Manuscript Library, Yale University.

Figure 4.2. **Wharton's home, The Mount, in Western Massachusetts where she lived from 1902–1912.** Beinecke.

gradual progression from tame and controlled to wild and potentially dangerous, or from the beautiful to the sublime, in the terms of Edmund Burke, allowed Wharton to indulge her love of both order (the beautiful) and mystery (the sublime).[71]

Indeed, in the book she describes Italian gardens in amorous, passionate, and mysterious terms, feelings she sought to evoke in her Lenox landscape:

> The traveler returning from Italy, with his eyes and imagination full of the ineffable Italian garden-magic, knows vaguely that the enchantment exists; that he has been under its spell, and that it is more potent, more enduring, more intoxicating to every sense than the most elaborate and glowing effects of modern horticulture; but he may not have found the key to the mystery.[72]

While Wharton loves Italian landscapes and uses a variety of words to express this devotion—"ineffable," "potent," "enduring," "intoxicating"—she also determines to control her emotion by way of understanding, or decoding, the Italian "garden-magic." Unlike the average traveler to Italy who has not "found the key to the mystery," Wharton provides the reader with that key. She explains the "skillful blending" of the three factors of Italian garden composition: marble, water, and verdure.[73] When Wharton tries to pinpoint exactly what it is that makes the Italian garden so "magical" and "intoxicating," she answers that it is a "deeper harmony of design": "However much other factors may contribute to the total impression of charm [...] by eliminating them one after another, by *thinking away* the flowers, the sunlight, the rich tinting of time, one finds that, underlying all these, there is the deeper harmony of design which is independent of any adventitious effects."[74] Wharton offers a fascinating prescription for elimination, the same elimination of excess that she sought in her decoration of houses and in her fiction. She embraces nature, and in particular the Italian garden, because of its underlying, structural harmony: a harmony that then emanates from within.

Once inside, the main rooms of the Mount—dining room, living room, and library—extend from the gallery, which runs from the stairwell at one end to Teddy's study at the other. The dining and living rooms were graced with arched French doors that opened onto the wide terrace and were furnished with pieces from Land's End and Wharton's New York City brownstone, mainly eighteenth-century Italian and French antiques. The two formal rooms featured ornate moldings and scrollwork designed by Codman and tapestries set into the walls. While the rooms were elegant and formal, they were neither overly grand nor cavernous. Like the rooms at Park Avenue, they offered intimacy and the chance for Wharton to entertain small groups of people; she preferred gatherings of six to ten rather than the large formal dinner parties then the custom in Lenox, Newport, and New York. Once asked by decorator Elsie de Wolfe why she did not have a larger dining room table and a greater number of chairs, Wharton reputedly replied, "There are but eight people [...] whom I care to have dine with me."[75]

Lying in the far northeast corner of the main floor and enjoying wide views of the formal flower garden and acreage beyond, Wharton's library remains one of the most fascinating rooms of the house. Unlike the three other main rooms on the floor (the dining and living rooms as well as Teddy's den), the room is not light, white, and airy, but warm and dark. Oak bookcases were built into three walls, one of which housed a hidden liquor cabinet and another, a concealed door that leads to Teddy's adjacent den. Wharton and Codman espouse the treatment of built-in bookcases in their book: "The plan of building bookcases into the walls is the most decorative and the most practical [...] the best examples of this treatment are found in France [...] and instead of being detached pieces of furniture, the bookcases are an organic part of the wall's decoration."[76] The walls also featured elaborate scrollwork and garlands designed by Codman, and the room's primary furniture, aside from the bookcases, consisted of a heavy desk, chairs, and a large fireplace.

Wharton's selection of books and maintenance of her library are also significant, for in both she was very much like a male scholar. Her library was based on a number of requirements: "a broad and firm foundation of books of reference constantly replenished and kept up to date; all the still *living* classics, in Greek, Latin and the principal modern languages, and an annual influx of the best in current letters."[77] Wharton even criticized the libraries of highly erudite friends like Henry James and Howard Sturgis, saying they "had nothing near to a library than a few dozen shelves of heterogeneous volumes," adding, "even in houses commonly held to be 'booky' one finds, nine times out of ten, not a library but a book-dump."[78] One whose library she did admire and felt was most like her own (but was "even bigger and more important") was Bernard Berenson's, a friend of hers who lived in Paris.[79] In her library, Wharton conversed and drank with the likes of James, Winthrop, and Walter Berry—usually the only woman in a group of highly accomplished intellectual men. In each of these ways—its use and furnishings—the room was highly unusual in its day.

In Wharton's fiction, contrary to what we witness in her life, women rarely benefit from the luxury of having their own library and women who read books, such as Ellen Olenska in *The Age of Innocence*, are ostracized by society for being too bohemian or cerebral. By contrast, gentlemen almost always have a library to retreat to. In this atypical house, however, Wharton's library garners a far more prominent location in the overall scheme than Teddy's den, which lay behind Wharton's library on the north, dark side of the house—a clear indicator of Wharton's domination at the Mount. Further, Teddy's den measured only fourteen by eighteen feet in contrast to Wharton's library, which measured twenty by twenty-five.

The evolution of the plans for Wharton's library and Teddy's den is as compelling as the fact that Wharton had a library at all. Before being dismissed as architect, Codman conceived Teddy's den at the center of the main floor, as his initial sketch for the Mount reveals. In the drawing, the den is surrounded on one side by the dining room and on the other by the library, thus the male-owner's room remains at the center of the main floor of the house, not unlike Thomas Jefferson's library at Monticello. Wharton discarded Codman's plan, however, and in redesigning the house with Hoppin, placed Teddy's den on the north side of the house. Of course, we cannot help but speculate that Wharton's increasingly strained relationship with Teddy at this time affected her decision to place his room on the dark side of the house. Curious as well is the detail that in Codman's original wall embellishments for Teddy's study, he placed the head of a woman facing east (that is, toward Wharton's library) in the medallion surrounded by swags above the fireplace and mirror. A Roman emperor's head crowned with leaves and facing west (away from Wharton's library) ultimately replaced the female head. Why, we may never know, but perhaps Wharton replaced the female head with a male one to masculinize the image of Teddy's study. In any case, Teddy had little say in the overall scheme and location of his den. When it came time to consider drawings with Hoppin, Wharton was usually the only one present, and changes to the plans are made in her handwriting. As Lewis asserts in his biography, "Edith Wharton was herself the one who supervised the manifold concerns of life at the Mount, and she reveled in every detail of it."[80]

As a whole, Wharton's library is far more intriguing than Teddy's den, not only because of its more prized location, larger scale, and abundance of books, but also because, for a woman's space, it is decidedly masculine with its dark wood and heavy leather chairs; in a sense, the room offers Wharton precisely the type of space she would inhabit were she a male author. In fact, her library resembles those that Howells used in his Beacon Street townhouse and New York City apartment—each epitomizes a masculine reading and writing room. The room and its three walls of built-in bookcases attracted such notice that they were written about in the local newspaper, *Berkshire Resort Topics*, in 1904. Teddy's den, by contrast, featured cream-colored walls with white molding and ceiling, an oak parquet floor, and several paintings; the Roman head was one of its few masculine elements. While the room was apparently furnished with a desk and a dark leather chair, it did not contain bookcases like those found in Wharton's library.[81]

In spite of a common contemporary assumption that Wharton composed her novels in her library—so believed because she posed for publicity photographs there—the author did all of her writing upstairs in her bedroom, another incongruity of the house. Here, in a corner room on the second floor, she propped herself up in bed surrounded by her many terriers, and wrote in the morning, usually from eight to noon. The bedroom sat directly above her library in the northeast corner of the house, and thus was sun-filled in the morning and offered beautiful views. Wharton established a "quiet and systematic kind of life" at the Mount, where, she recalled in her autobiography, for over ten years, "[she] lived and gardened and wrote contentedly."[82]

~   ~   ~

When Wharton moved into the Mount in late 1902, she was a woman on the verge of coming fully into her own, intellectually and literarily. Over the course of the next decade, she produced a number of her most important works: *The Valley of Decision* in 1902, *The House of Mirth* in 1905, *The Hermit and the Wild Woman and Other Stories* in 1908, *Ethan Frome* in 1911, and *The Reef* in 1912. *Ethan Frome* was the novel believed to contain her most intense and private emotions and whose main character was modeled most closely on her own psyche. It was written at a time when Wharton was increasingly frustrated in her marriage and in love with Morton Fullerton. By 1911, however much Wharton enjoyed her life at the Mount, she decided it was time for a move. That year she rented an apartment in Paris and determined to leave Teddy; he had grown mentally unstable and abusive and could not be counted on in any way. She wanted to live alone and far away from burdensome gossip and social obligations. In the fall of 1912, the Mount was sold and Wharton's divorce was finalized in 1913.

For the next six years, until the end of the First World War, Wharton dwelled in an apartment on the Rue de Varenne. By 1919, she "wanted first of all, and beyond all, to get away from Paris, away from streets and houses altogether and for always, into the country, or at least the near-country of a Paris suburb."[83] This desire brought her to a suburb about ten miles north of Paris, the small town of St.-Brice-sous-Forêt, where she bought a ramshackle but beautiful house called Pavillon Colombe. A few months later she agreed to rent (and eventually buy) a similarly run-down château in the south of France, a few miles east of Toulon. She spent the whole of 1920 begging off engagements as she superintended the cleaning up of the two houses, clearing out the gardens, planning new plantings, and settling into her two "shacks."[84] From the time Wharton divorced Teddy, her life increasingly revolved around her two loves: her houses and her writing; once her houses were fully realized (a process that took several years), Wharton focused more and more intently upon her fiction. "The core of my life was under my own roof[s], among my books and my intimate friends," she wrote in her autobiography. "Above all it was in my work, which was growing and spreading, and absorbing more and more of my time and my imagination."[85]

The Decoration of Fictional Houses

Like Wharton's interiors at the Mount, which emphasize fitness and proportion—two of the primary attributes of successful home decoration that Wharton and Codman underscore in their decorating manual—the author conceived streamlined and simple interiors in her novels to call attention to good characters. She confirms her preference for simplicity and integrity in her book on decoration:

> The simplest and most cheaply furnished room (provided the furniture be good of its kind, and the walls and carpet unobjectionable in color) will be more pleasing to the fastidious eye than one in which gilded consoles and cabinets of buhl stand side by side with cheap machine-made furniture, and delicate old marquetry tables are covered with trashy china ornaments."[86]

In the same way that Wharton felt sound architecture was a moral dictum (as expressed in her decorating manual), she used her fiction to illustrate how morally good characters live in contrast to those who are corrupt or vulgar. Simply furnished rooms are "more pleasing" than those overcrowded with an abundance of superficially decorated pieces, just as Wharton's "dull" characters—the word she uses to characterize a woman such as Gerty Farish in *The House of Mirth*—appear in more positive terms than their wealthy counterparts. Judy Trenor, who dwells at Bellomont amidst similar "gilded consoles" and "tables covered with trashy china ornaments," is depicted in morally inferior terms to the simpler characters in the book. She cannot, for example, "sustain life except in a crowd" and knows "no more personal emotion than that of hatred for the woman who presumed to give bigger dinners or have more amusing house-parties than herself" (34). Epitomizing the superficiality of the Gilded Age, Mrs. Trenor hides behind a glittery façade that cloaks her weak moral character.

Gerty, by contrast, evinces ingenuity and resourcefulness through her modest apartment, which "sparkle[s] with welcome" (122). Wharton notes the "ingenuity with which [Gerty] had utilized every inch of her small quarters," mainly by "improvising"—a sign of her self-sufficiency (122). Later in the novel, we encounter Nettie Struther, who, like her surroundings, "is alive with hope and energy" (243) and, in spite of hardship, puts forth a "beaming countenance" (244); she is generous, passionate, and strong. Her kitchen, though "extraordinarily small," is "miraculously clean" and "a fire shone through the polished flanks of the iron stove" (244). Upon leaving Nettie, and her welcoming, homey environment, Lily feels "stronger and happier" too (246).

Wharton's depiction of Nettie, her baby, and her small home, resonates with the illustration of a good Christian home in Beecher and Stowe's manual *The American Woman's Home*. Despite poverty and other troubles, Nettie manages to create a clean and moral home that suggests her goodness. The encounter with Nettie opens Lily's eyes and serves as a lesson: finally, in the meanest of circumstances, Lily has realized not only what it means to give spontaneously, but also that beautiful interiors do not necessarily equate with beautiful people. Even though Gerty's dull face might "invite a dull fate" (128), she is a morally sound person who chooses to do good even when she doesn't want to. When Lily arrives at her place late one night seeking consolation, Gerty jumps to her friend's aid in spite of a waver of hesitation: "Gerty's compassionate instincts, responding to the swift call of habit, swept aside all her reluctances. Lily was simply someone who needed help—for what reason, there was no time to pause or conjecture" (129). Both Gerty's and Nettie's homes positively affect those who enter them, no matter how simple, dull, or modest they may be. In fact, Wharton suggests that it is because of their modesty and simplicity that the rooms benefit their inhabitants.

When Wharton contrasts Charity Royall's home-life with that of the hapless Mountain people of North Dormer in her novella *Summer* (1917), she again imbues a simple abode with goodness. Mr. Royall's red house—especially when seen *vis à vis* the Mountain people's ramshackle dwellings—seems "the very symbol of household order" (57). Wharton conjures "the scrubbed floor and dresser full of china, and the peculiar smell of yeast and coffee and soft-soap" (57). Here, cleanliness and order trump any shortcomings Charity or Lawyer Royall may have, and as we learn by the end of the book, both characters ultimately behave in morally good and charitable ways. The description of Royall's clean and tidy house also evokes the model home laid out in *The American Woman's Home* with its "high-backed horsehair chairs," "rows of books," and "faded rag carpets"—emblems of modesty and warm domesticity. Royall's house, like Gerty's and Nettie's, showcases a dictum that George Santayana, a contemporary of Wharton's, observes is usually foreign to Americans at home, but is well worth following: "[One must] be poor in order to be simple."[87]

"My Two Gardens": Pavillon Colombe and Sainte-Claire Le Château, France

The "near-wreckage" of the two French residences that she purchased in 1919 did not faze the unstoppable Wharton. Both had been uninhabited for years, the one on the Mediterranean coast for over half a century. She had an enormous amount of repair and refurbishing to undertake on both places and yet wrote excitedly to a friend: "I am thrilled to the spine, I feel as if I were going to get married—to the right man at last!"[88] For Wharton, two houses to renovate meant the beginning of a new life, and once again, she was about to embark on one. Within a year, Wharton turned Pavillon Colombe, in the Parisian suburbs, and Sainte-Claire le Château, on the southern coast of France, into "superb domestic creations," and enjoyed her life like never before: "I'm getting as lively as a cricket, and go bustling up and down mountains like an English old maid," she wrote Bernard Berenson of her life in Hyères.[89] By the end of 1920, she sat back and basked in the final achievement of a beautiful villa outside of Paris and a Mediterranean castle: "The heavenly beauty and the heavenly quiet enfold me," she wrote Berenson, "and I feel that this really is the *Cielo della Quieta* [Heavenly Peace and Quiet] to which the soul aspires after its stormy voyage."[90] Wharton would divide her time evenly between the two residences for the rest of her life: December through May in the south, June through November in the north. Each November, Wharton spent two weeks at the Hôtel de Crillon in Paris while her household staff packed up one house and moved its contents to the other, and she continued to travel and sightsee until the end of her years.[91]

In her letters of the post-war years, when Wharton was in her late fifties and sixties, one senses an unparalleled desire to live: to wrest from life all that it offers. It is as if, after a twenty-five year marriage and then divorce, a much-delayed literary career and then fame and fortune, Wharton finally came out of her shell and fully into her own. Her letters are excited, impassioned, breathless, full of dashes, exclamations, abbreviations, postscripts, and above all, humor regarding her past travails. When she describes the amount of work it took to restore Pavillon Colombe and Sainte-Claire le Château, she does so with vivid, tantalizing images: "Every domestic detail has become a kind of Matterhorn, over which one has to be roped & hooked & hoisted, with every chance of perishing in an avalanche or down a precipice on the way; and I see myself, for the next year, with a perpetual rope around my waist, and perpetual spikes in my soles."[92] Wharton was ready for anything, even a metaphorical climb of the Matterhorn. She wrote Berenson a letter indicating her mind-set: "[H]aving had one or two knocks on the head, [I am] still able to sit up and find life [...] well worth the trouble of getting born."[93] Nothing stopped Wharton as she approached her sixtieth birthday. During the 1920s alone, she wrote fourteen volumes: five novels, four novellas, a collection of short stories, two travel books, a series of essays on fiction writing, and a volume of poetry. Between 1920 and 1924, she earned around three million dollars in today's currency, enough to take care of her two fully renovated houses, numerous gardens, four cars, and a household staff of seven or more, for the rest of life.

In spite of her relentless work and social schedule, Wharton found the time to indulge the great pleasure she took in her houses and gardens. At the end of her autobiography, written three years before she died, she had this to say of her two homes in France:

> At last I had leisure for the two pursuits which never palled, writing and gardening; and through all the years I have gone on gardening and writing. From the day when (to the scandal of the village!) I chopped down a giant araucaria on the lawn, until this moment, I have never ceased to worry and pet and dress up and smooth down my two or three acres; and when winter comes, and rain and mud possess the Seine Valley for six months, I fly south to another garden, as stony and soulless as my northern territory is moist and deep with loam.[94]

For Wharton, gardens were another domain to tame and control, and ultimately, like her interiors, to aestheticize. That she "worried over, petted, dressed up and smoothed down" her grounds, as if they were a collection of dolls, underscores this point. When Wharton discusses her attachment to the landscape, she writes that there was something in her "that was tremblingly and inarticulately awake to every detail of wind-warped fern and wide-eyed briar rose, yet more profoundly alive to a unifying magic beneath the diversities of the visible scene."[95] This is the same Wharton who is haltingly awake to the "hideous stone" of New York City brownstones and to the glorious beauty of a white and gold Louis XVIth commode. In these instances, Wharton is so overcome by the physical environment—whether nature's or her own, whether beautiful or hideous—that she becomes "inarticulate," much like her characters do when they attempt to express love for each other.[96] As important as her writing was at this time in her life, Wharton's passion remained for her houses and their gardens.

~   ~   ~

On the outside, Pavillon Colombe resembles none of Wharton's previous abodes: unlike the bulky Land's End and the regimented Mount, the "pleasure house," originally built in 1769 and named for a stage actress, sits on six acres of flat ground and is long and narrow, delicate and feminine. A series of arched doorways at the rear of the house lead to a nondescript wall behind which hide a goldfish pond, box hedges, flower and vegetable gardens, and other private enclaves typical of Wharton's "secret gardens." Wharton saw the property on a drive with her friend Elsina Tyler and promptly decided to buy it for the very undervalued postwar price of $10,000. On the inside, Wharton arranged Pavillon Colombe as she did her earlier residences with a particular eye to quietude for writing and gardens for musing. She threw herself into arranging classically ordered spaces, plotting furniture placement, making lists of accessories to purchase, and choosing wallpaper and slipcovers from samples sent by the Paris firm of Allioli. Wharton furnished Pavillon Colombe with about half of the belongings in her Rue de Varenne apartment. (The rest of her belongings from Paris, the Mount, and her mother, who died in 1901, went to the residence in the south). Her architect, Charles Knight, drew up plans to convert the old stable adjacent to the house into a summer cottage for guests, and Wharton sketched garden plans to fit the new layout. No record of the cost of renovation exists, but it took a full year, and at Wharton's death in 1937, the property was valued at one million francs.[97]

The well-proportioned and well-defined interiors of the public rooms at Pavillon Colombe recall the Mount's, and once the renovation was complete, Wharton settled into a similar pattern of writing in the morning, walking in the afternoon, visiting with friends over tea or luncheon in the late afternoon, and reading by the fire in the evenings. More and more time was devoted to writing, as Wharton ultimately acknowledged in a letter to her sister-in-law, Minnie Jones: "Writing is my business as well as my passion," not a sentiment she evinced when she first moved to the Mount in 1902. To suit her writing needs (secretaries, typists) and hobbies of driving about, gardening, and entertaining, Wharton employed a permanent staff of seven (compared to ten at the Mount) and an additional seasonal staff that included twenty more gardeners, footmen, and kitchen helpers. Thus, even though Wharton was a single woman, she was almost never alone.

Where Pavillon Colombe appears light and feminine, Sainte-Claire le Château (or Ste. Claire, as Wharton referred to it) epitomizes a dark and menacing castle. A rambling, two-story, turreted and castellated fourteenth-century château, it is the last place one would imagine Wharton living after studying the light airiness of her Newport home, the Mount, and the Pavillon Colombe. Wharton's friend Robert Norton described the place as "pure Albrecht Durer" after the German painter, and in its dark mysteriousness, the comparison is apt. Finally, Wharton could reign over a huge domain all her own, with neither a husband nor society to encroach upon her. The mansion and its surrounding property were immense, comprising several acres and twenty-eight terraced gardens designed by Wharton herself.[98]

The greatest appeal of the château for Wharton was, once again, the sheer physical beauty of the setting—a setting that of all of her properties, past and present, most resembled the Italian landscape. Her letters describing the Mediterranean castle overflow with adoration for the air, sun, sea, and vegetation, and recall her early descriptions of Italy and New York in their precision:

> The little house is delicious, so friendly and comfortable, and full of sun and air; but what overwhelms us all—though we thought we knew it—is the endless beauty of the view, or rather the views, for we look south, east, and west, "miles and miles," and our quiet-colored end of evening presents us with a full moon standing over the tower of the great Romanesque church just below the house, and a sunset silhouetting the Iles d'Or in black on a sea of silver.[99]

In typical fashion, Wharton minimizes her estate by referring to it as a "little house," most likely because its size was simply not of consequence to her; it was of course very large and featured a series of rooms on the main floor that echoed those at the Mount, only there were more of them. As she continued in the letter to her sister-in-law, she affirmed what was important to her: "It is good to grow old—as well as to die—'in beauty'; and the beauty of this little place is inexhaustible."[100] In letters to Bernard Berenson, Morton Fullerton, and Gaillard Lapsley, Wharton referred to the place as the *cielo della quieta*, a heaven of peace and quiet, and implored them to visit. To Fullerton she writes: "Ste. Claire is no mere parterre of heaven; it is the very *cielo della quieta* that Dante [...] found above the Seventh Heaven [...] I've found the Great Good Place."[101] Sainte-Claire le Château was for Wharton what Lamb House was for Henry James, heaven, and she borrows his phrase to describe it. It provided her with all the beauty and rapture that she sought in each of her previous abodes.

Once a convent, the castle remained unoccupied for over fifty years, so one can only imagine the state it was in when Wharton first saw it. Yet she was inspired and undaunted by the extraordinary amount of work it would take to refurbish the place. Enthusiastically she told the Berensons of her plans to enlarge and modernize the house, which included the outfitting of a prominent library with built-in bookcases and long reading tables, the place where Wharton housed her now-impressive library and researched her novels.[102] On the second floor, Wharton added four ample guest rooms, and on the exterior, several highly-detailed gardens, an orchard, and a large terrace from which to gaze into the hills and the stars as she used to do at the Mount. Wharton herself chose every one of the hundreds of varieties of flowers, plants, and shrubs for her gardens, writing detailed lists for her secretary, who would type them up and send them to various suppliers throughout Europe. Throughout 1920 and on and off for the next few years, Wharton's trusty chief of operations, Alfred White, oversaw the work, which included a complete overhaul of the interior as well as the addition of garages, staff quarters, roads, and twenty-eight gardens for which soil was imported. The total cost for the project, as for Pavillon Colombe, came to over one million francs (about $60,000 in Wharton's day or over $600,000 today).[103]

How Wharton found the time to oversee such a large undertaking and write several important works of fiction and non-fiction, not to mention keep up correspondence with friends as well as travel, is incomprehensible even to the modern-day workaholic, yet such achievement attests to her utter zest for life and unflagging energy in her later years. Perhaps she could work so relentlessly and so quickly for the very reason that she finally dwelled in not one but two houses that were completely her own—financially and aesthetically—in a country she loved. In fact, Wharton biographer Shari Benstock has documented that Wharton expressly wrote *The Age of Innocence* at this time—late 1919 to early 1920—in order to make money for her house renovations. The novel was written in record time from August 1919, when Wharton first spotted the two French residences, to March 1920, when the renovations were fully underway. Published in October 1920, the book was her most successful to date, earning her $50,000 in its first two years and a Pulitzer Prize. But the most satisfying thing about the book was neither the money nor the fame it brought her. It was, in Wharton's words, that it enabled her "to build walls and plant orange-orchards."[104]

EPILOGUE

Where the Houses Stand Today

In spite of each individual's inevitable impermanence, architecture can offer permanent testimony to the past. Though the lives of the four authors discussed in this book were transient, often restless, and collectively involved moves to eight states, three countries, and over forty properties, a remarkable number of their dwellings still stand. In Cambridge today, one can follow a path—as I have many times—from Howells's first house at 41 Sacramento Street, across Massachusetts Avenue to 3 Berkeley Street, and around the corner to 37 Concord Avenue. From there, one can take the commuter rail or walk, as Howells and James did, to Belmont and peer through the woods to Redtop, still standing in all its glory, meticulously maintained by its current proud owners.

Or, one can take Interstate 95 along the Connecticut coastline into Rhode Island, and drive by Wharton's former Pencraig Cottage on Harrison Avenue and Land's End, both in the still-prominent resort town of Newport, and made dignified by the work of Edith Wharton and Ogden Codman, Jr. One can drive north from Boston to the Stone Cabin in Andover, Massachusetts, where Stowe displayed the wares of her travels in Europe in the 1850s, and where the current Dean of Students of Phillips Academy resides. Drive further north and east, and the tourist will find the solid white Greek Revival house in Brunswick, Maine, where Stowe wrote *Uncle Tom's Cabin*, and the cottage in Kittery Point, Maine, where Howells spent the last decades of his life working from a library that continues to face the Atlantic Ocean. Yet, of these many properties, only one (and one of the more modest ones)—37 Concord Avenue—alerts the passerby to the significance of the home's early owner with a blue historic marker. The others remain anonymous and unacknowledged, like millions of dwellings across the American landscape; their secret histories known solely by their contemporary owners and a handful of historians.

Only very rarely has the individual's home become a museum: Stowe's Forest Street House in Hartford, Connecticut; Wharton's Mount in Lenox, Massachusetts; and James's Lamb House in Rye, England. Of the dozens of domiciles discussed in these pages, these three alone are open to the public. In some cases, the houses have disappeared: Stowe's Oakholm and Mandarin, Florida, properties; Wharton's pair of New York City brownstones; James's first apartment in London; and many of the New York City hotels and apartments that Howells inhabited at the turn of the century. In other instances, a surviving property is unrecognizable, such as Howells's brick townhouse at 302 Beacon Street in Boston's Back Bay. Once a three-story building with a dormered attic floor, the current structure has five full stories. The stairs and front door have been relocated and the windows are larger than the originals and no longer feature iron grills on the first floor. The only evidence of the original building's distinction is its neighbor, number 300, which has also been modified, but less so. Though both Howells and George Santayana lived at 302 Beacon Street, no sign recalls them; rather, new owners have renovated and reconfigured the townhouse to make it their own.

This is, of course, the point: to make a house one's own. Since most houses—and the majority of those that the authors of this study lived in—have been inhabited by others, it is necessary that they be changed to reflect each new inhabitant's residency, however temporary that stay may be. The most basic means of transformation is furniture—what the French call "les meubles" or "the movables"— and interior decoration: painting the walls, hanging new curtains, laying down carpets. But if we can somehow change the "immeuble"— the "immobile" building itself—by taking down some walls (as Wharton did at Land's End), adding a front porch (as Stowe did to the Andover house), or enclosing an open space (as James did with his Garden Studio)—so much the better. Altering a structure seems to signify possession. We convert spaces to match our tastes, values, and standards; we edit them as if they were pieces of writing. Perhaps this is why it was essential to each author to renovate (literally, to "renew" or to "revive") a favorite property. For Stowe, Howells, and Wharton, so-called "dream houses" fell short of their dreams, but properties that already existed and that they could "revive" or "revise" on their own terms, served them best: Stowe's Forest Street house; Howells's Kittery Point refuge; Wharton's two French estates; and James's Lamb House. These four individuals were writers, after all, and they spent their lives revising, editing, rewriting—houses and manuscripts.

The great majority of us live in structures erected by people we never knew, inhabited by ghosts from different generations—an unsettling realization given our love of our own individuality and personalities. Often we do not know the men or women who built the houses we live in, why they were built, or even when, but still we purchase them and attempt to make them ours. Stowe, Howells, and Wharton were among the very privileged who are able to design and build their own houses from the ground up, though each did so only once. They were able, in a sense, to take the act of authorship and apply it to architecture. Effectively, they wrote the one custom-made house that they each lived in, and they entitled their masterpieces: Oakholm, Redtop, the Mount. James, conversely, though fully engaged with the material world, never desired a house of his own making; he was the least attached to the domestic realm and seemed to dwell the most completely in his work.

~   ~   ~

The business of making a home one's own is an enormous industry today. Dozens of so-called "shelter" magazines line the newsstands, catering to the public's desire for "doing over" or "doing up" their houses. Many of these magazines survive from the late nineteenth century, when the practices of domestic architecture and house decoration began to thrive; these include the *Ladies' Home Journal* (1883), *House Beautiful* (1896), and *House & Garden* (1901), to name a few. The four authors discussed in this book also advanced ideals about the home in their writing—mainly by treating houses, their location, and their decoration so consistently and intensely in their work. The numerous residences in their novels—from Lillie's Newport house in Stowe's *Pink and White Tyranny*, to Lapham's Back Bay mansion, James's Gardencourt, and the various mansions and modest apartments of Wharton's *The House of Mirth*—suggest ways of acquiring and decorating a home as well as the significance of these activities.

In spite of perfecting the tasteful and meaningful home in their works of fiction, the authors' attempts in their personal lives to erect or run similarly significant households did not always materialize. This may well be the greatest lesson we have to glean from the four authors in this study: that, in spite of their tremendous legacies as authors, in their real lives, at home, they were people. For their work, Stowe, Howells, James, and Wharton survive as authors—truly, authorities—but in their homes, behind closed doors, they tended to be like all of us: messy, disorganized, whimsical, impatient, erratic.

In reality, each author desired, purchased, and dwelled in a so-called dream house and played an important role in its design, location, and construction. These structures were extensions of the authors themselves: Stowe's Oakholm—built in Hartford, Connecticut, from 1862 to 1864—uses, with its many lancet-arched windows and cross gables, the Gothic Revival to express her fanciful and spiritual nature; Howells's Redtop—constructed from 1876 to 1878 in Belmont, Massachusetts—follows the organic Shingle Style with its variegated colors and textures and pays homage to the author's love of nature; Wharton's Mount in Lenox, Massachusetts—designed from 1900 to 1902—mirrors her authoritative demeanor with its classical symmetry and vast white exterior. While James did not design and build his own ideal home, as the other authors did, he hired an architect to transform his final residence, Lamb House, on the southeastern coast of England. There, among other additions, he converted a detached building into a "Garden Studio," where he wrote during the summer months engulfed in sunshine, quietude, and the ocean breeze—his dream come true.

As dissimilar as these dream houses are physically, they share important philosophical similarities and attest to characteristics common among writers: each house reflects a desire for refuge—a place where the author could write peacefully and in solitude. Each house is located on the outskirts of towns or cities: Oakholm, a few miles from the center of Hartford; Redtop, from Boston and Cambridge; the Mount, from Lenox; Lamb House, from London. While isolated and surrounded by land (a few acres in the case of Oakholm and Redtop and over a hundred in the case of the Mount), the houses were situated in areas that enabled the authors to participate in a literary or professional circle. In Hartford, for example, Stowe lived in an area known as Nook Farm where her brother-in-law and fellow authors Mark Twain and Charles Dudley Warner resided. Howells chose Belmont because it was accessible to his *Atlantic Monthly* office and to Cambridge where friends like Charles Eliot Norton and James Russell Lowell lived, and boasted an artistic community of its own. Wharton had the financial means to live wherever she wanted. Lenox provided both social and professional stimulation; wealthy aristocrats and intellectuals alike owned homes in the Berkshires. Henry James was perhaps the least concerned with neighbors: when he chose to live at Lamb House in Sussex county, England, he knew no one, but loved the sea air and simple life afforded by the location. Most of all, his remote outpost enabled him to write prolifically.

While these residences provided ample quietude and desired garden space, fulfilling notions of success and contentment, none remained long in the authors' possession. Except for James, who owned Lamb House until he died, the others soon became overwhelmed by the time and money required to maintain their personal palaces. Stowe sold Oakholm after living there for only six years; Howells sold Redtop after four; and Wharton sold the Mount after a decade. In spite of the energy and personality invested in these places, these three authors were not able to keep them; curiously, when they relocated to already-existing dwellings, Stowe, Howells, and Wharton seemed far more content.

The decision to include a study or library at home—a place to read and write—was also significant. The two male writers, Howells and James, dedicated separate rooms to their craft, acknowledging its importance in their lives. When Howells designed his Belmont house with his wife and her architect brother, he placed his library near the center of the ground floor, according it more space and prominence than the dining room or parlor. Just off the entry hall, it is the first room one sees upon entering the front door. From here, Howells could look out on the activity of his household: he could see the front hall, the dining room, even the stairs to the second floor. In his case, life and work flowed together. By contrast, the unmarried James set up his London apartments on Bolton Street and De Vere Gardens almost entirely as work studios, using the central and spacious parlor in each as his study. His home-life, in a sense, took place outside the home in literary clubs and at the estates of friends.

Unlike the men, Stowe and Wharton chose to write in remarkably non-literary environments: Wharton, sequestered in her bedroom, and Stowe, at the kitchen table. While no one was privy to Wharton's acts of authorship—she sat in bed with a pen and paper—Stowe's entire family, including servants, could observe hers. Stowe wrote amidst chaos, wherever she was, whenever she had time, and drew, for her content, on the activity of the household.

In spite of numerous false starts, each author ultimately found contentment at home, usually (and ironically) by maintaining a degree of flux. In traveling between two residences, they accommodated the different facets of their personalities. An urban dwelling met the needs of the mind; a seaside home fed the soul. Stowe moved to a more manageably-sized house on Forest Street in Hartford when she was sixty years old and lived there for six months each year; during the winter she relocated to her house in Florida. Howells acquired two residences as well: a cottage on the coast of Maine and a New York City apartment, which, like Stowe's houses, offered him the best of both worlds—city stimulation and country isolation. Wharton fled the United States for France after deciding to leave her husband, and also acquired two properties—one north of Paris, the other on the Mediterranean coast—between which she traveled for the rest of her life. Even James, who was the least attached to physical houses, spent the last five years of his life vacillating between a small apartment in London and the removed, coastal Lamb House.

~ ~ ~

Today we continue to build dream houses, but like Stowe, Howells, and Wharton, often we cannot handle the financial, social, and domestic burdens of them. In life as in literature, the fulfillment of the dream—the house—becomes the receptacle for all other unfulfilled wishes. When Stowe and Howells moved to smaller abodes and James and Wharton fled to more remote locations, they reclaimed their privacy, and, most importantly, their senses of home.

The message we can take away from Stowe's experience at Oakholm, Howells's at Redtop, Wharton's at the Mount—and perhaps from millions of other Americans in search of an ideal home—is that dream houses might best remain what they are: dreams. Ultimately, the authors of this study did not *need* to inhabit houses of their own design—something James avoided throughout his adult life. When Stowe, Howells, and Wharton moved to houses not built expressly for them, they were freed from expectations and burdens and could focus on what captivated James all along: the house of fiction. We can be thankful that they managed to arrive at that door after all.

~ ~ ~

When I began this book in graduate school, in the form of my doctoral dissertation, it was hard for me to imagine that I too might one day own a home. Because of the amount of time my husband and I spent studying and working on houses, I had somehow convinced myself that I would spend my life researching how other people lived, but would never find the time to ponder how *I* actually wanted to live. Thus, I would remain a lifelong renter. Furthermore, because I regularly taught classes on the meaning of the American Dream (which, ostensibly, included home ownership) I spent a lot of time deconstructing the myth that home ownership provides happiness. Hadn't Stowe, Howells, and Wharton shown me clearly enough that dream houses more often than not turned into nightmares, and that houses in general frequently became no more than repositories for a hefty load of financial and maintenance concerns? Ultimately, I questioned whether owning a home was worth its costs and sacrifices, and my husband and I prided ourselves on the freedom we felt we had as renters to "drop everything" and move whenever we wanted because we weren't burdened with an outsized mortgage.

All of this changed on the eve of my fortieth birthday when I successfully defended my dissertation and graduated from Boston University with a doctorate and a 400-page manuscript. Suddenly, room opened up inside me where the thought of buying a house could lodge. Maybe, like Wharton, who wrote her first novel just prior to turning forty (and who decided to design and construct her most important residence, the Mount, the same year), I could now make space for another substantial project, having just completed one.

For me, finding the house I was going to buy and knowing so the minute I saw it, was similar to the way many people find their life partner: they just know. I think this is how Stowe felt when she saw the home on Forest Street in Hartford, and the way that Howells felt when he laid eyes on his cottage in Kittery Point, Maine; these were the places for which the authors had waited their entire lives. And while Stowe's and Howells's last residences could not compare aesthetically with the custom-designed houses that preceded them— Oakholm in the case of Stowe and Redtop for Howells—and neither of their last, far more modest houses was named, these final dwelling places remained their homes until the day each author died.

My house too exists without its own special moniker; frankly, it's not the type of place one would name. I have come to see this as a good thing: modest, simple, and straightforward, our house lives up to the only name that really matters: it is *home*.

NOTES

Introduction

1. In informal studies I have conducted in the undergraduate liberal arts classroom, I have found that many of my students believe a black woman wrote *Uncle Tom's Cabin*. No student I have encountered in six years of teaching has been able to cite another title by Stowe.

2. These two books examine the private lives of groups of authors but do not expose an overriding preoccupation with the home. See Samuel Schreiner, Jr., *The Concord Quartet: Alcott, Emerson, Hawthorne, Thoreau, and the Friendship that Freed the American Mind* (New York: Wiley, 2006) and Susan Cheever, *American Bloomsbury: Louisa May Alcott, Ralph Waldo Emerson, Margaret Fuller, Nathaniel Hawthorne, and Henry David Thoreau: Their Lives, Their Loves, Their Work* (New York: Simon & Schuster, 2006).

3. See Eric Hobsbawm's trilogy of the "long nineteenth century," which became a defining work of his chosen period, from 1789 to 1914: *The Age of Revolution* (1962), *The Age of Capital* (1975), and *The Age of Empire* (1987). On the professionalization of an American domestic architecture, there are a number of useful sources to consult, including, but not limited to, Dell Upton's "Pattern Books and Professionalism: Aspects of the Transformation of Domestic Architecture in America, 1800–1860," *Winterthur Portfolio* 19 (Summer/Autumn 1984) and Mary Woods' *From Craft to Profession: The Practice of Architecture in Nineteenth-Century America* (Berkeley: University of California Press, 1999). On the professionalization of authorship, see Lawrence Buell, *New England Literary Culture: From Revolution to Renaissance* (Cambridge and New York: Cambridge University Press, 1986) and Daniel Borus, *Writing Realism: Howells, James, and Norris in the Mass Market* (Chapel Hill, University of North Carolina Press, 1989).

4. Historians as diverse as Erving Goffman and Alan Trachtenberg have elucidated how the house evolved into a theater for the presentation of a newly self-conscious individual; in the words of Trachtenberg, particularly in the late nineteenth century, the house became the marker of one's "economic individuation." See Erving Goffman, *The Representation of Self in Everyday Life* (Garden City, N.Y.: Doubleday, 1959) and Alan Trachtenberg, *The Incorporation of America: Culture and Society in the Gilded Age* (New York: Hill and Wang, 1982), especially pages 5–6.

5. Kenneth Lynn's 1961 introduction to an edition of *Uncle Tom's Cabin* proposes that Stowe's novel is "a tear-jerker with a difference." By this Lynn means that "the novel's sentimentalism continually calls attention to the monstrous actuality [slavery] which existed under the very noses of its readers." Lynn claims that Stowe's novel departs from sentimental tradition in that it "aroused emotions not for emotion's sake alone but in order to facilitate the moral regeneration of an entire nation." See Kenneth S. Lynn, *Uncle Tom's Cabin, Or, Life Among the Lowly* (Cambridge, MA: The Belknap Press of Harvard University, 1962).

6. HBS to Hattie Stowe, no date, [May 1861]. Harriet Beecher Stowe Letters [A/S892; A/S892a; A/S892b]. Arthur and Elizabeth Schlesinger Library on

the History of Women in America, Harvard University. Hereafter referred to as Schlesinger.

7. French poet Charles Baudelaire refers to the city wanderer as a *flâneur* in his 1861 poem, *"Tableaux Parisiens"* [Parisian Sketches], in his collection of poems, *Les Fleurs du Mal* [*The Flowers of Evil*], (1861; rpt., New York: Penguin, 1993).

8. See chapter three for more on James's "house of fiction."

Chapter One

1. During the antebellum decades (1820–1860), the era known for "the cult of true womanhood" and "the cult of domesticity," women were expected to assert their virtue through four primary traits: piety, purity, submissiveness, and domesticity. In the domestic arena, this meant upholding the nuclear family and the home as provinces of safety and virtue in a world of uncertainty and competition. See Linda Kerber, *Women of the Republic: Intellect and Ideology in Revolutionary America* (Chapel Hill: University of North Carolina Press, 1997) and Nancy Cott, *The Bonds of Womanhood: 'Woman's Sphere' in New England, 1780–1835*, second edition (New Haven: Yale University Press, 1997).

2. Lyman Beecher married three times and had eleven children; his seven sons all became congregational clergymen. Daughters and in-laws also achieved renown: HBS, her sister Catharine, brother Henry, and sister-in-law Eunice (wife of Henry) authored several dozen books among them. Eunice Beecher, like Stowe and Catharine, wrote manuals of household advice and edited a monthly magazine on the subject for one year. Stowe lived with her father until she married Calvin Stowe in 1836, except from 1826 to 1831 when Lyman Beecher lived in Boston, during which time Stowe attended her sister Catharine's school in Hartford.

3. For future reference, the names and dates of Stowe's seven children are the following: The twins, Harriet "Hattie" Beecher (1836–1907) and Eliza Tyler (1836–1912); Henry Ellis (1838–1857); Frederick William (1840–unknown); Georgiana "Georgie" May (Mrs. Henry Freeman Allen, 1843–1890); Samuel Charles "Charley" (1848–1849); and Charles Edward (1850–1934). Four of Stowe's seven children did not outlive her, and one, Charley, died when he was a year and a half old in 1849. The oldest twin daughters did not marry, while Stowe's other daughter, Georgiana, died prematurely at age 47. Two other sons, Henry and Charles, died at nineteen and at around age thirty, respectively. It bears mention up front that while Stowe provided incessant counsel to her three daughters, her sons received advice of a different kind: to join the ministry. Of Stowe's four sons, her only surviving one, Charles, fulfilled her hope and become a minister. Stowe, in a manner, rewarded Charles for his career choice; she bought him a house in Hartford after he spent one year living on the third floor of the Forest Street house from 1883–1884 while he was pastor at Hartford's Windsor Avenue Congregational Church. He was also the primary beneficiary and executor of his mother's will. By virtue of his sex and his profession, Charles was never subjected to the domestic admonitions of his mother.

4. Stowe's father, her seven brothers, and her husband became ministers. For additional biographical information on the Stowe family, see Constance Mayfield Rourke, *Trumpets of Jubilee* (1927) and Lyman Beecher Stowe, *Saints, Sinners, and Beechers* (1934), as well as Charles E. Stowe and Lyman Beecher Stowe, *Harriet Beecher Stowe: The Story of her Life* (Boston: Houghton Mifflin Company, 1911), 66–67. Hereafter referred to as *HBS: The Story of her Life*.

5. On the history of women's education during the first half of the 19th century, see Lynn Gordon, *'From Seminary to University:' Gender and Higher Education in the Progressive Era* (New Haven: Yale University Press, 1990).

6. Between 1860 and 1880, the amount of money paid to magazine writers tripled. On the rise in writers' salaries and the professionalization of authorship in the mid-nineteenth century, see Lawrence Buell, *New England Literary Culture: From Revolution to Renaissance* (Cambridge and New York: Cambridge University Press, 1986).

7. Alexander Jackson Davis (1803–1892) published *Rural Residences* in 1838. Andrew Jackson Downing (1815–1852) wrote four influential books including the popular *Cottage Residences* (1842) and *The Architecture of Country Houses* (1850). For more on Downing, see David Schuyler, *Apostle of Taste: Andrew Jackson Downing, 1815–1852* (Baltimore: Johns Hopkins University Press, 1996).

8. The Beecher family worked together for their causes, promoting each other's work in their publications. Catharine Beecher's numerous titles include *The Moral Instructor for Schools and Families, Containing Lessons on the Duties of Life* (1838), *Treatise on Domestic Economy* (1841), *Letters to Persons who are Engaged in Domestic Service* (1842), *Miss Beecher's Domestic Receipt-Book* (1865) and others; Eunice Beecher's publications included the magazine she edited, *The Mother at Home,* and *Household Magazine,* which ran from January to December 1869; *Motherly Talks with Young Housekeepers* (1873), *All Around the House, or How to Make Homes Happy* (1878), and *The Law of a Household* (1912).

9. HBS to James T. Fields, November 1864. Emphasis original. Huntington. James T. Fields (1817–1881) was editor of the *Atlantic Monthly* from 1861 to 1871. He succeeded James Russell Lowell (editor from 1857–1861) and preceded William Dean Howells (editor from 1871 to 1881). His wife, Annie Fields (1834–1915), also an editor and writer, was a close friend of Stowe's.

10. Battle wounds suffered by Frederick Stowe are detailed in *HBS: The Story of Her Life,* 190–196; the effects he suffered as a result of the war are detailed on pages 205, 213, 277–279. No one knows for certain where or when Frederick Stowe died.

11. Undated letter from HBS to Calvin Stowe, attributed to the 1840s. Quoted in *The Life and Letters of Harriet Beecher Stowe,* Annie Fields, ed. (Boston: Houghton Mifflin, 1897), 110. Hereafter referred to as *Life and Letters of HBS*.

12. Stowe and her sister Catharine advocate the "good temper in the housekeeper" in chapter 16 of *The American Woman's Home,* ed. Nicole Tonkovich (1869; rpt., New Brunswick, New Jersey: Rutgers University Press, 2002), 162–166. All further references are to this edition and are noted parenthetically in the text. Stowe also warns against irritability as well as other negative personal traits in *Little Foxes*.

13. *Life and Letters of HBS,* 172.
14. Built in 1807, the Brunswick, Maine, house contains Federal and Greek Revival elements; the latter include the pilasters and entablature surrounding the front door. The Stowes had little to do with the appearance of the Brunswick house because they leased it for only two years from its owner. Stowe confirms in a letter to her sister-in-law, Mrs. George Beecher [Sarah Buckingham Beecher], the extent to which owner John Titcomb took responsibility for all house-related jobs in Brunswick: "[John Titcomb] is part owner and landlord of the house I rent...Being of ingenious turn, he does painting, gilding, staining, upholstery jobs, varnishing, all in addition to his primary trade of carpentry." *Life and Letters of HBS,* 126.
15. HBS to Hattie Stowe, no date, [May 1861]. Schlesinger.
16. In spite of an ongoing misconception that Stowe received a pittance for *Uncle Tom's Cabin,* she earned $10,000 after the publication of the novel, a sum based on the 300,000 copies sold in its first year of publication and her agreement to a fixed ten percent royalty rate; to be sure, she could have earned much, much more, but $10,000—over $250,000 in 2009—was a very substantial sum nonetheless. See *Life and Letters of HBS,* 37, and Hedrick, *Harriet Beecher Stowe,* 223. Some accounts state that the book sold "almost half a million copies" its first year such as Joseph Van Why, *Harriet Beecher Stowe's House in Nook Farm, Hartford* (Hartford: Stowe-Day Foundation, 1970).
17. This information comes from the Phillips Academy Survey of Buildings, courtesy the resident of the house in 2004. Stowe tried to have two servants, but more often than not only had one because she had such a difficult time finding and keeping reliable girls.
18. "Andover Advertiser," March 5, 1853. The owner of the house gave a transcribed copy of the article to me, August 2004.
19. Stowe, *Sunny Memories of Foreign Lands* (Boston: Phillips, Sampson, and Company, 1854), 149.
20. *Sunny Memories,* 159.
21. *Life and Letters of HBS,* 188.
22. To her sister-in-law Stowe wrote: "My pictures are all framed and you have no idea how pretty they look." HBS to Mrs. George Beecher [Sarah Buckingham], November 11, 1853. Acquisitions Folder. Stowe Center Library. This letter includes a sketch by Stowe of the various items and their placement; sadly, it is too faded and fragile to be reproduced.
23. From an undated, unidentified typed article entitled "Mrs. Stowe in Andover," attributed to Agnes Park. Schlesinger.
24. See Van Wyck Brooks, *The Dream of Arcadia: American Writers and Artists in Italy, 1760–1915* (New York: Dutton, 1958), xi.
25. See *HBS: The Story of Her Life,* 175.
26. *Sunny Memories,* 423; *Life and Letters of HBS,* 172.
27. Stowe's inability to discipline her children was complicated perhaps by the sudden death of her second oldest child, Henry Ellis, who drowned while she was on her second tour of Europe in 1857. Stowe felt guilty for not having been at home during the ordeal, though she arrived soon thereafter. Her guilt may have prevented her from exerting a strict hand over her children, but evidence shows that she had as difficult a time disciplining her children before as she did after Henry's death.

28. Quoted in *HBS: The Story of Her Life,* 212.

29. Van Why, 3. The Hartford directories show Octavius Jordan living and working as an architect in Hartford from 1849 to 1865. After this year, he disappears and nothing more has been learned of him.

30. See Marion Grant Hepburn and Ellsworth Strong, *The City of Hartford, 1784–1984* (Hartford: Connecticut Historical Society, 1986), 138–145.

31. *Life and Letters of HBS,* 294.

32. David Schuyler, *Apostle of Taste: Andrew Jackson Downing, 1814–1852* (Baltimore: Johns Hopkins University Press, 1996), 101.

33. Quoted in Schuyler, 100.

34. I am indebted to David Schuyler and his book, *Apostle of Taste,* from which the material in this and the preceding paragraphs is drawn, and for elucidating some of the connections between Beecher, Hale, Stowe, and Downing. I also thank him for his comments on an earlier version of this chapter.

35. *Life and Letters of HBS,* 293. Though they hardly knew each other, Stowe and Hawthorne were competitive with each other. When Hawthorne visited England in the early 1850s to promote *The House of Seven Gables,* he felt he was ignored while Stowe was treated "like a Queen" for *Uncle Tom's Cabin.* She booked passage on the boat he was taking home from England in 1860 so she could pick his brain. See *HBS: The Story of Her Life,* 187.

36. For details regarding the materials and decorative ornamentation of Oakholm, see "The Home of an Authoress," *The Hartford Times,* May 16, 1863. Quoted in Myron Stachiw, Thomas Paske, et al., *Historic Structures Report for the Harriet Beecher Stowe House* (Hartford, CT: Stowe Center Library, 2002), 23. Hereafter *Historic Structures Report.* I thank the staff of the Stowe Center Library for making this unpublished document available to me.

37. Andrew Jackson Downing, *The Architecture of Country Houses* (1850; rpt., New York: Dover, 1969), 25, 40. For further reading on Downing, see Schuyler, *Apostle of Taste,* and Adam Sweeting, *Reading Houses and Building Books: A. J. Downing and the Architecture of Popular Antebellum Literature, 1835–1855* (Hanover, N. H.: University Press of New England, 1996).

38. Dawn Adiletta, curator of the Harriet Beecher Stowe House on Forest Street in 2004, confirms that no floor plan for Oakholm has been found, and thus, that the number of rooms and bathrooms remains uncertain.

39. William Dean Howells, *My Mark Twain* (1910; rpt., Mineola, New York: Dover Publications, 1997), 37. Of course, Stowe did not "invent" the greenhouse. The man responsible for that was English gardener and landscape designer, Joseph Paxton (1803–1865), who developed the first "glass houses" in the 1830s in order to maximize sunlight. Paxton went on to design the Crystal Palace for the World's Fair of 1851.

40. Harriet Beecher Stowe, *Uncle Tom's Cabin,* ed. Elizabeth Ammons (1852; rpt., New York: W. W. Norton & Co., 1994), 247. All further references are to this edition and are noted parenthetically in the text.

41. As early as 1840, Stowe wrote to her husband, "If I am to write, I must have a room to myself, which shall be *my* room," foreshadowing by a half-century Virginia Woolf's now-famous plea. Quoted in *Life and Letters of HBS,* 104. Emphasis original.

42. HBS to George Buckingham Beecher, [November 12, 1863]. Emphasis original. Stowe Center Library.
43. HBS to Hattie, Eliza, and Georgiana Stowe, October 3, 1863. Stowe Center Library.
44. *HBS: The Story of Her Life,* 213.
45. *HBS: The Story of Her Life,* 213.
46. HBS to James Fields, October 27, 1863. Huntington.
47. HBS to James Fields, October 27, 1863. Huntington.
48. In the first edition of *House and Home Papers,* one finds opposite the title page a list of "Mrs. Stowe's Writings." The copyright page also includes her name. See Crowfield, Christopher. [pseud]. *House and Home Papers* (Boston: Ticknor and Fields, 1865).
49. Crowfield, 18, 181.
50. Crowfield, 182.
51. See Joan Hedrick, *Harriet Beecher Stowe, A Life* (New York: Oxford University Press, 1994), 314. Hereafter referred to as *HBS, A Life.*
52. Crowfield, 72.
53. Crowfield, 164–165.
54. On the consumerism and capitalism of the era following the Civil War, see Alan Trachtenberg's *The Incorporation of America: Culture and Society in the Gilded Age* (New York: Hill and Wang, 1982). On the evolution of the house from a site of production to an emblem of consumption in the mid-nineteenth century, see Jan Cohn's *The Palace or the Poorhouse: The American Home as a Cultural Symbol* (East Lansing: Michigan State University Press, 1979).
55. Details on the Florida property are drawn from Olav Thulesius, *Harriet Beecher Stowe in Florida, 1867–1884* (Jefferson, North Carolina: McFarland and Company, 2001) and from *Life and Letters of HBS,* 302–303.
56. Quoted in Hedrick, *HBS, A Life,* 330.
57. *Life and Letters of HBS,* 302.
58. *HBS: The Story of Her Life,* 224.
59. *HBS: The Story of Her Life,* 224.
60. The floor plan and exact number of rooms remain unknown and the house no longer stands. From letters, I have pieced together that Stowe and her husband had separate rooms, Aunt Eunice had her own room, and the twins shared a room, which means that there were at least four small bedrooms in the house.
61. Harriet Beecher Stowe, *Palmetto Leaves* (1872; rpt. Gainesville: University Press of Florida, 1999), 37.
62. Florida provided an invaluable refuge for Eunice Beecher during the time when her husband was accused of adultery in what became known as the Beecher-Tilton scandal; the scandal became public in 1872.
63. *Palmetto Leaves,* 26.
64. For more on Stowe as an early realist, see Kenneth Lynn's introduction to *Uncle Tom's Cabin* (Harvard, 1962) and Robyn Warhol's essay, "Poetics and Persuasion: *Uncle Tom's Cabin* as a Realist Novel," *Essays in Literature,* 13 (Fall, 1986).
65. See *HBS, A Life,* 293.
66. *HBS, A Life,* 333.
67. HBS to Hattie and Eliza Stowe, August 1869. Schlesinger.

68. Stowe wrote her daughters: "The problem is to set a good table and make palatable food at least expense. If you can find pleasure in being helpful, then you can help me, but if you do it with pain, disgust, weariness, it will be improbable [...] to help up my spirits." HBS to Hattie and Eliza Stowe, August 1869. Schlesinger.

69. Stowe, *Pink and White Tyranny* (1869; rpt., New York: Plume, 1988). All further references are to this edition and are noted parenthetically in the text.

70. HSB to James T. Fields, n.d. [before November 9], [1864], Fields Papers, Huntington.

71. On the competing types of consumption see Rachel Naomi Klein, "Harriet Beecher Stowe and the Domestication of Free Labor Ideology," *Legacy*, 18: 2 (2001), from which I learned much.

72. Bound Book, 1878–1879. Day Collection, Stowe Center Library.

73. HBS to James Fields. June 3, 1864. Huntington. Howells and Wharton abandoned their dream houses for similar—and additional—reasons.

74. Stowe wrote: "If it please God this shall be the last season that my family shall be scattered wanderers, sick in hotels and boarding houses, and other people's families—it is not respectable and there must put an end to this." Stowe to Hattie and Eliza Stowe, September 23, 1872. Acquisitions, Stowe Center Library.

75. HBS to Hattie and Eliza Stowe, September 23, 1872. Acquisitions, Stowe Center Library.

76. See Grant and Strong, *The City of Hartford, 1784–1984.*

77. *Historic Landscape Report,* 41.

78. This information is drawn from Hartford Directories and appears in the *Historic Structures Report*, Appendix III.

79. *Historic Structures Report,* 40.

80. HBS to Hattie and Eliza Stowe, September 23, 1872. Acquisitions, Stowe Center Library.

81. Curator of the Forest Street house, Dawn Adiletta, provided the square footage of the houses in an interview on August 30, 2004. The house built by Chamberlin on the North side of the Stowe house in 1880 was 8,000 square feet.

82. Joseph Twitchell wrote the entry on Harriet Beecher Stowe in *Authors At Home*, and described the pamphlets in her front hall: "...In the hall [of the Forest Street house], [the visitor] would find there the twenty-six folio volumes of the 'Affectionate and Christian Address of Many Thousands of Women in Great Britain and Ireland to their Sisters of the United States of America,' pleading the cause of the slave." See J. L. and J. B. Gilder, *Authors at Home* (New York: A. Wessels Co., 1905), 318–319. Joseph Twitchell (1838–1918), a Hartford-based Congregationalist clergyman, was a friend of the Stowes and Mark Twain.

83. Descriptions of the Forest Street interiors are based upon period photographs, reproduction photographs, and the curators and house interpreters with whom I spoke. The house has been restored to match as closely as possible how it looked when Stowe lived there. Stowe was a prolific painter; many of her works still hang in the house. In *House and Home Papers* (92), Stowe promotes an artist by the name of "Morvillier," but no literature on a nineteenth-century painter of this name seems to exist.

84. Thomas Schlereth, *Victorian America: Transformations in Everyday Life* (New York: HarperCollins, 1991), 141.
85. HBS to Hattie and Eliza Stowe, from Mandarin to Hartford, no date [circa May 1872]. Schlesinger. The placement and description of the furniture are based upon Stowe's sketch of the rooms which appears in this letter; sadly her pencil drawing is too light to reproduce.
86. Gilder, *Authors at Home*, 317–318.
87. It is important to note the complete title of their work, for only there, buried in the lengthy subtitle does one find the word "Christian," an indispensable aspect of the Beecher home. The complete title reads: *The American Woman's Home: or, Principles of Domestic Science; being a guide to the formation and maintenance of economical, healthful, beautiful, and Christian homes.* The book used Catharine Beecher's earlier manual, *Treatise on Domestic Economy* (1841), as its frame and included chapters from Catharine's other publications, especially *Letters to the People on Health and Happiness* (1855). It also incorporated material from Stowe's *House and Home Papers*. See Tonkovich, "Introduction," *The American Woman's Home*, xviii.
88. See Tonkovich, "Introduction," *The American Woman's Home*, xiv-xv.
89. Bound book, 1878–1879. Day Collection. Stowe Center Library. The accounts show payments to numerous individuals, including a Frank, Nelly, Anthony, Bella, Mrs. Howe, Munson, Mrs. Chase, and others.
90. Bound book, 1878–1879. Day Collection. Stowe Center Library. Stowe grew many of her own fruits and vegetables, especially in Florida, and canned much of the produce for the winter months.
91. Joseph Van Why, *Nook Farm* (Hartford: Stowe-Day Foundation, 1975), 25.
92. Many of Stowe's immediate relations lived too far away for her to see, but she corresponded with her brothers Henry (who died in 1887), Charles (in 1893), and Edward (in 1895), and with Eunice, who died in 1897. Beecher family members were remarkably long-lived for the time.
93. Stowe, *House and Home Papers,* 30.

Chapter Two

1. William Dean Howells [hereafter WDH] to Aurelia H. Howells, Sept. 21, 1918. Quoted in George Arms et al., eds. *Selected Letters of William Dean Howells.* 6 vols. (Boston: Twayne Publishers, 1979–1983), VI: 140–141. (Letters quoted from the six volumes hereafter are referred to as *Selected Letters* and include the volume and page number from which the letter is drawn).
2. After Howells died in 1920, the house became the property of his son John Mead and daughter Mildred and upon their deaths, passed to John's sons, William White Howells and John Noyes Mead Howells. They bequeathed the residence to Harvard University in 1979. For future reference, Howells's wife was the former Elinor Gertrude Mead (1837–1910); his three children (one of whom died in her twenties) were: Winifred, or, "Winny" (1863–1889); John Mead (1868–1959); and Mildred, or, "Pilla" (1872–1966).

3. WDH to William Cooper Howells [hereafter WCH], October 26, 1859. William Dean Howells and Family Papers, Houghton Library, Harvard University (hereafter abbreviated as Houghton). Emphasis original.

4. WDH to Charles Eliot Norton [hereafter CEN], Sept. 24, 1876, *Selected Letters*, II: 139–140.

5. Though Howells did not dwell year-round at the Maine house, he considered it his "home for old age," and spent several months there every year between the purchase in 1902 and his death in 1920. Thus, it was the most consistently inhabited of all of his houses.

6. Howells lived in at least fifteen different apartments or hotels in New York City between 1888 and 1909. For a complete list, see *http://www.wsu.edu/~campbelld/howells/howellsaddresses.htm*.

7. That the house was relatively new in 1866 is attested to by Howells's description of the neighborhood in *Suburban Sketches*. He writes that his house is "almost new and in perfect repair" and that the neighborhood is young: "All round us carpenters were at work building new houses." See Howells, *Suburban Sketches* (Boston: James R. Osgood and Company, 1875), 13–14. Though the house still stands, the surrounding neighborhood has changed dramatically. No longer bucolic, it is a semi-urban environment with houses close together. The Cambridge Historical Commission in Cambridge, Massachusetts, confirms that the house at 41 Sacramento Street was built circa 1857, following a period of development in the area beginning in 1852. Rail service was opened along old omnibus routes in Cambridge at Harvard Station in 1856 and in Somerville at Porter Station in 1858. The street railway quickly became a way of life for suburban dwellers like Howells and his family; within a year, the Cambridge and Porter railroads were carrying an estimated 5,000 passengers a day, mainly to Boston. See Henry C. Binford, *The First Suburbs: Residential Communities on the Boston Periphery, 1815–1860* (Chicago: University of Chicago Press, 1985), 146–149.

8. WDH to Edmund Stedman, Feb. 20, 1866, *Selected Letters*, I: 251–252; WDH to CEN, May 25, 1866, *Selected Letters*, I: 253–254; and WDH to Thomas Higginson, Nov. 20, 1866, *Selected Letters*, I: 270. The letters detail Howells's move to Sacramento Street as well as the financial assistance he received from Norton and his father-in-law to secure the Sacramento Street house.

9. After the birth of John, the family moved temporarily to Boston so Elinor could be closer to doctors and to economize. Howells explained the move and the need to reduce expenses in a letter to his father in November 1868: "Now, with the wet nurse we keep three women, and the house-keeping is beyond my means [. . .] As boarding rooms are cheaper, I'm resigned to it, though of course, we'd rather keep house," Houghton.

10. WDH to CEN, May 25, 1866, *Selected Letters*, I: 253–254.

11. Descriptions of the Sacramento Street interiors are drawn from Howells's letters to his friends and family in which he described his new house. See, for example, *Selected Letters*, I: 253–254 and I: 307.

12. WDH to WCH, February 8, 1866, *Selected Letters*, I: 250.

13. WDH to Henry James [hereafter HJ], June 26, 1869, *Selected Letters*, I: 328–332. "A Doorstep Acquaintance" first appeared in the *Atlantic* in April 1869; "A Pedestrian Tour" appeared in November 1869.

14. WDH to HJ, January 2, 1870, *Selected Letters*, I: 350–355. "A Romance of Real Life" appeared in the *Atlantic* in March 1870. Howells met and befriended the young Henry James in the mid 1860s (c.1865) when HJ first submitted work to the *Atlantic Monthly*; his first piece was published in the magazine in March 1865. At this time, both WDH and HJ were living in Cambridge, James at his parents' homestead near Harvard University at 20 Quincy Street and Howells on Sacramento Street. Though the two authors did not see each other frequently after HJ moved abroad in the 1870s, they remained lifelong friends.

15. WDH to WCH, December 20, 1868, *Selected Letters*, I: 309–310.

16. WDH, *A Modern Instance*, (1882; rpt., New York: Penguin Books, 1984), 51. Emphasis original.

17. See, for example, Howells's notebook from Columbus, Ohio, 1857–1858, and his notebook containing notes for Silas Lapham, both at the Houghton Library.

18. In March 1868, Howells wrote his family, "Bliss is appalling from its insecurity. The fact that we're all very well just now increases our trepidation." See WDH to WCH family, March 6, 1868, *Selected Letters*, I: 292–293, and WDH to WCH, April 18, 1869, *Selected Letters*, I: 322–324.

19. By the turn of the century, he had only his wife and daughter Mildred to support and his net worth exceeded $100,000. See Howells's "Business Papers," Houghton Library. This income was derived from many different sources: the Cambridge house (37 Concord Avenue) valued at $10,000; cash in several different banks ($13,000); stocks and bonds ($23,000); life insurance ($27,000); and plates for Harpers and Houghton Mifflin ($5,000). Howells figured his net worth each year, and each year between 1890 and the first decade of the twentieth century, it steadily increased.

20. See WDH to CEN, Nov. 7, 1869, *Selected Letters*, I: 344–347.

21. Anywhere from 30,000 Irish in 1865 to a high of 77,000 in 1873 immigrated each year. See the *Historical Statistics of the United States: Colonial Times to 1970, Bicentennial Edition*, Part 1 (Washington, D.C.: U.S. Department of the Census, 1975).

22. WDH to WCH family, March 6, 1868, *Selected Letters*, I: 292. Adjusted for inflation, $10,000 is about $177,000 in 2009 currency.

23. Elinor Mead Howells [hereafter EMH] to Victoria Howells, September 11, 1870, quoted in *If Not Literature: Letters of Elinor Mead Howells*, Ginette de B. Merrill and George Arms, eds. (Columbus: Ohio State University Press, 1988), 130. Hereafter referred to as *Letters of EMH*. Richard Henry Dana (1815–1882), author and antislavery activist, was famous for his book, *Two Years Before the Mast* (1841).

24. The deed to the land is dated July 30, 1872, and signed by Howells, the purchaser, and Theophilus Parsons, the seller. See Howells, Box Am 1784. 3(26), Houghton. See also "37 Concord Avenue," Cambridge Historical Commission, for details regarding the property.

25. Ethel Fiske, ed., *The Letters of John Fiske* (New York: Macmillan Company, 1940), 362–364. John Fiske (1842–1901) was a philosopher and historian who lived in Cambridge.

26. Additional details regarding the new house and EMH's touches such as the monogramming are found in *Life in Letters of William Dean Howells*,

Mildred Howells, ed., two volumes (1928; rpt., New York: Russell & Russell, 1968), I: 177. Hereafter referred to as *Life in Letters*.

27. WDH to HJ, Sept. 1, 1872, *Life in Letters*, I: 171–172.
28. *A Modern Instance*, 26.
29. Thorstein Veblen (1857–1929), a contemporary of Howells, coined the term "invidious comparison" in his work, *The Theory of the Leisure Class* (1899; rpt., New York: Modern Library, 2001), chapter two.
30. WDH to HJ, January 2, 1870, *Selected Letters*, I: 350–352.
31. In "A Pedestrian Tour," Howells takes note of the hundreds of mansard-roofed houses cropping up and adds: "I turn [. . .] northward, up a street upon which a flight of French-roof houses suddenly settled a year or two since, with families in them, and many outward signs of permanence, though their precipitate arrival might cast some doubt on this. I have to admire their uniform neatness and prettiness, and I look at their dormer-windows with the envy of one to whose weak sentimentality dormer-windows long appeared the supreme architectural happiness." *Suburban Sketches*, 61.
32. Hamlin Garland, "William Dean Howells's Boston," *Boston Evening Transcript*, May 22, 1920. The house, still standing, has been converted into condominiums and altered quite a bit.
33. *A Modern Instance,* 49.
34. EMH to Susan Warner, [Oct. 29, 1877], *Letters of EMH*, 188–189.
35. WDH to WCH, Nov. 24, 1877, *Selected Letters*, II: 179–180 and WDH to WCH, Jan. 9, 1875, *Selected Letters*, II: 87–88.
36. Wharton, *A Backward Glance*, (1933; rpt., New York: Charles Scribner's Sons, 1964), 146–147.
37. Gwendolyn Wright, *Building the Dream* (Boston: MIT Press, 1981), 96.
38. Charles Fairchild (1838–1910) was a paper manufacturer and then banker in Boston. He was also an art collector and a friend and patron of many writers and artists. See Ginette de B. Merrill, "Redtop and the Belmont Years of W. D. Howells and His Family," *Harvard Library Bulletin*, vol. XXVIII, Number 1, January 1980, 35n4, 38. Details regarding the neighborhood in which the house was located are drawn from *Belmont: The Architecture and Development of the Town of Homes* (Belmont, MA: Belmont Historic District Commission, 1984), especially 56 and 76. I owe a special debt of gratitude to Ginette de B. Merrill and her husband, who have dwelled at Redtop since 1976 and who kindly welcomed me into their home, providing me not only with an extended tour of the house and gardens, but with information regarding the original details of the house.
39. Howells named the house "Redtop." On one occasion, Elinor referred to it as "Shingleside." See Merrill, 39.
40. Among the new magazines devoted to building houses in the country were *American Homes* (1871) and *The American Home* (1877). The *Atlantic Monthly*, reviewer of H. Hudson Holly's *Modern Dwellings in Town and Country* (1878), complained of an over-emphasis on "the rural branch" of houses, so great was the emphasis on country houses in the late 1870s.
41. Elinor's brother, William Rutherford Mead (1846–1928), was an architect working in New York with Charles Follen McKim (1847–1909) and McKim's brother-in-law, William B. Bigelow. McKim, Mead & Bigelow disbanded shortly after Annie Bigelow abandoned McKim in 1878. In 1879, Stanford

White (1853–1906) joined the firm and the firm's name, McKim, Mead & White, was established. See Richard Guy Wilson, *McKim, Mead, & White, Architects* (New York: Rizzoli, 1983).

42. In late 1877, Elinor reprimanded her brother for drawing up a faulty plan because he "didn't know the lay of the land," quoted in Merrill, 37. On June 15, [1878], she wrote to him, "I got no letter from you this morning so I conclude you are too indignant to write," *Letters of EMH*, 203–204.

43. The other quotations on the library walls were Thomas Hardy's "Far From the Madding Crowd" and Goethe's "Uber Allen Gipfeln Ist Ruh," meaning "Over Every Hilltop is Peace."

44. See Merrill, 33–35, and *Letters of EMH*, 182–211.

45. Susan Goodman and Carl Dawson, *William Dean Howells: A Writer's Life* (Berkeley: University of California Press, 2005), 295.

46. WDH to Charles Fairchild, Oct. 6, 1881, *Selected Letters*, II: 298–299.

47. J. L. and J. B. Gilder, *Authors at Home: Personal and Biographical Sketches of Well-known American Authors* (New York: A. Wessels Company, 1905), 195.

48. Bainbridge Bunting in *Houses of Boston's Back Bay: An Architectural History, 1840–1917* (Cambridge, MA: Belknap Press of Harvard University, 1967), 173.

49. George Santayana, *Persons and Places* (New York: Charles Scribner's Sons, 1944), 141–142. The earliest extant photograph of number 302 dates from 1920 and ran in the *Saturday Evening Transcript* (May 22, 1920), but the building appears to have been altered even by this date. The newspaper's photograph shows four stories plus a basement and attic, while Santayana's and Gilder's descriptions suggest three primary floors, not four.

50. As Bunting confirms, Gothic Styles made up 19 percent of the Back Bay's town houses; while Queen Anne and Romanesque Styles were very infrequent, with 8 and 4 percent of each, respectively. See Bunting, 173.

51. Gilder, 196.

52. Both Gilder, in 1889, and Santayana, from memory, provide detailed descriptions of the building's layout and the surrounding neighborhood. See Gilder, 195–209; and Santayana, 140–147. These chapters remain particularly helpful because the building was entirely remodeled and turned into a five-unit apartment building in 1933 by J. B. Brown (see Bunting, 407).

53. Santayana, 142.

54. Santayana, 142.

55. Howells, *The Rise of Silas Lapham*, (1885; rpt., New York: W. W. Norton & Co., 1982), 49. All future references to this book are to this edition and are noted parenthetically in the text.

56. WDH to HJ, August 22, 1884, *Selected Letters*, III: 108–110.

57. Bunting, 20. Bunting's description of the cultural background of the neighborhood reveals that the monotony of the Back Bay's streets matched the conservative, discrete quality of the families with "old money" who lived there. See Bunting, 9–20.

58. Anon., "The Tyranny of Things," Contributor's Club, *Atlantic Monthly* (January 1906): 715–717.

59. Though Howells wrote these words to his father on August 20, 1869, they were a recurring refrain in his letters until he bought his Maine cottage in 1902.
60. This analysis is drawn from looking at period photographs of the interior of the house that are located in the Howells collection at Houghton and that appear in *Selected Letters* and *Letters of EMH*.
61. WDH to Anne Howells Fréchette, Jan. 17, 1913, *Selected Letters*, VI: 27. Emphasis original.
62. WDH to WCH, February 2, 1890, *Selected Letters*, III: 271–272.
63. WDH to WCH, August 10, 1884, *Life in Letters*, I: 363–364.
64. William Dean Howells, "A Traveler from Altruria," in *The Altrurian Romances*, Clara and Rudolf Kirk, eds. (1893; rpt., Bloomington: Indiana University Press, 1968), 94–95. WDH serialized the novella in *Cosmopolitan* from November 1892 to October 1893.
65. "A Traveler from Altruria," 95.
66. WDH to HJ, July 1, 1910, *Selected Letters*, V: 323–324.
67. WDH to WCH, Nov. 22, 1891 and WDH to WCH, Oct. 18, 1891, *Selected Letters*, III: 326 and 321. The Howellses lived on Beacon Street for three years, from 1884 to 1887. They sold the property in 1887, and for the next two years they traveled the East coast and New York state, trying to find a doctor who could cure daughter Winny. After she died in 1889, the Howellses moved temporarily back to Boston (renting an apartment on Commonwealth Avenue) to be near their son John who was at Harvard. At the end of 1891, they returned to New York on as permanent a basis as was possible for them.
68. In a letter to Charles Eliot Norton, Howells describes the unexpected offer he had received to be the editor of *Cosmopolitan* and the terms of his position. While WDH intended to keep the job for many years, he left the position after only six months, a sign, perhaps, of his new resolve to live life on his own terms. See WDH to CEN, Dec. 12, 1891, *Selected Letters*, III: 327–328.
69. WDH referred to the family's search for a summer house as a "wild goose chase" as well. See WDH to Aurelia Howells, July 28, 1895. Houghton.
70. On occasion, the Howellses rented an individual house in the city rather than an apartment, but these were harder to come by and, increasingly, the elderly couple preferred buildings with elevators and prepared meals, as Howells explained to his father: "It will be more difficult running a house than a flat, and the stairs are very trying for both Elinor and me," WDH to WCH, Dec. 20, 1891, *Life in Letters*, II: 20.
71. The history of the New York City apartment building is drawn from three sources: Elizabeth Cromley, *Alone Together: A History of New York's Early Apartments* (Ithaca: Cornell University Press, 1990), especially 128–143; M. Christine Boyer, *Manhattan Manners: Architecture and Style, 1850–1900* (New York: Rizzoli, 1985), especially 154–165; and Paul E. Groth, *Living Downtown: The History of Residential Hotels in the United States* (Berkeley: University of California Press, 1994).
72. *A Hazard of New Fortunes* (1890; rpt., New York: Penguin Books, 2001), 57.
73. Betsy Klimasmith, *At Home in the City: Urban Domesticity in American Literature and Culture, 1850–1930* (Durham, University of New Hampshire Press, 2005), 165.

74. *A Hazard of New Fortunes,* 84.
75. Klimasmith, *At Home in the City*, 165.
76. According to Elizabeth Cromley, the expected rate for a twelve-room apartment was $2,500 a year. See *Alone Together*, 129, 131. M. Christine Boyer notes that in spite of a great deal of development on the upper-west and upper-east sides of Manhattan in the 1880s and 1890s, in 1892, there remained 1,612 vacant lots between 59th and 72nd Streets—an area where Howells frequently stayed. This statistic might explain why, when he chose to buy, he did so in a building on West 57th Street, a thoroughfare amidst a more developed area. See Boyer, *Manhattan Manners*, 217.
77. In *A Hazard of New Fortunes*, Howells made fun of apartment names when he sent the March family looking for the superintendent of an apartment called the Xenophon. The man could not be found, and the Marches were told to look for him at the Herodotus or the Thucydides next door. I wish to thank Elizabeth Cromley for pointing out this clever detail in *Alone Together*, 142.
78. Except for the Dakota, none of the apartment buildings mentioned here still stand.
79. WDH to Charles Eliot Norton, July 1901, *Selected Letters*, IV: 292.
80. WDH to Aurelia Howells, July 28, 1895, Houghton.
81. WDH to Samuel Clemens, Oct. 20, 1902, *Selected Letters*, V: 38.
82. WDH to HJ, Oct. 7, 1902, *Selected Letters*, V: 35.
83. WDH to Aurelia Howells, Oct. 4, 1903, *Selected Letters*, V: 65–66.
84. While the date of its construction and its architect are unknown, the house has belonged to Harvard University since 1979 when the Howells family bequeathed it to the school. I thank the inhabitants at the time of my visit for their generosity in letting me explore and take pictures of the grounds and the residence.
85. The few extant photographs of Howells's library in Kittery Point are small and dark and are not effectively reproduced. One view of the library can be seen in *Letters of EMH*, 283.
86. WDH to Sir George Trevelyan, May 24, 1905, *Selected Letters*, V: 121–122.
87. At this point in his life, Howells had a yearly income of about $14,000 (about $300,000 today), which he could "run up to $20,000" if he chose by "writing outside." This income was derived from the following sources: $5,000 yearly from the "Easy Chair;" $5,000 yearly from the rent of houses; $3,500 yearly from the rent of the New York apartment on West 57th street; $1,500 yearly in royalties from old books; and the remainder from city bonds, trusts, interest, and savings. See WDH to Mildred Howells, Nov. 2, 1915, *Selected Letters*, VI: 86.
88. WDH to CEN, Oct. 25, 1894, *Selected Letters*, IV: 78.
89. WDH to Mrs. J. G. (Laura) Mitchell, Feb. 9, 1914, *Life in Letters*, II: 332–333.

Chapter Three

1. James was only the third owner of the early Georgian brick house that had been in the Lamb family for nearly 150 years (from approximately 1722 to 1864). Francis Bellingame, a Rye lawyer, owned the home for thirty-three years before James began to lease the house in 1897; James bought the

house in 1899 and owned it until his death in 1916. He bequeathed the house to his nephew, Henry James, Jr., the son of William, whose wife, Mrs. Henry James, Jr., gave the house to the National Trust of England in 1950. See H. Montgomery Hyde, *The Story of Lamb House, Rye: The Home of Henry James* (Rye, Sussex: Adams of Rye Limited, 1966).

2. Henry James [hereafter HJ] to William James [hereafter WJ] Feb. 28 [1877], quoted in Leon Edel, ed., *Henry James Letters*, Volume II, 1875–1883 (Cambridge: Belknap Press of Harvard University, 1975), 102. Hereafter referred to as *HJ Letters*, II. Each of the four volumes of *HJ Letters* edited by Edel will hereafter be referred to as *HJ Letters*, followed by the volume number.

3. In his letters, James writes of "inhaling" and "appropriating" the old world and of "soaking" in England. See HJ to the James Family, November 1, [1875], in Leon Edel, ed., *Henry James Letters*, Volume I, 1843–1875 (Cambridge: Belknap Press of Harvard University, 1974), 484. Hereafter referred to as *HJ Letters*, I. Also see HJ to WJ, February 28, [1877], *HJ Letters*, II: 102.

4. HJ to William James, February 28 [1877], *HJ Letters*, II: 100; HJ to Grace Norton, *HJ Letters*, II: 135. Grace Norton (1834–1926) was the unmarried sister of Charles Eliot Norton (1827–1908), coeditor of the *North American Review* and the *Nation*, and professor of art history at Harvard beginning in 1873. HJ remained close friends with both Grace and Charles until their deaths.

5. HJ to WDH, March 30, [1877]. *HJ Letters*, II: 105.

6. Leon Edel, in his masterful and psychologically probing five-volume biography of James, posits that only after 1890 was James ready to commit to friendships and to his own life, and therefore a home. In the years after 1890, Edel writes, James dined out less, curtailed his country visits, and focused on his literary, London friends. See Edel, *Henry James*, vols. 1–5 (Philadelphia: J. B. Lippincott, 1952–1972). James wrote famously about constructing the house of fiction in his preface to the New York Edition of *The Portrait of a Lady* (1908). These words appear as the epigraph to the chapter: "The house of fiction has in short not one window, but a million—a number of possible windows not to be reckoned, rather; every one of which has been pierced, or is still pierceable, in its vast front, by the need of the individual vision and by the pressure of the individual will." See Henry James, *The Portrait of a Lady*, ed. Robert E. Bamburg (1908; rpt., New York: W. W. Norton, 1995), 7. All further references are to this edition and are noted parenthetically in the text. Of the four authors in this study, James was the only one never to build a dream house, but in a sense, his house of fiction can be considered his "dream house."

7. James explained to his friend Grace Norton why he did not wish to marry: "I am attached to [my life], I am used to it—it doesn't in any way paralyze or incapacitate me (on the contrary), and it doesn't involve any particular injustice to any one, least of all to myself." HJ to Grace Norton, November 7, [1880], *HJ Letters*, II: 314. James moved into Lamb House in 1897 as noted in the first paragraph of this chapter, as a leasee of the property, but he did not actually buy the place until 1899.

8. Mrs. James T. Fields (Annie Fields), wife of the American publisher and good friend to Harriet Beecher Stowe, described James's residence in this way after paying him a visit. Quoted in Hyde, *The Story of Lamb House*, 52.

9. Studies that emphasize HJ's particular way of viewing the world and his vision include the following: Ralph F. Bogardus, *Pictures and Texts: Henry James, A. L. Coburn, and New Ways of Seeing in Literary Culture* (Ann Arbor: University of Michigan Press, 1984); Laurence Holland, *The Expense of Vision: Essays on the Craft of Henry James* (Princeton: Princeton University Press, 1964); William Vance, "Reading the Campagna: 'Silence Made Visible,'" in *America's Rome* (New Haven: Yale University Press, 1989), 136–146; and the two issues of *The Henry James Review* devoted solely to the "art" of Henry James: "Jamesian Arts," *The Henry James Review* 23 (2002); and "More Jamesian Arts," *The Henry James Review* 24 (2003).

10. When James was twenty-three, he wrote to Thomas Sergeant Perry that he tried to be all of these things, as if telling himself. These also became the traits that James is perhaps best known and appreciated for as a writer. See HJ to Thomas Sergeant Perry, September 15 [1866], *HJ Letters*, I: 65. In *The Art of Fiction*, James wrote of "guessing the unseen from the seen." See Walter Besant with Henry James, *The Art of Fiction* (Boston: Cupples, Upham and Co., 1885), 66.

11. HJ to Sarah Butler Wister, August 10 [1873], emphasis original, *HJ Letters*, I: 399.

12. The father of Henry James, Sr., William James of Albany, New York, left an estate valued at three million dollars when he died in 1832. From this, Henry senior received a large parcel of real estate in Syracuse that yielded him about $10,000 a year. He accordingly found himself "leisured for life." See Leon Edel, *Henry James: The Untried Years*, 1843–1870 (Philadelphia and New York: J. B. Lippincott Company, 1953), 20–21. Hereafter referred to as *Untried Years*. This volume of Edel's five-volume biography of Henry James details James's family background and the history of Henry James, Sr.'s, inheritance, which was originally only $1,200 a year. See Edel, 20.

13. Henry James was the second son of the five children of Henry James, Sr. (1811–1882) and Mary Robertson Walsh (1810–1882). Their other four children were William (1842–1910), a Harvard professor and philosopher; Garth Wilkinson "Wilkie" (1845–1883), who died of alcoholism; Robertson "Bob" (1846–1910), who lived in Milwaukee and was also an alcoholic; and Alice (1847–1892), who never married and died of cancer at age forty-five.

14. James's upbringing was markedly transient: the family was living at Washington Place in New York City when Henry James was born in 1843. When he was one year old, the family moved to Paris for a year. In 1845, the family returned to the United States and lived in Albany, New York, and New York City, settling, finally, into a house at 58 West 14th Street. In 1855, when Henry was twelve, the family moved back to Paris and moved about Europe for three years. In 1858, they again returned to the United States and settled in Newport, Rhode Island. The family returned to Europe in 1859 for another year and returned to Newport in 1860. In 1862, the young Henry James, now 19, joined his older brother, William (who was attending Harvard's Divinity School), in Cambridge, Massachusetts, and attended Harvard Law School. Neither HJ nor WJ enlisted in the Civil War, though

their two younger brothers, Wilkie and Bob, did. His parents, missing their two sons, moved from Newport to Cambridge in 1864, residing first in Ashburton Place, and finally at 20 Quincy Street—the first and last "family home." Henry and his brother William soon moved into the family house at Quincy Street. These numerous moves are chronicled in Edel, *Untried Years*, and in Edel, *Henry James: A Life* (New York: Harper & Row, 1985), especially 59–70 [hereafter referred to as *Henry James*].

15. James's two Newport friends became influential in their fields: John La Farge (1835–1910), a painter and stained glass artist, and Thomas Sergeant Perry (1845–1928), a critic, editor, and translator (Perry's sister Margaret married John La Farge); his close friend from Cambridge, Oliver Wendell Holmes, Jr. (1841–1935), became a Supreme Court Justice. James remained friends with all three men throughout his life.

16. "The Story of a Year," *Atlantic Monthly* (1865), March, XV: 257–281.

17. HJ to Thomas Sergeant Perry, September 20 [1867], *HJ Letters*, I: 77.

18. Besant and James, *The Art of Fiction*, 66.

19. This is not to suggest that HJ was completely free from issues regarding his sexuality and/or by complicated relationships with men and women, as recent biographers have illuminated. See especially, Sheldon M. Novick, *Henry James: The Young Master* (New York, Random House, 1996), and Paul Fisher, *House of Wits: An Intimate Portrait of the James Family* (New York: Henry Holt, 2008), 352–356, 393–397.

20. Besant and James, *The Art of Fiction*, 54. Emphasis original.

21. Both were James's expressions: the "house of fiction," as we have already seen, was his way of referring to the building of a text. The "house of life" was James's way of referring to his upbringing, which was grounded in experiences rather than in formal education. See Edel, *Untried Years*, 80.

22. Leon Edel, *Henry James: The Conquest of London*, 1870–1881 (Philadelphia and New York: J. B. Lippincott Company, 1962), 182. Hereafter referred to as *Conquest of London*.

23. Edel, *Conquest of London,* 197.

24. HJ to Mrs. Henry James, Sr. Christmas Eve [1876]. *HJ Letters*, II: 85–88.

25. James had resided near the Bolton Street apartment, at 7 Half Moon Street, when he toured Europe as a man of twenty-five, eight years earlier, so he was familiar with the neighborhood. James's housemaid, Louisa, prepared his meals and cleaned, but did not live in the apartment. These details are drawn from H. Montgomery Hyde, *Henry James at Home* (New York: Farrar, Straus, & Giroux, 1969), 3–8.

26. Edel, *Conquest of London*, 271–272.

27. James noted retrospectively in his journal: "[I walked] for exercise, for amusement, for acquisition and above all I always walked home at evening's end. One walked of course with one's eyes greatly opened." Quoted in Edel, *Henry James*, 206.

28. HJ to Alice James, December 13 [1876], *HJ Letters*, II: 82.

29. HJ to Alice James, December 13 [1876], *HJ Letters*, II: 82.

30. Edel, *Conquest of London,* 272.

31. HJ to Mrs. Henry James, Sr., Christmas Eve [1876], *HJ Letters*, II: 85–86; HJ to William Dean Howells, December 18 [1876], *HJ Letters*, II: 84–85.

32. *Roderick Hudson* was serialized in the *Atlantic Monthly* from January to December 1875; *The American* ran in the *Atlantic* throughout 1876. *The*

Europeans was published in the *Atlantic* from July to October 1878. Howells was editor of the magazine at this time. Prior to *Roderick Hudson*, James published *Watch and Ward* in the *Atlantic* from August to December 1871 but did not revise it for book publication until the fall of 1877. James also published *A Passionate Pilgrim*, in January, 1875, with Houghton, Osgood & Company. James Ripley Osgood (1836–1892), who launched his own publishing house, J. R. Osgood Company, in 1871, published *Roderick Hudson* in November 1875, as well as other early works by HJ.

33. HJ to Grace Norton, January 15, 1874, *HJ Letters*, I: 429, and, HJ to Alice James, December 13 [1876], *HJ Letters*, II: 82.

34. HJ to WJ, November 31, [1872], *HJ Letters*, I: 312–313. James uses the French verb "flânant," from "flâner," meaning to stroll, to saunter, or to hang about.

35. HJ to Mrs. Henry James, Sr., Christmas Eve [1876], *HJ Letters*, II: 86–88.

36. Charles Baudelaire wrote about the "flâneur" in his 1861 poem "Tableaux Parisiens" ["Parisian Sketches"] in his collection of poems, *Les Fleurs du Mal* (1861; rpt., *The Flowers of Evil*, trans. by James McGowan, New York: Penguin, 1993).

37. Walter Benjamin, *The Arcades Project* (1940; rpt., Cambridge: Belknap Press of Harvard University Press, 1999), 10, 423.

38. In his letters, James writes of "working off" impressions by thinking through them on lengthy walks, and advises friends to do the same, telling Grace Norton, for example, "Whenever you are afflicted with an excess of impressions remember whitherward to work them off." HJ to Grace Norton, July 16, 1871, *HJ Letters*, I: 258.

39. The first mention of an art object that James acquired is made in 1899 when he orders a bust of a young boy from Hendrik Andersen, a young sculptor who lived in Italy. See HJ to Hendrik Andersen, July 19, 1899, *HJ Letters*, IV, 108.

40. HJ to Henry James, Sr., September 19 [1877], *HJ Letters*, II: 139.

41. Benjamin, *The Arcades Project*, 423.

42. HJ to Mrs. John Rollin Tilton, April 3 [1878], *HJ Letters*, II: 163, 164n2.

43. From biographies and letters, it appears that James's closest friends were those he left behind in Cambridge: his family members (especially his brother William and sister Alice), to whom he wrote regularly; Charles Eliot Norton and his sister Grace; and three women whose lives were cut short: Mary "Minny" Temple (1845–1870), a cousin of the James family and with whom HJ spent time in Newport, Rhode Island, as a boy; Elizabeth "Lizzie" Boott (1846–1888), who was reared in Florence by her father Francis Boott and who married the painter Frank Duveneck; and Constance Fenimore Woolson (1840–1894), an American regionalist writer and grand-niece of James Fenimore Cooper who lived in Italy and England. For an in-depth discussion of HJ's relationship with Minny Temple and Constance Fenimore Woolson, see Lyndall Gordon, *A Private Life of Henry James: Two Women and His Art* (London: Chatto & Windus, 1998). See also Novick's 2-volume biography of HJ and Fisher, *House of Wits*.

44. HJ mentions dinners or breakfasts at these clubs early on in letters home; see, for example, HJ to Mrs. Henry James, Sr., Christmas Eve [1876], *HJ Letters*, II: 86 and 109. On the creation of the Rabelais Club (1879–1889), a

literary dining club, and its founder, Charles Godfrey Leland, see HJ to WJ, March 4 [1879], *HJ Letters*, II: 217 and *HJ Letters*, III, 162.

45. To James's dismay he was not elected to the very elite Athenaeum Club—"the foremost modern literary club in England"—until much later in his life; he was consoled, however, by being elected a member of the equally fine Reform Club. James wrote to his sister, Alice, that he took up with the St. James's Club "in default of the acutely missed Athenaeum." See HJ to Alice James, December 29 [1877], *HJ Letters*, II: 147. The St. James's Club, located near James's apartment at 106 Piccadilly, was founded in the mid-1700s, and was known for embracing "many with an intimate knowledge of foreign countries, and even the Far East," and, in exchange for elitism, offered its members "one of the most agreeable and sociable clubs in London." For locations and descriptions of the clubs, including the quotation on the St. James's Club, see Ralph Nevill, *London Clubs: Their History and Treasures* (London: Chatto & Windus, 1911), especially 215–218; and George Woodbridge, *The Reform Club, 1836–1978: A History from the Club's Records* (New York and Toronto: Clearwater Publishing Company, 1978).

46. Nevill, 232–233, and Charles Graves, *Leather Armchairs: The Book of London Clubs* (New York: Coward-McCann, 1964), 56.

47. It is no wonder that James enjoyed his meals at the Reform Club, prepared as they were by the famous French chef, Alexis Soyer, who immigrated to England in the early nineteenth century and became known as "one of the great cooks of history," (Nevill, 233).

48. HJ to Henry James, Sr., May 29 [1878], *HJ Letters*, II: 175.

49. The subject of James's finances has been much scrutinized in the numerous biographies of him. It appears that he struggled financially for the first five or so years that he lived in Europe (roughly 1875–1880). However, though he often took the liberty of drawing on his father's letter of credit for him, he was extremely fastidious in repaying his father, usually by having money owed him for publications sent directly to Henry, Sr. in Cambridge. In the case of the dues for the Reform Club, James added in the letter to his father: "I can easily and promptly repay you the money and shall in the course of a strictly limited time do so," *HJ Letters*, II: 176.

50. Graves, *Leather Armchairs,* 56–59. HJ to Henry James, Sr., May 29 [1878], *HJ Letters*, II: 176.

51. HJ to Henry James, Sr., May 29 [1878], *HJ Letters*, II: 176.

53. James refers to the museums of his youth as "palaces of art" in his autobiography, *A Small Boy and Others* (1913). See also Edel, *Untried Years*, 80.

54. Though James's American friends, and the elder women with whom he socialized in London, yearned for him to become engaged—and circulated rumors to this effect—James's relationships with women remained platonic. Countless letters by James mention these types of individuals, such as one to his mother dated July 6 [1879]. See HJ to Mrs. Henry James, Sr., *HJ Letters*, II: 247–250. In some cases, James's American friends, such as Charlotte Temple, sister of the deceased Minnie Temple, married into the English aristocracy. Leon Edel also notes that James befriended such people for their conversation and their impressions. See *HJ Letters*, II: 250n2. In recent years, James has been the subject of a number of books on queer and gender studies, which identify him as the prototypical late-nineteenth early-

twentieth-century homosexual. His status as a flâneur corroborates these theories. See Eric Haralson, *Henry James and Queer Modernity* (Cambridge and New York: Cambridge University Press, 2003); Peggy McCormack, ed., *Questioning the Master: Gender and Sexuality in Henry James's Writings* (Newark: University of Delaware Press, 2000); and John R. Bradley, ed., *Henry James and Homo-erotic Desire* (New York: St. Martin's Press, 1999).

55. HJ to Mrs. Henry James, Sr., November 28 [1880], *HJ Letters*, II: 318. John Bright (1811–1889) was the son of a Quaker cotton spinner, whose Quaker beliefs shaped his politics. He fought for an end to social, political, or religious inequalities between individuals and peoples. Lord Northbrook (1826–1904) was Governor General and Viceroy of India from May 1872 to April 1876. A liberal of the school of Gladstone, Lord Northbrook, like Rosebery, believed in less government interference and was in favor of keeping the colonial state undisturbed by unwarranted changes. Both Bright and Northbrook were liberals like Rosebery. Rosebery broke with the Liberal party in 1905, however, because he opposed Irish Home Rule.

56. HJ to Mrs. Henry James, Sr., November 28 [1880], *HJ Letters*, II: 317–318.

57. HJ to Mrs. Henry James, Sr., November 28 [1880], *HJ Letters*, II: 319.

58. HJ to Mrs. Henry James, Sr., November 28 [1880], *HJ Letters*, II: 319.

59. Ariana Wormeley Randolf Curtis and her husband, Daniel Sargent Curtis (1825–1908), a Boston lawyer and banker and a relation of the artist John Singer Sargent, were the parents of the artist Ralph Wormeley Curtis. An unfortunate incident with a Boston judge led Mr. Curtis to move his family to Europe where he eventually acquired the Palazzo Barbaro. The palazzo inspired a number of artistic and literary works, and the Curtis family itself was the subject of Sargent's *An Interior in Venice* (1898) which depicts the palazzo. Mr. Curtis died in Venice at the age of eighty-three.

60. Mrs. Isabella Stewart Gardner (1840–1924), the Boston hostess and art collector, was commonly called "Mrs. Jack" after her husband, John L. Gardner, whom she married in 1860. She later built the Isabella Stewart Gardner Museum in Boston in the form of a Venetian palace, and furnished it with the objects acquired while she stayed in Italy.

61. The descriptions of the Palazzo Barbaro are drawn from photographs and from *Henry James, Letters from the Palazzo Barbaro*, Rosella Mamoli Zorzi, ed. (London: Pushkin Press, 1998); Elizabeth Anne McCauley, ed., *Gondola Days: Isabella Stewart Gardner and the Palazzo Barbaro Circle* (Boston: Isabella Stewart Gardner Museum, 2004); Hugh Honour and John Fleming, *Venetian Hours of Henry James, Whistler, and Sargent* (Boston: Little, Brown, 1991); and Edel, *Middle Years*, 324–325.

62. See Leon Edel, "Introduction," *HJ Letters*, III: xiv.

63. William H. Gass, "The High Brutality of Good Intentions," *Accent*, XVIII (Winter, 1958), 62–71.

64. Gass, 62–71.

65. Edel asserts that HJ used Osterley Park as the model for the mansions in his short stories "The Covering End" and "The Lesson of the Master." See *HJ Letters*, III: 123n2. For the original title of *The Spoils*, see HJ to Horace Scudder, September 3, 1895, *HJ Letters* IV: 18, 22–23.

66. Quoted in Charles Feidelson, "The Moment of *The Portrait of a Lady*," in *Portrait*, 712.

67. HJ to Mrs. John "Jack" Gardner, January 29, [1880]. *HJ Letters*, II: 265–266.

68. Even before this, James had written to his parents: "Endure my absence yet a while longer and I will return to you primed for immortality," and to his sister: "I shall immortalize myself: *vous allez voir* [you'll see]." See HJ to his parents, February 27, 1874, *HJ Letters*, I: 433; and HJ to Alice James, April 18 [1874], I: 438.

69. Feidelson, 715.

70. Edel, "Italian Hours," *HJ Letters*, III: 144.

71. HJ to Grace Norton, January 4 [1879], *HJ Letters*, II: 209.

72. James was famously insecure about his career—at times highly assured of his skill, and at others, profoundly dismayed by his inability to sell. He also suffered for many years (particularly in the 1870s and 1880s) from a number of ailments including indigestion and constipation, which he described as "the bane of his existence," and as young man, resented being the "mere junior" to his father's senior position as Henry James. See Edel, *Untried Years*, 50–58.

73. Mr. Touchett has wisely realized the passion that comes from holding on to something, while Ralph and Isabel have not yet. The senior Touchett's assertion implicates Isabel, who, at this early stage, is a rootless orphan who will reject the marriage proposals of Lord Warburton and Caspar Goodwood. Her ultimate decision to remain with the villainous Gilbert Osmond, in the novel's last chapter, however, suggests that by this time, she has learned James's lesson: that anything held onto and worked on long enough can become a work of art.

74. This travel sketch appears in "Italy Revisited" (1877; reprinted in *Italian Hours* (New York: Grove Press, 1959), 123–125, 146–147, 162–163, 213. See also Van Wyck Brooks, *The Dream of Arcadia: American Writers and Artists in Italy, 1760–1915* (New York: Dutton, 1958).

75. HJ, *Notes of a Son and Brother* (1914), 65.

76. On the overly relaxing environment in Italy, see HJ to Henry James, Sr. March 30 [1880], *HJ Letters*, II: 277. Laurence Holland has written about Henry James and his resemblance to Gilbert Osmond. I repeat a few of these likenesses here in a different context: to illuminate how James dwelled— literally found a dwelling place—through his characters and their houses. See Laurence Holland, *The Expense of Vision*, 28–42.

77. HJ to Elizabeth Boott, December 11 [1883], *HJ Letters*, III: 17. On the subject of Osmond's autonomy, it bears noting that I mean not that he is truly an independent person, but rather, that his sense of himself conveys a sense of "forced" autonomy.

78. HJ to Grace Norton, [no date], *HJ Letters*, II: 406.

79. HJ to Grace Norton, July 23, 1887, *HJ Letters*, III: 195.

80. HJ to WJ, December 9, 1885 and March 9, 1886, *HJ Letters*, III: 106, 114.

81. HJ to Francis Boott, [no date], *HJ Letters*, III: 120. See also Edel, *Middle Years*, 158–161.

82. Edel characterizes these two novels in this manner in *Middle Years*, 192.

83. Details of the publication of *The Tragic Muse* are drawn from *Middle Years*, 253–264.

84. In 1890, James received seventy pounds from Macmillan for *The Tragic Muse*, instead of his usual 200 to 250 pounds because, based on past performance, the publishing house did not think the novel would sell. See *Middle Years*, 264–265.

85. HJ to Mrs. Edward Compton, March 15, 1895, *HJ Letters*, III: 520–521. Mrs. Compton's husband, Edward, ran the Compton Comedy Company, which specialized in staging romantic plays. James sent him his adaptation of *The American* and *Guy Domville* in 1893. When Compton asked for a "happy ending" to the latter, James added a fourth act, but Compton did not like it and did not think the play would succeed with English audiences. He was right. See Edel, *HJ Letters*, III: 412–413n1.

86. HJ to WJ, September 30, 1895, *HJ Letters*, IV: 19.

87. The small apartment was located at 21 Carlyle Mansions, SW, in Chelsea, on the Thames.

88. HJ to Edmund Gosse, October 15, 1912, *HJ Letters*, IV: 630.

89. Edel, *HJ Letters*, IV: 570.

90. HJ to Arthur Benson, September 25, 1897, *HJ Letters*, IV: 57. James knew Benson (1862–1925), the English born essayist and poet, from London.

91. Edward Prioleau Warren (1856–1937) found James the Rye property and later worked as his architect when James undertook alterations. HJ to Edward Warren, September 15, 1897, *HJ Letters*, IV: 56.

92. James's preferred designation for the house and the location of the property in Rye was "my little corner." See, for example, HJ to Paul Bourget, [no date], *HJ Letters*, IV: 140.

93. HJ to Rudyard Kipling, September 16, 1899, *HJ Letters*, IV: 120.

94. HJ to Henry James, III, July 26, 1904, *HJ Letters*, IV: 309.

95. The details of the house, its layout, and alterations, are drawn from Hyde, *The Story of Lamb House*, 16–18, 40–63.

96. Quoted in Hyde, *Lamb House*, 53.

97. HJ to Mrs. William James, May 22, 1900, *HJ Letters*, IV: 142.

98. HJ to Henrietta Reubell, [no date], *HJ Letters*, IV: 218.

99. Though Horace Fletcher (1849–1919), an American businessman from Lawrence, Massachusetts, had no formal medical training, he became very well known for his writing and lectures on popular nutrition. Numerous celebrities of the time, including James, Upton Sinclair, and John D. Rockefeller, followed his advice. See also HJ to WJ, May 6, 1904, *HJ Letters*, IV: 307n3.

100. HJ to WJ, May 6, 1904, *HJ Letters*, IV: 307.

101. HJ to Mrs. Humphrey Ward, September 25, 1906, *HJ Letters*, IV: 415–416.

102. HJ to WJ, October 17, 1907, *HJ Letters*, IV: 468.

103. HJ to Ellen Emmet Rand, November 2, 1908, *HJ Letters*, IV: 501.

104. After MacAlpine, James hired Mary Weld, who left his employ to get married in 1906. His final typist was Theodora Bosanquet, who worked for James for ten years, and after his death became a writer and editor.

105. HJ to Mrs. William James, January 5, 1913, *HJ Letters*, IV: 647.

106. Paul Bourget (1852–1935), a French novelist and critic, was friends with both Edith Wharton and Henry James. He gave Wharton a letter of introduction to James, which Wharton used to call upon James in 1902 when she visited London. Wharton and James exchanged work from this time forward.

107. HJ to Jessie Allen, October 22, 1904, The Mount, Lenox, Mass., *HJ Letters*, IV: 329. Emphasis original. In the same letter, James wrote of the Mount, "Here I am in an exquisite French *chateau* perched among Massachusetts mountains [...] and filled exclusively with old French and Italian furniture

and decorations." For more on Edith Wharton and her life at the Mount, see Chapter 4.

108. HJ to Jessie Allen, March 28, 1907, Hotel Guichard, Pau, Basses Pyrenees, [France], *HJ Letters*, IV: 441.

109. HJ to Mr. and Mrs. Edward Wharton, August 11, 1907, *HJ Letters*, IV: 455; HJ to Mrs. W. K. Clifford, February 17, 1907, *HJ Letters*, IV: 435; and HJ to George and Fanny Prothero, April 13, 1907, *HJ Letters*, IV: 445.

110. HJ to Mr. and Mrs. William James, September 4, 1896, *HJ Letters*, IV: 36. For more on Fullerton and his relationship with EW, see Chapter 4.

111. Biltmore, located in Asheville, North Carolina, was designed by Richard Morris Hunt and built from 1889 to 1895. During the summer of 1889, Vanderbilt and Hunt visited Waddesdon Manor in Buckinghamshire, England, where James had been a frequent visitor. Built from 1877 to 1883, with a wing added from 1888 to 1889, Waddesdon, though smaller, inspired the design of Biltmore. The two palaces share similar principal facades, a projecting pavilion on the north side, and a spiral stair tower. See John M. Bryan, *G. W. Vanderbilt's Biltmore, The Most Distinguished Private Place* (New York: Rizzoli, 1994), 42; and Mrs. James de Rothschild, *The Rothschilds at Waddesdon Manor* (New York: Viking Press, 1979).

112. HJ to Edith Wharton, February 8, 1905, *HJ Letters*, IV: 346–347. Emphasis original.

113. HJ to Edmund Gosse, February 16, 1905, *HJ Letters*, IV: 352.

114. HJ to W. E. Norris, December 23, 1907, *HJ Letters*, IV: 483. James referred to life at Waddesdon Manor as one of "gilded bondage." See HJ to Grace Norton, August 23, 1885, *HJ Letters*, III: 98.

115. Edel, "Revisions," *HJ Letters*, IV: 363.

116. Alvin Langdon Coburn (1882–1966) was a young American photographer whose work had attracted considerable attention in London and been highly praised by George Bernard Shaw. On his working relationship with HJ, see *Alvin Langdon Coburn, Photographer: An Autobiography* (New York: F. A. Praeger, 1966) and Leon Edel, *Henry James: The Master, 1901–1916* (Philadelphia and New York: J. B. Lippincott Company, 1972), 333–338.

117. HJ to Grace Norton, August 1910, *HJ Letters*, IV: 564.

118. HJ to Paul Bourget, December 23, 1898, *HJ Letters*, IV: 91. Emphasis original.

119. HJ to Morton Fullerton, November 19, 1907, *HJ Letters*, IV: 475. Emphasis original.

Chapter Four

1. Edith Wharton and Ogden Codman, Jr., *The Decoration of Houses* (1897; rpt., New York: W. W. Norton & Co., 1998), 116. Hereafter abbreviated as *DH*. In this decorating manual, written by Wharton and her friend and decorator, Ogden Codman, Jr., the authors promoted a layout where the stairs cannot be seen from the vestibule, writing, "The staircase in a private house is for the use of those who inhabit it; the vestibule or hall is necessarily used by persons in no way concerned with the private life of the inmates," 116. Wharton knew the Boston-born Codman (1868–1951) from their summers in Newport, Rhode Island, and enlisted him to help her decorate her Newport, Rhode Island, and New York City homes before they

collaborated on the book. Wharton and Codman are hereafter usually referred to by their initials, EW and OC.

2. R. W. B. and Nancy Lewis, eds. *The Letters of Edith Wharton* (New York: Collier Books, 1988), 252. Hereafter referred to as *EW Letters*.

3. Edith Wharton, *A Backward Glance* (New York: D. Appleton and Co., 1934), 122. Hereafter abbreviated as *ABG*.

4. See chapter one of this book for a discussion of Stowe's Hartford, Connecticut, residence, Oakholm, and chapter two for a discussion of Howells's Belmont, Massachusetts, residence, Redtop. Neither dwelling can compare with Wharton's in terms of the inaccessible layout.

5. The unusual fact that Wharton had a library at all and that it garnered a far more prominent position in the house's layout than her husband's den will be discussed later in the chapter.

6. Wharton began writing poetry as a young girl; her mother had a volume of these verses privately printed by the Newport, Rhode Island, publisher, C. E. Hammett, Jr., in 1878 when Wharton was sixteen years old. Her next published work, which she co-authored with Codman, *The Decoration of Houses*, came nearly two decades later, in 1897. In 1899, at age thirty-seven, Wharton published her first collection of short stories, *The Greater Inclination*, and published her first novel, *The Valley of Decision*, in 1902, when she was forty years old.

7. In her autobiographical essay, "A Little Girl's New York," published posthumously, Wharton writes that her early critical eye was proof of her "intolerable self assurance." (*Harper's Magazine*, March, 1938), 363.

8. Beatrix Jones Farrand to Gaillard Lapsley, August 18, 1937. Quoted in Shari Benstock, *No Gifts From Chance: A Biography of Edith Wharton*, (New York: Charles Scribner's Sons, 1994), 461. Hereafter abbreviated as *NGFC*. Wharton's niece, Beatrix Jones Farrand (1872–1959), was the only child of Wharton's eldest brother Harry and his wife Mary "Minnie" Cadwalader Jones. She married the historian, Max Farrand, became an influential landscape designer, and was the first woman member of the American Society of Landscape Architects. Gaillard Lapsley (1871–1949), a historian and fellow of Trinity College at Cambridge University, England, was selected by Wharton to be the literary executor of her estate.

9. Of these significant residences, only one, the Mount, exists as a house museum and is open to the public. Land's End in Newport still stands and is privately owned; I was able to access the house thanks to the hospitality of the current owners. The Pavillon Colombe, north of Paris, is privately owned, while Ste. Claire le Château on the Côte d'Azur (a former convent) is closed to the public, though the gardens are open. Wharton's adjoining brownstones in New York City (882–884 Park Avenue) have been razed.

10. EW to Bernard Berenson, March 14 [1912], *EW Letters*, 268.

11. Quoted in Hermione Lee, *Edith Wharton* (New York: Knopf, 2007), 411.

12. *ABG*, 177; *EW Letters*, 277n1.

13. EW to Bernard Berenson, January 27, 1919, *EW Letters*, 421.

14. Wharton expresses these two sides of herself in a letter to Morton Fullerton in 1908. See EW to Fullerton, no date, *EW Letters*, 151. In her autobiography, Wharton also writes of her "two lives," the real and the unreal, the latter created by her fiction. See *ABG*, 205.

15. *ABG*, 21.

16. *ABG*, 5.
17. Details regarding Wharton's childhood are drawn from a number of sources: her autobiography, *A Backward Glance*; her autobiographical essay, "A Little Girl's New York," which details Wharton's father hunched over his desk writing bills and her mother's habits as a born "shopper" (361); several biographies of Wharton, particularly R. W. B. Lewis's, *Edith Wharton: A Biography* (New York: Harper & Row, 1975), hereafter referred to as *EW*; Shari Benstock's *No Gifts From Chance: A Biography of Edith Wharton*; Cynthia Griffin Woolf's, *A Feast of Words: The Triumph of Edith Wharton* (New York: Scribner's, 1977); Hermione Lee's *Edith Wharton* (New York: Knopf, 2007); and Wharton's numerous letters and journals, housed in the Edith Wharton Collection at Beinecke Rare Book and Manuscript Library, Yale University [hereafter Beinecke], some of which are collected in Lewis's *EW Letters*.
18. "A Little Girl's New York," 358.
19. For the details of the furnishings and decoration of the West 23rd Street brownstone, see "A Little Girl's New York," as well as the extensive collection of period photographs housed in the Edith Wharton Collection at Beinecke.
20. In her autobiography, Wharton refers to her writing life as "her secret garden" and asserts that from the time she was a young girl, she had a highly "peopled inner world." See *ABG*, 197.
21. "A Little Girl's New York," 357.
22. *ABG*, 128.
23. *ABG*, 54–55.
24. *ABG*, 54.
25. *ABG*, 29.
26. *ABG*, 44.
27. Gaston Bachelard, *The Poetics of Space* (New York: Orion Books, 1958), introduction, xvi–xviii.
28. Richard Guy Wilson, "Edith and Ogden: Writing, Decoration, and Architecture," in *Ogden Codman and the Decoration of Houses*, Pauline Metcalf, ed. (Boston: The Boston Athenaeum and Godine Publishers, 1988), 153–156.
29. EW to OC, [1895], Historic New England (formally the Society for the Preservation of New England Antiquities). I am especially grateful to Laura Condon, head archivist and librarian at Historic New England, for pointing me in the direction of the invaluable Codman Family Papers, which contains numerous letters between Wharton and Codman on the decoration of her several residences between 1885 and 1915.
30. Bachelard, xxxvii.
31. Wharton, "The Fullness of Life," *Scribner's* 14 (December 1893), 700.
32. Edith Wharton, *The House of Mirth*. Ed. Elizabeth Ammons (New York: Norton, 1990), 118. All further references are to this edition and are noted parenthetically in the text.
33. *ABG*, 28.
34. Edith Wharton, *The Age of Innocence* (New York: D. Appleton & Co., 1920), 235. See also Robert A. M. Stern et al., *New York 1880: Architecture and Urbanism in the Gilded Age* (New York: The Monacelli Press, 1999), 577–580, for a useful discussion of Wharton and her relatives who, during the

1870s and 1880s, built marble mansions in New York City upon which Wharton based many of the residences in her New York fiction. As Stern points out, Wharton also based her depiction of Sillerton Jackson in *The Age of Innocence* upon her close friend and aesthetic advisor, Egerton Winthrop. See Stern, 612.

35. In an undated letter from EW to OC, Wharton writes: "The older I grow the more I feel that I would rather live in Italy than anywhere—the very air is full of architecture—*'la ligne'* [the line] is everywhere." EW to OC [no date]. Historic New England.

36. *ABG*, 363.

37. Richard Guy Wilson also has called houses surrogates for Wharton: "In a very real sense architecture and decoration became surrogates [for an unsatisfying marriage]." See Wilson, "Edith and Ogden: Writing, Decoration, and Architecture," 138.

38. These were reasons given by the local Newport paper, *Town Topics*, in 1881. Quoted in *NGFC*, 46.

39. Daily Diary, Oct. 11, 1927, and EW to Elsina Tyler, 1927. Beinecke. Walter Berry (1859–1927) was a distant cousin of Wharton's and a Harvard and Columbia educated lawyer who practiced in New York, Washington, D.C., and ultimately, Paris. Though Wharton felt great affection for Berry, she was afraid of losing his friendship if they married (though there is no evidence that he proposed to her). She and Berry remained close friends until his death in 1927. For more on Walter Berry, see Leon Edel, "Walter Berry and the Novelists: Proust, James, and Edith Wharton," *Nineteenth-Century Fiction*, Vol. 38, No. 4 (March 1984): 514–528.

40. *ABG*, 326. Teddy Wharton (1850–1928) originally intended to become a banker, but preferred hunting and fishing, and after his marriage to Edith, whose income was higher than his, he became leisured for life. When he died in 1928, estranged from Wharton from whom he had been divorced since 1913, he left his money to his nurse.

41. Morton Fullerton (1865–1952) was born and educated in the United States and moved to London as a young man. He worked for the *London Times* before moving to Paris, where he eventually joined the staff of *Le Figaro*. He was also a friend of Henry James's. Wharton and Fullerton had an affair from 1908 to 1910. The anxiety that this relationship caused Wharton is apparent from her letters to him throughout 1910. See *EW Letters*, 206–214.

42. Each of these men was reputable for his education and knowledge in the arts: Ogden Codman as an interior decorator; Egerton Winthrop, a descendant of John Winthrop and well-known as a connoisseur of the arts; and Charles McKim, as an architect trained at the Ecole des Beaux-Arts in Paris and at the office of H. H. Richardson, who became a partner in the highly successful New York City firm of McKim, Mead, & White.

43. *ABG*, 92–94. For a more complete discussion of Egerton Winthrop's Richard Morris Hunt-designed house (and its decoration) on East 33rd Street in New York City, and his aesthetic influence upon Wharton, see Stern, 611–612.

44. Bernard Berenson (1865–1959), the American art critic and connoisseur of Italian art, and his wife Mary Berenson, were close friends with the English critic and essayist, Percy Lubbock (1879–1965), and his wife Lady Sybil; both were also friends with Henry James.

45. In later years, when she was in her fifties, Wharton enjoyed friendships with several women: the daughters of Charles Eliot Norton, Sara and Elizabeth ("Lily") whom Wharton had known since her youth; sister-in-law Mary "Minnie" Cadwalader Jones; niece Beatrix Cadwalader Jones; and Mary Berenson. In *No Gifts From Chance*, Benstock refers to Wharton's mother's "icy disapproval," 57.

46. The money was bequeathed to her by a distant cousin named Joshua Jones, whom Wharton had never met, when she was twenty-five years old, and amounted to an outright sum of $120,000 in 1888 (nearly three million dollars in today's currency), which secured her and Teddy's future financial health once and for all. Apparently the money was intended for Edith Wharton's father, a cousin of Joshua Jones, but his will stipulated that if George Frederic was deceased, the money was to be split equally among his children. Thus, Edith and her two brothers received equal sums. Wharton's father had died in 1885, when Wharton was twenty-three. See Lewis, *EW*, 59.

47. *ABG*, 106.

48. Architect John Hubbard Sturgis who designed Land's End was Codman's uncle. Land's End was the first project on which Wharton enlisted the professional services of Codman, a friend who traveled in the same Newport, RI, social circles as she. In spite of some difficulties in their friendship, particularly when it came to designing the Mount in 1900 and 1901, Codman became one of Wharton's closest friends. Like she, he bought a house in France, and was one of the few people Wharton saw in the months preceding her death. See *NGFC*, 455. For Wharton's description of the house as "incurably ugly" and for details on the additions she and Codman made to Land's End, see *ABG*, 106.

49. EW to OC, April 23, 1895. Historic New England.

50. *DH*, 1.

51. *DH*, 1.

52. *ABG*, 116.

53. *ABG*, 200.

54. *EW Letters*, 44.

55. This letter from EW to OC is dated May 4th, but does not have a year. Presumably it is from 1892, as she purchased the house in November 1891. Historic New England.

56. EW to OC, May 4, 1892. Historic New England. Emphasis original.

57. These details (including the price of the house) are drawn from Lewis, *EW*, 67.

58. Very little is known of the exact configuration of the two townhouses, as sources confirm. See, for example, Theresa Craig, *Edith Wharton: A House Full of Rooms*, 81–82, and Wilson, "Edith and Ogden: Writing, Decoration, and Architecture," 147.

59. EW to OC, [May 1895]. Historic New England. Emphasis original.

60. EW to OC, [June 1895]. Historic New England. Emphasis original.

61. *DH*, 3.

62. EW to OC, June 7 [no year], Aix-les-Bains. Historic New England.

63. Gaston Bachelard, *The Poetics of Space*, introduction, xviii.

64. Quoted in Lee, *EW*, 136.

65. OC to Sarah Codman, [No date] 1901. Historic New England.

66. OC to Sarah Codman, [No date] 1901. Historic New England.
67. OC to Sarah Codman, 1901. Historic New England.
68. *DH*, 6.
69. *ABG*, 124–125.
70. EW to Bernard Berenson, August 6 [1911], *EW Letters*, 251–252.
71. See Edmund Burke, *A Philosophical Enquiry into the Origin of Our Ideas of the Sublime and Beautiful* (1756; rpt: New York: Penguin, 1999).
72. EW, *Italian Villas and Their Gardens*, 6.
73. EW, *Italian Villas and Their Gardens*, 5.
74. EW, *Italian Villas and Their Gardens*, 5. Emphasis original.
75. This story may be apocryphal, but is related by Elsie de Wolfe in her autobiography, *After All* (New York: Harper & Brothers, 1935), 107–108.
76. *DH*, 148–149.
77. *ABG*, 327. Emphasis original.
78. *ABG*, 327.
79. *ABG*, 327. Wharton's library was even more unusual because the author based its conception upon libraries belonging to men. There is a dearth of scholarship on the subject of libraries that belong to women, although some mention is made of the advent of private female spaces in Thomas Schlereth's *Victorian America: Transformations in Everyday Life* (New York: Harper Collins, 1991), and in Jessica Foy and Schlereth, eds., *American Home Life, 1880–1930: A Social History of Spaces and Services* (Knoxville, University of Tennessee Press, 1994). A provocative study of male and female spaces at home is Cheryl Robertson's "Male and Female Agendas for Domestic Reform: The Middle-Class Bungalow in Gendered Perspective," *Winterthur Portfolio* 26, no. 2/3 (1991), 123–141.
80. Lewis, *EW*, 149. Wharton would also find out that during his frequent and lengthy absences from the Mount, Teddy was visiting with mistresses in the Wharton's New York City apartment or in Boston, where his mother kept an apartment for him. Thus, it is fair to assume he was not very involved in many decisions including architectural ones.
81. The information regarding the furnishings of the two rooms is drawn from Scott Marshall, *The Mount, Home of Edith Wharton: A Historic Structure Report* (Lenox, Massachusetts: Edith Wharton Restoration, Inc., 1997), 78–80. The den, which was referred to by this name, is the only room of the main floor of the Mount for which no period photographs exist, thus the exact furnishings of the room are unknown. The *Berkshire Resort Topics*, however, reported on the dark leather chairs and the color of the walls in 1904. See Marshall, *The Mount*, 79.
82. Wharton refers to her life at the Mount as "quiet and systematic" in a letter to Sara Norton, 1901 (*EW Letters*, 46) and to her happiness at the Mount in *ABG*, 125.
83. *ABG*, 362.
84. Wharton referred to the two properties as "shacks," which of course they were not, and used the "Var & S & O" as shorthand for the two regions of France in which the houses were located: Var, in the south of France, and Seine-et-Oise (named for the intersection of the Seine and Oise Rivers), in the north. See *EW Letters*, 429–430.
85. *ABG*, 293.
86. *DH*, 26.

87. As quoted in Carol Singley, *Edith Wharton: Matters of Mind and Spirit,*" (New York: Cambridge UP, 1998), 33.

88. *EW Letters*, 417.

89. *EW Letters*, 421.

90. *EW Letters*, 434. With thanks to Dr. Flora Vaccarino, Yale University, who provided the translation from Italian.

91. *NGFC*, 372.

92. *EW Letters*, 430.

93. EW to Bernard Berenson, January 27, 1919, *EW Letters*, 421–422.

94. *ABG*, 363.

95. *ABG*, 54.

96. See, for example, Newland Archer rendered speechless around Ellen Olenska in *The Age of Innocence* and Charity Royall reduced to stammering with Lucius Harney in *Summer*.

97. Details regarding the purchase and cost of the Pavillon Colombe are drawn from *NGFC*, 350–352.

98. The total cost of the project according to the real estate documents was $60,000, over $600,000 in 2009 dollars. Details on the gardens and the hundreds of varieties of plants, shrubs, and flowers that Wharton planted can be found in the Edith Wharton Collection at Beinecke. Wharton was able to buy the property and fund its restoration very cheaply due to the depreciation of real estate following World War I.

99. EW to Minnie Cadwalader Jones, 1920, *EW Letters*, 436.

100. EW to Minnie Cadwalader Jones, 1920, *EW Letters*, 436.

101. EW to Morton Fullerton, [June 12, 1921], *EW Letters*, 443. Wharton's evocation of "The Great Good Place" refers to Henry James's short story by the same name, which ran in *Scribner's Magazine* in January, 1900.

102. The list of books housed at Ste. Claire upon Wharton's death abounds in gardening and horticulture books (many in French) and in European novels, including those by Charles Dickens, George Eliot, and Gustav Flaubert. The catalogue also includes nearly all of Henry James's work. Though Wharton wrote a novel called *Hudson River Bracketed* (1929) at this time—a novel whose title refers to a style of domestic architecture of the Hudson River Valley, New York—the catalogue does not include titles by Hudson River architects, Andrew Jackson Downing or Andrew Jackson Davis. See the "Catalogue of Wharton's Library," Beinecke.

103. Details on the renovation and cost of Sainte-Claire le Château are drawn from *NGFC*, 352.

104. Details about the writing and the sales of *The Age of Innocence* are drawn from *NGFC*, 357–363. EW to Bernard Berenson, January 1921. Beinecke.

SELECTED BIBLIOGRAPHY

Collections

Codman, Ogden, Jr. and Family. Papers. Historic New England, Boston, Massachusetts.

Fields, James Thomas. Papers and Addenda (FI 1–5637). The Huntington Library, Art Collections, and Botanical Gardens, San Marino, California.

Howells-Fréchette Family. Papers (mssHM 27527–27619). The Huntington Library, Art Collections, and Botanical Gardens, San Marino, CA

Howells, William Dean and Family. Papers (bMS Am 2023). Houghton Library, Harvard University, Cambridge, Massachusetts.

James, Henry and Family. Papers (bMS Am 1237). Houghton Library, Harvard University, Cambridge, Massachusetts.

Letters to the Norton Family. Papers (bMS Am 1088.1). Houghton Library, Harvard University, Cambridge, Massachusetts.

Stowe, Harriet Beecher and Family. Papers. Schlesinger Library, Radcliffe College, Cambridge, Massachusetts.

Stowe, Harriet Beecher and Family. Papers. The Harriet Beecher Stowe Center Library, Hartford, Connecticut.

Wharton, Edith. Collection (YCAL MSS 42). Yale Collection of American Literature, Beinecke Rare Book and Manuscript. Library, Yale University, New Haven, Connecticut.

Winterthur Museum, Library, and Gardens, Wilmington, Delaware.

Primary Sources

Arms, George, Christopher K. Lohmann, et al. *Selected Letters of W. D. Howells*. 6 vols. Boston: Twayne, 1976–1983.

Baedeker, Karl. *London and its Environs*. Leipsic: Karl Baedeker, 1881.

Banks, F. R. *The Penguin Guide to London*. Harmondsworth, Middlesex: Penguin Books, 1958.

Baudelaire, Charles. *Les Fleurs du Mal*. 1861. Reprint; New York: Penguin, 1993.

Beecher, Catharine, E. *A Treatise on Domestic Economy*. 1841. Reprint; New York: Schocken Books, 1977.

Beecher, Catharine E. and Harriet Beecher Stowe. *The American Woman's Home*. 1869. Reprint; Hartford: Stowe-Day Foundation, 1975.

Beecher, Henry Ward. *Norwood, or, Village Life in New England*. New York: Charles Scribner's and Co., 1868.

Bellamy, Edward. *Looking Backward, 2000–1887*. 1888. Reprint; New York: Bedford Books of St. Martin's Press, 1995.

Belmont Historic District Commission. *Belmont: The Architecture and Development of the Town of Homes*. Belmont, MA: Belmont Historic District Commission, 1984.

Benjamin, Walter. *The Arcades Project*, trans. Howard Eiland and Kevin McLaughlin. 1940. Reprint; Cambridge: Belknap Press of Harvard University, 1999.

Bentzon, Thomas. "Family Life in America." *Forum* 21 (March 1896): 1–20.

Besant, Walter with Henry James. *The Art of Fiction*. Boston: Cupples, Upham and Co., 1885.

Blackall, C. "The Wholesale Architect as Educator." *American Architect and Building News* 46 (November 1894): 44–45.

Child, Lydia Maria. *The American Frugal Housewife*. 1833. Reprint; Boston: Hendee & Co., 1980.

Coburn, Alvin Langdon. *Alvin Langdon Coburn, Photographer: An Autobiography*. New York: F. A. Praeger, 1966.

_____. *Men of Mark*. New York: Mitchell Kennerley, 1913.

Cook, Clarence. *The House Beautiful: Essays on Beds and Tables, Stools and Candlesticks*. New York: Scribner, Armstrong, 1878.

Davis, Alexander Jackson. *Rural Residences*. 1837. Reprint; New York: Da Capo Press, 1980.

De Wolfe, Elsie. *After All*. New York: Harper & Brothers, 1935.

_____. *The House in Good Taste*. New York: The Century Co., 1914.

Downing, Andrew Jackson. *The Architecture of Country Houses*. 1850. Reprint; New York: Dover Publications, 1969.

_____. *Cottage Residences*. 2nd edition. New York: Wiley and Putnam, 1844.

Dreiser, Theodore. "How He Climbed Fame's Ladder: William Dean Howells Tells the Story of His Long Struggle for Success and his Ultimate Triumph." *Success*. New York, April, 1898.

Eastlake, Charles. *Hints on Household Taste in Furniture, Upholstery and Other Details*. 1868. Reprint; New York: Dover Publishing, 1986.

Edel, Leon, ed. *The Diary of Alice James*. Boston: Northeastern University Press, 1999.

_____. *The Letters of Henry James*. 4 vols. Cambridge: Belknap Press of Harvard University, 1974–1984.

Fagan, Louis. *The Reform Club: Its Founders and Architect*. London: B. Quaritch, 1887.

Fields, Annie, ed. *Life and Letters of Harriet Beecher Stowe*. Boston: Houghton Mifflin, 1897.

Fiske, Ethel, ed. *The Letters of John Fiske*. New York: Macmillan Co., 1940.

Gibson, Louis H. *Beautiful Houses: A Study in House-Building*. New York: Thomas Y. Crowell & Sons, 1895.

Gilder, J. L. and J. B. *Authors at Home: Personal and Biographical Sketches of Well Known American Authors*. New York: A. Wessels Company, 1905.

Gilman, Charlotte Perkins. *Home: Its Work and Influence*. New York: McClure, Phillips & Co., 1903.

Hawthorne, Nathaniel. *The House of Seven Gables*. 1851. Reprint; New York: Penguin, 1996.

Howells, William Dean. *The Altrurian Romances*. Clara and Rudolf Kirk, eds. 1893. Reprint; Bloomington: Indiana University Press, 1968.

_____. *Criticism and Fiction*. New York: Harper Publishers, 1891.

_____. *The Early Prose Writings of William Dean Howells, 1853–1861*. Thomas Wortham, ed. Athens: Ohio University Press, 1990.

_____. *A Hazard of New Fortunes*. Everett Carter, ed. 1889. Reprint; Bloomington: University of Indiana Press, 1976.

_____. *Interviews with William Dean Howells*. Ulrich Halfmann, ed. Arlington, Texas: American Literary Realism, 1973.

_____. *Life in Letters of William Dean Howells*. Mildred Howells, ed. 1928. Reprint; New York: Russell & Russell, 1968.

_____. *Literature and Life*. New York: Harper Publishers, 1911.

_____. *The Minister's Charge*. 1887. Reprint; New York: W. W. Norton, 1985.

_____. *A Modern Instance*. 1882. Reprint; New York: Penguin Books, 1996.

_____. *My Literary Passions*. New York: Harper Publishers, 1895.

_____. *The Rise of Silas Lapham*. 1885. Reprint; New York: W. W. Norton, 1982.

_____. *Suburban Sketches*. Boston: James R. Osgood, 1875.

_____. *Venetian Life*. 1866. Reprint; New York: W. W. Norton & Co., 1982.

_____. *Years of My Youth*. New York: Harper Publishers, 1916.

_____. *The World of Chance*. New York: Harper, 1893. Reprint; New York: W. W. Norton, 1976.

James, Henry. *The American*. 1877. New York: W. W. Norton & Co., 1978.

_____. *The American Scene*. New York: Harper and Brothers, 1907.

_____. *The Art of the Novel, Critical Prefaces*. New York: Charles Scribner's Sons, 1934.

_____. *The Future of the Novel: Essays on the Art of Fiction*. Leon Edel, ed. New York: Vintage Books, 1956.

_____. *The Golden Bowl*. 1904. New York: Alfred A. Knopf, 1992.

_____. *Italian Hours*. 1877. Reprint; New York: Grove Press, 1959.

_____. *Letters from the Palazzo Barbaro*. Rosella Mamoli Zorzi, ed. London: Pushkin Press, 1998.

_____. *The Portrait of a Lady*. Robert E. Bamburg, ed. 1881. Reprint; New York: W. W. Norton, 1995.

_____. *Roderick Hudson*. 1875. Boston: Houghton Mifflin Company, 1977.

_____. *The Sacred Fount*. 1901. New York: Penguin Books, 1990.

_____. *A Small Boy and Others*. New York: Charles Scribner's Sons, 1913.

_____. *The Spoils of Poynton*. 1897. New York: Penguin Books, 1985.

_____. *The Wings of the Dove*. New York: C. Scribner's Sons, 1902.

James, William. *Pragmatism: A New Name for Some Old Ways of Thinking*. New York: Longman, Green & Co., 1897.

Lubbock, Percy, ed. *The Letters of Henry James*. 2 vols. New York: Octagon Books, 1970.

McCarthy, Justin. *Reminiscences*. London: Harper & Brothers, 1899.

Merrill, Ginette de. B. and George Arms, eds. *If Not Literature: The Letters of Elinor Mead Howells* (Columbus: Ohio State University, 1988).

Monteiro, George and Brenda Murphy, eds. *John Jay—Howells Letters: The Correspondence of John Milton Hay and William Dean Howells, 1861–1905*. Boston: Twayne, 1980.

Nevill, Ralph. *London Clubs: Their History and Treasures*. London: Chatto & Windus, 1911.

Polley, G.H. *Italian Renaissance Architecture & Decoration*. 1890. Reprint; Boston: Houghton Mifflin and Co., 1990.

Powers, Lyall, H. *Henry James and Edith Wharton, Letters: 1900–1915*. New York: Charles Scribner's Sons, 1990.

Praz. Mario. *The House of Life*. Angus Davidson, trans. London: Methuen, 1964.

Riis, Jacob. *How the Other Half Lives: Studies Among the Tenements of New York*. 1890. Reprint; New York: Penguin, 1997.

Ruskin, John. *The Seven Lamps of Architecture*. New York: Century & Co. 1859.

_____. *The Stones of Venice* (complete). New York: Century & Co. 1884.

Santayana, George. *Persons and Places*. New York: Charles Scribner's Sons, 1944.

Schuyler, Montgomery. *American Architecture & Other Writings*. New York: Century & Co., 1892.

Smith, Henry Nash and William M. Gibson. *Mark Twain—Howells Letters: The Correspondence of Samuel L. Clemens and William D. Howells, 1872–1910.* Cambridge, MA: Harvard University Press, 1960.

Stowe, Harriet Beecher. *Agnes of Sorrento*. Boston: Ticknor and Fields, 1862.

_____. *House and Home Papers*. Boston: Ticknor and Fields. 1865.

_____. *Little Foxes*. Boston: Ticknor and Fields, 1865.

_____. *The Minister's Wooing*. 1859. Reprint; New York: Penguin Books, 1999.

_____. *My Wife and I: Or, Harry Henderson's Story*. Boston: Houghton, Mifflin, & Co. 1871.

_____. *Palmetto Leaves*. Boston: James R. Osgood & Co., 1873.

_____. *The Pearl of Orr's Island*. Boston: Ticknor and Fields, 1862.

_____. *Pink and White Tyranny: A Society Novel*. 1869. Reprint; New York: Plume, 1988.

_____. *Poganuc People*. 1878. Reprint; Hartford: Stowe-Day Foundation, 1977.

_____. *Sunny Memories of Foreign Lands*. Boston: Phillips, Sampson, and Co., 1854.

_____. *Uncle Tom's Cabin, Or, Life Among the Lowly*. Elizabeth Ammons, ed. 1852. Reprint; New York: W. W. Norton & Co., 1994.

_____. *We and Our Neighbors: Or, The Records of an Unfashionable Street*. New York: J. B. Ford & Co., 1875.

Van Westrum, A. Schade. "Mr. Howells and American Aristocracies." *Bookman* 25 (March 1907): 67–73.

Vaux, Calvert. *Villas and Cottages*. New York: Harper and Brothers, 1857.

Veblen, Thorstein. *The Theory of the Leisure Class*. 1899. Reprint; New York: Modern Library, 2001.

Wheeler, Candace. *Household Art*. New York: Harper & Brothers, 1893.

Wharton, Edith. *The Age of Innocence*. 1920. Reprint; New York: Charles Scribner's Sons, 1970.

_____. *A Backward Glance*. New York: D. Appleton-Century Co., 1934.

_____. *The Custom of the Country*. New York: Charles Scribner's Sons, 1913.

_____. *Ethan Frome*. 1911. Reprint; New York: Signet Classics, 1980.

_____. *French Ways and Their Meaning*. New York: D. Appleton and Co., 1919.

_____. *The Fullness of Life*. New York: The Century Press, 1917.

_____. *The House of Mirth*. 1905. Reprint; New York: Signet Classics, 2000.

_____. *Hudson River Bracketed*. New York: D. Appleton, 1929.

_____. *Italian Villas and Their Gardens*. New York: The Century Press, 1904.

_____. *The Letters of Edith Wharton*. R. W. B. Lewis and Nancy Lewis, eds. New York: Collier Books, 1988.

_____. "A Little Girl's New York." *Harper's Magazine* (March 1938): 355–365.

_____. *Summer*. 1917. Reprint: New York: Collier Books, 1992.

_____. *The Writing of Fiction*. New York: Octagon Press, 1925.

Wharton, Edith, and Ogden Codman, Jr. *The Decoration of Houses*. New York: Charles Scribner's Sons, 1897.

Wolfe, Elsie de. *After All*. London: William Heinemann Ltd., 1935.

Secondary Sources

Aaron, Daniel. *Studies in Biography*. Cambridge: Harvard University Press, 1978.

Ames, Kenneth L. "American Decorative Arts/Household Furnishings." *American Quarterly* 35:3 (1983): 280–303.

_____. "Material Culture as Non-Verbal Communication: A Historical Case Study." *Journal of American Studies* (1981): 619–46.

_____. "Meanings in Artifacts: Hall Furnishings in Victorian America." *Journal of Interdisciplinary History* 9:1 (Summer 1978): 19–46.

Anesko, Michael. *Letters, Fictions, Lives: Henry James and William Dean Howells*. New York: Oxford University Press, 1997.

Aslet, Clive. *The American Country House*. London & New Haven: Yale University Press, 1990.

_____. *The Last Country Houses*. New Haven: Yale University Press, 1982.

Auchincloss, Louis. *Reading Henry James*. Minneapolis, University of Minnesota Press, 1975.

Axelrod, Alan, Ed. *The Colonial Revival in America*. New York: W. W. Norton & Co., 1985.

Bachelard, Gaston. *The Poetics of Space*. New York: Orion Books, 1958.

Baker, John Milnes. *American House Styles: A Concise Guide*. New York: W. W. Norton, 1994.

Banta, Martha. *Imaging American Woman: Idea and Ideals in Cultural History*. New York: Columbia University Press, 1987.

Barbour, James and Tom Quirk, eds. *Biographies of Books: The Compositional Histories of Notable American Writings*. Columbia, MO: University of Missouri Press, 1996.

Baxter, Annette. "Howells' Boston and Wharton's New York." *Midwest Quarterly 4*, (Summer 1962): 353–361.

Bell, Millicent, ed. *The Cambridge Companion to Edith Wharton*. Cambridge and New York: Cambridge University Press, 1995.

Benstock, Shari. *No Gifts From Chance: A Biography of Edith Wharton*. New York: Charles Scribner's Sons, 1994.

Bentley, Nancy. *The Ethnography of Manners: Hawthorne, James and Wharton*. Cambridge and New York: Cambridge University Press, 1995.

Binford, Henry C. *The First Suburbs: Residential Communities on the Boston Periphery, 1815–1860*. Chicago: University of Chicago Press, 1985.

Blackmar, Elizabeth. *Manhattan for Rent, 1785–1850*. Ithaca: Cornell University Press, 1989.

Bogardus, Ralph, F. *Pictures and Texts: Henry James, A. L. Coburn, and New Ways of Seeing in Literary Culture*. Ann Arbor: University of Michigan Press, 1984.

Borus, Daniel, H. *Writing Realism: Howells, James and Norris in the Mass Market*. Chapel Hill: University of North Carolina Press, 1989.

Boyer, M. Christine. *Manhattan Manners: Architecture and Style, 1850–1900*. New York: Rizzoli, 1985.

Bradley, John R., ed. *Henry James and Homo-erotic Desire*. New York: St. Martin's Press, 1999.

Brodhead, Richard. *Cultures of Letters: Scenes of Reading and Writing in Nineteenth-Century America*. Chicago: University of Chicago Press, 1993.

Bronner, Simon, ed. *Consuming Visions: Accumulation and Display in America, 1880–1920*. New York: W. W. Norton & Co., 1989.

Brooks, Peter. *The Melodramatic Imagination: Balzac, Henry James, Melodrama, and the Mode of Excess.* New York: Columbia University Press, 1985.

Brooks, Van Wyck. *The Confident Years, 1885-1915.* (vol. 5 of *Makers and Finders: A History of the Writer in America, 1800–1915*). New York: E. P. Dutton & Co., 1952.

_____. *The Dream of Arcadia: American Writers and Artists in Italy, 1760–1915.* New York: Dutton, 1958.

Brown, Bill. *A Sense of Things: The Object Matter of American Literature.* Chicago, University of Chicago Press, 2003.

Brown, Gillian. *Domestic Individualism: Imagining Self in Nineteenth-Century America.* Berkeley: University of California Press, 1990.

Bryan, John M. *G. W. Vanderbilt's Biltmore: The Most Distinguished Private Place.* New York: Rizzoli, 1994.

Buell, Lawrence. *New England Literary Culture: From Revolution to Renaissance.* Cambridge and New York: Cambridge University Press, 1986.

Bunting, Bainbridge. *Houses of Boston's Back Bay: An Architectural History, 1840–1917.* Cambridge: Belknap Press of Harvard University, 1967.

Burroughs, John. "The Vanity of Big Houses." *Cosmopolitan* 41 (May 1906): 89–93.

Bushman, Richard. *The Refinement of America: Persons, Houses, Cities.* New York: Vintage Press, 1993.

Cady, Edward H. *The Realist at War: The Mature Years, 1885–1920, of William Dean Howells.* Syracuse: Syracuse University Press, 1958.

_____. *The Road to Realism: The Early Years, 1837–1885, of William Dean Howells.* Syracuse: Syracuse University Press, 1956.

Cawelti, John G. "The Self-Made Man and Industrial America." In *Apostles of the Self-Made Man.* Chicago: University of Chicago Press, 1965.

Chandler, Marilyn R. *Dwelling in the Text: Houses in American Fiction.* Berkeley: University of California Press, 1991.

Cheever, Susan. *American Bloomsbury: Louisa May Alcott, Ralph Waldo Emerson, Margaret Fuller, Nathaniel Hawthorne, and Henry David Thoreau: Their Lives, Their Loves, Their Work.* New York: Simon & Schuster, 2006.

Clark, Clifford E., Jr. *The American Family Home, 1800–1960.* Chapel Hill: University of North Carolina Press, 1986.

_____. "Domestic Architecture and the Cult of Domesticity in America, 1840–1870." *Journal of Interdisciplinary History* 7:1 (Summer 1976): 33–56.

Cohn, Jan. "The Houses of Fiction: Domestic Architecture in Howells and Edith Wharton." *Texas Studies in Literature and Language* 15:3 (Fall 1973): 49–72.

_____. *The Palace or the Poorhouse: The American Home as a Cultural Symbol.* East Lansing: Michigan State University Press, 1979.

Colquitt, Clare, et al., eds. *A Forward Glance: New Essays on Edith Wharton.* Newark: University of Delaware Press, 1999.

Cott, Nancy. *The Bonds of Womanhood: 'Woman's Sphere' in New England, 1780–1835,* second edition. New Haven: Yale University Press, 1997.

Craig, Theresa. *Edith Wharton: A House Full of Rooms: Architecture, Interiors, and Gardens.* New York: Vintage Books, 1996.

Cromley, Elizabeth. *Alone Together: A History of New York's Early Apartments.* Ithaca: Cornell University Press, 1990.

DiMaggio, Paul. "Cultural Entrepreneurship in 19th Century Boston." *Media, Culture and Society* 4 (1982): 33–50.

Dimock, Wai-Chee. "Debasing Exchange: Edith Wharton's *The House of Mirth.*" In Shari Benstock, *Edith Wharton: The House of Edith.* New York: St. Martin's Press, 1993.

_____. "Gender, the Market, and the Non-Trivial in James." *The Henry James Review* 15:1 (Winter 1994): 24–30.

_____, ed. *Rethinking Class: Literary Studies and Social Formations.* New York: Columbia University Press, 1994.

Douglas, Ann. *The Feminization of American Culture.* New York: Alfred Knopf & Co., 1977.

Downing, Antoinette, F. and Vincent Scully, Jr. *The Architectural Heritage of Newport, Rhode Island, 1640-1915.* New York: C. N. Potter, 1967.

Edel, Leon. *Henry James: A Life.* New York: Harper & Row, 1985.

_____. *Henry James: The Untried Years: 1843–1870.* Philadelphia: J. B. Lippincott & Co., 1953.

_____. *Henry James: The Conquest of London: 1870–1881.* Philadelphia: J. B. Lippincott & Co., 1962.

_____. *Henry James: The Middle Years: 1882–1895.* Philadelphia: J. B. Lippincott & Co., 1962.

_____. *Henry James: The Treacherous Years: 1895–1901.* Philadelphia: J. B. Lippincott & Co., 1969.

_____. *Henry James: The Master: 1901–1916.* Philadelphia: J. B. Lippincott & Co., 1972.

_____. "Walter Berry and the Novelists: Proust, James, and Edith Wharton," *Nineteenth-Century Fiction*, Vol. 38, No. 4 (March 1984): 514–528.

Elliott, Michael A. and Claudia Stokes. *American Literary Studies: A Methodological Reader.* New York: New York University Press, 2003.

Esch, Deborah, ed. *New Essays on* The House of Mirth. Cambridge, England: Cambridge University Press, 2001.

Fisher, Philip. *Hard Facts: Setting and Form in the American Novel.* New York: Oxford University Press, 1987.

_____. *Making and Effacing Art: Modern American Art in a Culture of Museums.* Cambridge, MA: Harvard University Press, 1991.

Fourmy Cutrer, Emily. "Visualizing Nineteenth-Century American Culture," *American Quarterly* 51:4 (1999): 895–909.

_____. "A Pragmatic Mode of Seeing: James, Howells, and the Politics of Vision," in *American Iconology*, David C. Miller, ed. New Haven: Yale University Press, 1993.

Fox, Richard W. and Jackson Lears, eds. *The Culture of Consumption: Critical Essays in American History, 1880–1980.* New York: Vintage Books, 1983.

Foy, Jessica and Thomas Schlereth, eds. *American Home Life, 1880–1930: A Social History of Spaces and Services.* Knoxville: University of Tennessee Press, 1994.

Frank, Ellen Eve. *Literary Architecture: Essays Toward a Tradition.* Berkeley: University of California Press, 1979.

Frazier, David L. "Howells' Symbolic Houses: The Plutocrats and Palaces." *American Literary Realism 10*, (Summer 1977): 267–279.

Freedman, Jonathan. *The Cambridge Companion to Henry James.* Cambridge and New York: Cambridge University Press, 1996.

Friedman, Alice. *Women and the Making of the Modern House: A Social and Architectural History.* New York: Henry N. Abrams, 1998.

Fryer, Judith. *Felicitous Space: The Imaginative Structures of Edith Wharton and Willa Cather.* Chapel Hill: University of North Carolina Press, 1986.

Fuss, Diana. *The Sense of an Interior: Four Writers and the Rooms that Shaped Them.* New York: Routledge, 2004.

Gass, William. "The High Brutality of Good Intentions." *Accent* XVIII (Winter, 1958): 62–71

Gill, Richard. *Happy Rural Seat: The English Country House and the Literary Imagination.* New Haven: Yale University Press, 1972.

Girouard, Mark. *Life in the English Country House: A Social and Architectural History.* New Haven and London: Yale University Press, 1978.

_____. *Life in the French Country House.* London: Cassell and Co., 2000.

_____. *The Victorian Country House.* 1971. Reprint; New Haven: Yale University Press, 1979.

Goffman, Erving. *The Representation of Self in Everyday Life.* Garden City, New York: Doubleday, 1959.

Goodman, Susan and Carl Dawson. *William Dean Howells: A Writer's Life.* Berkeley: University of California Press, 2005.

Gordon, Lyndall. *A Private Life of Henry James: Two Women and His Art.* London: Chatto & Windus, 1998.

Gordon, Lynn. *'From Seminary to University:' Gender and Higher Education in the Progressive Era.* New Haven: Yale University Press, 1990.

Grant, Marion Hepburn and Ellsworth Strong. *The City of Hartford, 1784–1984.* Hartford: The Connecticut Historical Society, 1986.

Graves, Charles. *Leather Armchairs: The Book of London Clubs.* New York: Coward McCann, 1964.

Griffin, Susan M. *The Historical Eye: The Texture of the Visual in Late James.* Boston: Northeastern University Press, 1991.

Groth, Paul. *Living Downtown: The History of Residential Hotels in the United States.* Berkeley: University of California Press, 1994.

Handlin, David. *The American Home: Architecture and Society, 1815–1915.* Boston: Little, Brown & Co., 1979.

Haralson, Eric. *Henry James and Queer Modernity.* Cambridge and New York: Cambridge University Press, 2003.

Hatch, Nathan. *The Democratization of American Christianity.* New Haven: Yale University Press, 1989.

Hayden, Dolores. *The Grand Domestic Revolution.* Cambridge: MIT Press, 1981.

Hedrick, Joan. *Harriet Beecher Stowe, A Life.* New York: Oxford University Press, 1994.

Hewitt, Mark Alan. *The Architect and the American Country House, 1890–1940.* New Haven: Yale University Press, 1990.

Hobsbawm, Eric. *The Age of Revolution*: 1789–1848. 1962. Reprint; New York: Vintage, 1996.

_____. *The Age of Capital*: 1848–1875. 1975. Reprint; New York: Vintage, 1996.

_____. *The Age of Empire*: 1875–1914. 1987. Reprint; New York: Vintage, 1996.

Hoeller, Hildegard. *Edith Wharton's Dialogue with Realism and Sentimental Fiction.* Gainesville, FL: University Press of Florida, 2000.

Holland, Laurence. *The Expense of Vision: Essays on the Craft of Henry James.* Princeton, N. J.: Princeton University Press, 1964.

Horowitz, Daniel. *The Morality of Spending: Attitudes Toward the Consumer Society in America, 1875–1970*. Baltimore: Johns Hopkins University Press, 1985.

Honour, Hugh and John Fleming. *Venetian Hours of Henry James, Whistler, and Sargent*. Boston: Little, Brown, 1991.

Hyde, H. Montgomery. *Henry James at Home*. New York: Farrar, Straus & Giroux, 1969.

_____. *The Story of Lamb House, Rye: The Home of Henry James*. Rye, Sussex, England: Adams of Rye Limited, 1966.

James, Robert Rhodes. *Rosebery: A Biography of Archibald Philip, Fifth Earl of Rosebery*. London: Weidenfeld and Nicholson, 1963.

Kaplan, Amy. *The Social Construction of American Realism*. Chicago: University of Chicago Press, 1988.

Kelley, Mary. *Private Women, Public Stage: Literary Domesticity in Nineteenth Century America*. New York: Oxford University Press, 1984.

Kerber, Linda. *Women of the Republic: Intellect and Ideology in Revolutionary America*. Chapel Hill: University of North Carolina Press, 1997.

Kiely, Robert, ed. *Modernism Reconsidered*. Cambridge, MA: Harvard University Press, 1983.

Kilham, Walter H. *Boston After Bulfinch: An Account of its Architecture, 1800–1900*. Cambridge, MA: Harvard University Press, 1946.

Kirk, Clara Marburg. *W. D. Howells and Art in His Time*. New Brunswick, N.J.: Rutgers University Press, 1965.

_____. *W. D. Howells, Traveler From Altruria*. New Brunswick, N. J.: Rutgers University Press, 1962.

Klimasmith, Betsy. *At Home in the City: Urban Domesticity in American Literature and Culture, 1850–1930*. Durham, University of New Hampshire Press, 2005.

Lears, T. J. Jackson. *No Place of Grace: Anti-modernism and the Transformation of American Culture*. New York: Pantheon Books, 1981.

Leavitt, Sarah. *From Catharine Beecher to Martha Stewart: A Cultural History of Domestic Advice*. Chapel Hill: University of North Carolina Press, 2002.

Lee, Hermione. *Edith Wharton*. New York: Knopf, 2007.

Levine, Lawrence. *Highbrow, Lowbrow: The Emergence of Cultural Hierarchy in America*. Cambridge, MA: Harvard University Press, 1988.

Levine, Miriam. *A Guide to Writers' Homes in New England*. Cambridge, MA: Applewood Books, 1984.

Lewis, R. W. B. *The American Adam: Innocence, Tragedy and Tradition in the Nineteenth Century*. Chicago: University of Chicago Press, 1955.

_____. *Edith Wharton: A Biography*. New York: Harper & Row Publishers, 1975.

_____. *The Jameses: A Family Narrative*. New York: Farrar, Straus, & Giroux, 1991.

_____. "Writers at the Century's Turn." In *The National Book Award: Acceptance Speeches*. New York: W. W. Norton & Co., 1995.

Lockwood, Charles. *Bricks and Brownstone: The New York Row House, 1783–1929*. New York: McGraw Hill, 1972.

Lukacs, John. "The Bourgeois Interior," *American Scholar* 39: 4 (Autumn 1970): 620–631.

Lynn, Kenneth S. *William Dean Howells: An American Life*. New York: Harcourt Brace Jovanovich, 1971.

Marshall, Scott. *The Mount: Home of Edith Wharton. A Historic Structure Report.* Lenox, MA: Edith Wharton Restoration, Inc., 1997.

Mayhew, Edgar de N., and Minor Myers, Jr. *A Documentary History of American Interiors from the Colonial Era to 1915.* New York: Charles Scribner's Sons, 1980.

McCauley, Elizabeth Anne, ed. *Gondola Days: Isabella Stewart Gardner and the Palazzo Barbaro Circle.* Boston: Isabella Stewart Gardner Museum, 2004.

McCormack, Peggy, ed. *Questioning the Master: Gender and Sexuality in Henry James's Writings.* Newark: University of Delaware Press, 2000.

Merrill, Ginette de B. "Redtop and the Belmont Years of W. D. Howells," *Harvard Library Bulletin* 18:1 (January 1980): 33–57.

Metcalf, Pauline, ed. *Ogden Codman and the Decoration of Houses.* Boston: The Boston Athenaeum and Godine Publishers, 1988.

McCracken, Grant. *Culture and Consumption: New Approaches to the Symbolic Character of Consumer Goods and Activities.* Bloomington: Indiana University Press, 1988.

McWhirter, David. *Henry James's New York Edition: The Construction of Authorship.* Stanford: Stanford University Press, 1995.

Montgomery, Maureen. *Displaying Women: Spectacles of Leisure in Edith Wharton's New York.* New York: Routledge, 1998.

Mumford, Lewis. *The Brown Decades: A Study of the Arts of America, 1865–1895.* New York: Beacon Press, 1931.

Nettels, Elsa. *Language and Gender in American Fiction: Howells, James, Wharton and Cather.* London: Macmillan Press, 1997.

Novick, Sheldon M. *Henry James: The Young Master.* New York: Random House, 2007.

_____. *Henry James: The Mature Master.* New York: Random House, 2007.

Orvell, Miles. *The Real Thing: Imitation and Authenticity in American Culture, 1880–1940.* Chapel Hill: University of North Carolina Press, 1989.

Pease, Donald, ed. *New Essays on* The Rise of Silas Lapham. Cambridge, England: Cambridge University Press, 1991.

Porte, Joel, ed. *New Essays on* The Portrait of a Lady. Cambridge and New York: Cambridge University Press, 1990.

Ramsden, George, ed. *Edith Wharton's Library: A Catalogue.* Settrington, England: Stone Trough Books, 1999.

Rothschild, Mrs. James de. *The Rothschilds at Waddesdon Manor.* New York: Viking Press, 1979.

Schlereth, Thomas J. *Victorian America: Transformations in Everyday Life, 1876–1915.* New York: Harper Collins Publishers, 1991.

Schreiner, Samuel Jr., *The Concord Quartet: Alcott, Emerson, Hawthorne, Thoreau, and the Friendship that Freed the American Mind.* New York: Wiley, 2006.

Schuyler, David. *Apostle of Taste: Andrew Jackson Downing, 1814–1852.* Baltimore: Johns Hopkins University Press, 1996.

Scully, Vincent. *The Shingle Style and the Stick Style: Architectural Theory and Design from Richardson to the Origins of Wright.* New Haven: Yale University Press, 1955.

Seltzer, Mark. *Henry James and the Art of Power.* Ithaca: Cornell University Press, 1984.

Sharp, Honey. "A Garden Reawakened." *Berkshires Week.* (July 31, 2003).

Singley, Carol J. *Edith Wharton: Matters of Mind and Spirit*. Cambridge, England: Cambridge University Press, 1998.

———, ed. *A Historical Guide to Edith Wharton*. Oxford: Oxford University Press, 2003.

Sklar, Kathryn, K. *Catharine Beecher: A Study in American Domesticity*. New Haven: Yale University Press, 1973.

Stachiw, Myron, Thomas Paske, et al. *Historic Structures Report for the Harriet Beecher Stowe House. Prepared for the Harriet Beecher Stowe Center, December 31, 2001*. Hartford, CT: Harriet Beecher Stowe Center Library, 2002.

Stern, Robert A. M. et al. *New York 1880: Architecture and Urbanism in the Gilded Age*. New York: The Monacelli Press, 1999.

Stewart, Susan. *On Longing: Narratives of the Miniature, the Gigantic, the Souvenir, the Collection*. Durham: Duke University Press, 1993.

Stowe, Charles E. and Lyman Beecher Stowe. *Harriet Beecher Stowe: The Story of Her Life*. Boston: Houghton Mifflin, 1911.

Susman, Warren. *Culture as History: The Transformation of American Society in the Twentieth Century*. New York: Pantheon, 1984.

Sweeting, Adam. *Reading Houses and Building Books: A. J. Downing and the Architecture of Popular Antebellum Literature, 1835-1855*. Hanover, N.H.: University Press of New England, 1996.

Tanselle, G. Thomas. "The Architecture of *The Rise of Silas Lapham*." *American Literature* 37: 4 (January 1966): 430–457.

Thompson, Eleanor, ed. *The American Home: Material Culture, Domestic Space, and Family Life*. Winterthur: Winterthur Museum, 1998.

Thulesius, Olav. *Harriet Beecher Stowe in Florida, 1867–1884*. Jefferson, N.C.: McFarland and Co., 2001.

Tintner, Adeline. *Edith Wharton in Context: Essays on Intertextuality*. Tuscaloosa, AL: University of Alabama Press, 1999.

———. *Henry James and the Lust of the Eyes: Thirteen Artists in His Work*. Baton Rouge: Louisiana State University Press, 1993.

———. *The Museum World of Henry James*. Ann Arbor: UMI Research Press, 1986.

Trachtenberg, Alan. *The Incorporation of America: Culture and Society in the Gilded Age*. New York: Hill and Wang, 1982.

———, ed. *Critics of Culture: Literature and Society in the Early Twentieth Century*. New York: Hill and Wang, 1976.

Tuttleton, James W. "William Dean Howells: Equity as a Basis of Good Society." In *The Novel of Manners in America*. Chapel Hill: University of North Carolina Press, 1971.

———, et al., eds. *Edith Wharton: The Contemporary Reviews*. Cambridge, England: Cambridge University Press, 1992.

Upton, Dell. *Architecture in the United States*. Oxford: Oxford University Press, 1998.

———. "Pattern Books and Professionalism: Aspects of the Transformation of Domestic Architecture in America, 1800–1860." *Winterthur Portfolio* 19, Summer/Autumn 1984.

Van Why, Joseph. *Harriet Beecher Stowe's House in Nook Farm, Hartford*. Hartford: Stowe-Day Foundation, 1970.

———. *Nook Farm*. Hartford: Stowe-Day Foundation, 1975.

Vance, William. *America's Rome*. New Haven: Yale University Press, 1989.

Warhol, Robyn. "Poetics and Persuasion: *Uncle Tom's Cabin* as a Realist Novel," *Essays in Literature*, 13 (Fall, 1986).

White, Barbara. *Edith Wharton: A Study of the Short Fiction*. New York: Twayne Publishers. 1991.

Wilson, Richard Guy. *McKim, Mead, & White, Architects*. New York: Rizzoli, 1983.

Woodbridge, George. *The Reform Club, 1836–1978: A History from the Club's Records*. New York and Toronto: Clearwater Publishing, 1978.

Woods, Mary. *From Craft to Profession: The Practice of Architecture in Nineteenth-Century America*. Berkeley: University of California Press, 1999.

Woolf, Cynthia Griffin. *A Feast of Words: The Triumph of Edith Wharton*. New York: Scribner's, 1977.

Wright, Gwendolyn. *Building the Dream: A Social History of Housing in America*. Cambridge, MIT Press, 1983.

Yeazell, Ruth Bernard. *Henry James: A Collection of Critical Essays*. Englewood Cliffs, N.J.: Prentice Hall, 1994.

_____. *Language and Knowledge in the Late Novels of Henry James*. Chicago: University of Chicago Press, 1980.

INDEX

Studies on Themes and Motifs in Literature

The series is designed to advance the publication of research pertaining to themes and motifs in literature. The studies cover cross-cultural patterns as well as the entire range of national literatures. They trace the development and use of themes and motifs over extended periods, elucidate the significance of specific themes or motifs for the formation of period styles, and analyze the unique structural function of themes and motifs. By examining themes or motifs in the work of an author or period, the studies point to the impulses authors received from literary tradition, the choices made, and the creative transformation of the cultural heritage. The series will include publications of colloquia and theoretical studies that contribute to a greater understanding of literature.

For additional information about this series or for the submission of manuscripts, please contact:

Dr. Heidi Burns
Peter Lang Publishing
P.O. Box 1246
Bel Air, MD 21014-1246

To order other books in this series, please contact our Customer Service Department:

800-770-LANG (within the U.S.)
212-647-7706 (outside the U.S.)
212-647-7707 FAX

Or browse online by series at:

www.peterlang.com